*Find wholeness
and hope by telling
your stories.*

Diane Rooks

Spinning
Gold
out of
Straw

Spinning Gold out of Straw

How Stories Heal

Diane Rooks

Salt Run Press

Published by
Salt Run Press
151 Santa Monica Avenue
St. Augustine, Florida 32080
saltrunpress@storyjourney.com

Publisher's Cataloging-in-Publication

Rooks, Diane.
      Spinning gold out of straw : how stories heal / Diane
      Rooks. -- 1st ed.
      p. cm.
      Includes biographical references.
      LCCN 2001116811
      ISBN 0-9709598-4-2

      1. Mythology--Psychology. 2. Storytelling--
Psychological aspects. 3. Psychology--Biographical
methods. 4. Self-perception. 5. Rooks, Diane.
I. Title.

BL313.R66 2001   158
                              QBI01-700420

Printed in the United States of America

10 9 8 7 6 5 4 3 2 1

Cover by Linda Olsen

This book is printed on acid-free paper.

for David

July 2, 1964 -
September 29, 1993

with love and awe

⇒≫≪⇐

Contents

Stories ix
Acknowledgements xi
Introduction 1

1 open hearts and teach us to grieve 7

2 render meaning from chaos 31

3 penetrate barriers with images 49

4 preserve and perpetuate memories 63

5 validate listeners as individuals 79

6 connect us to the universe 95

7 expand imagination and creativity 117

8 enable growth and learning 139

9 transform pain 161

10 establish control and closure 177

11 restore the future 193

12 offer hope 209

Appendix 1 Research prospectus
            How and Why Stories Heal 225
Appendix 2 List of healing stories 241
Appendix 3 Research paper
            The Scottish View of Death and Dying 245
Bibliography 265

Stories

Story (*Poem) Title	Source	Chapter	Page
The Soldier	Buddhist monk	1	22
Oktoberfest	Rooks	1	27
Perfect Vision	Rooks	2	35
*Why	Vern Hotchkiss	2	46
A Fable	Jeanette Isley	3	58
*There's an Elephant in the Room	Terry Kettering	4	75
Jean	Rooks	5	81
Nora	Rooks	5	82
Alice	Rooks	5	84
J. D. Dupree	Clyde Annandale	5	92
Greevin'	Annette Bruce	6	110
Infinite Resource and Sagacity	Rooks	7	131
Not Presh	Rooks	8	140
Dates and Names	Rooks	8	144
Jonathan	Jay O'Callahan	8	156

The Day I Lost Granddaddy	John Taylor	9	165
*To Feel the Eggshell	Melissa Morphew	9	170
It's Hard for an Eight-Year-Old to Understand	Rooks	10	190
Boilie	Rooks	11	196
Heaven and Hell	Rooks (adapted)	11	200
MTC	Tommie Oakes	12	212

Acknowledgments

So many people have shared their lives and their stories with me and I would like to thank them all. I could not have written this book without them, especially those who agreed to be part of my research and so generously took their time and energy to answer my questions and send me additional resources. The writers and tellers of stories who completed the questionnaire were Sue Alexander, Tina Alston, Jeannine Auth, Joanne Banyon-Ward, Nancy Case, Louise Colln, Ginny Conrad, Donald Davis, Myra Davis, Jenna Eisenberg, Elizabeth Ellis, Mary Fears, Ada Forney, Avis Fox, Audrey Galex, David Holt, Christyna Jensen, Peggy Kenny, Susan Klein, Margaret Lawrence, John McLaughlin, Michael Parent, Christine Reese, Gail Rosen, Sarah Swanson, John Ward, and Carrie Wharton. In addition, many others offered insights and stories that contributed to my understanding.

I would like to thank Dr. John Taylor and Dr. Flora Joy for the help and encouragement they gave me to start the project. All of the students, faculty, and institute leaders that I met at East Tennessee State University contributed their enthusiasm for storytelling, which motivated me to pursue the writing.

The knowledge I gained from the many storytelling workshops I have taken through the years helped me to process how powerful the art of storytelling can be. Special insights came from Clyde Annandale, Donald Davis, Rex Ellis, Susan Klein, Doug Lipman, Rafe Martin, and Jay O'Callahan.

I am greatly indebted to Dr. Flora Joy, Dr. James Granade, Shirley Bryce, Jeannine Auth, Lynne Blow, Bill Cash, and my daughters

Kathi Jolley and Wendy Moreland, for struggling through the early revisions of the book and making comments and suggestions that forced me to re-examine and learn from my own words. In addition, Kathi spent many hours editing the text and designing the page layout. Thanks to Linda Olsen for her patience and talent in designing the cover. Special thanks go to my storytelling coach and friend, John McLaughlin, for his insights and constant encouragement and to Frank Green for teaching me so much about the craft of writing.

Most especially I would like to thank my daughters Kathi and Wendy, and my husband Wilton Rooks, for their help, guidance, understanding, and love.

Introduction

Stories have always been a part of my life. As a child, I frequently withdrew into a storybook world where a handsome prince rescued the princess and good won out in the end. When I found myself in an unpleasant situation, I could disappear for hours in the fantasy of a story. I believed everyone would live happily ever after, imagining myself as the princess being rescued from some awful situation if I could just hang on, let down my hair, sleep for twenty years, or fulfill the current requirement. Sometimes merely inventing the circumstances was enough to make me feel better. Being rescued was not important, although a dramatic ending created additional rewards.

My father was an alcoholic, so I looked for opportunities to escape. A collection of storybook dolls lined my bedroom wall, but I was not allowed to actually play with them. I would lie in bed and imagine being one of those beautiful women in an exotic, faraway land. Their magnificent clothes never got dirty, and their lives were adventurous and happy.

I have many wonderful memories of my friends and family. When my father was sober, life was great. However, my world grew dark in a hurry once he started to drink. Many years passed before I was able to look at that entire scene with any sort of understanding. I hated him so much at times that I wished he were dead. At other times, I absolutely worshipped him. Living with this Dr. Jekyll and Mr. Hyde created a lot of confusion in my mind. Never knowing which one he would be made me distrust relationships and people unless they were ones I created in a story—then I had control of the outcome. Continuing into my teenage years, I became better and better at escaping reality.

Fortunately, I did not turn to alcohol and drugs—maybe because they were not readily available or maybe I was too frightened of what my father might do to me if I did. I certainly hated what alcohol did to my father. I just relied on stories and my imagination more and more.

Eventually I was able to put out of my mind completely whatever situation existed when I left my house. At home I stayed upstairs in my room and avoided contact as much as possible. I developed a wonderful escape mechanism—deny, ignore and imagine.

I married at nineteen and moved away to an exciting new life. My husband was an ensign in the Navy and I followed his ship all over the Far East. After four years he left active duty and we returned home to settle down. Soon we were a typical suburban family complete with kids, pets, and a Ford LTD station wagon with fake wood paneling on the side. After nineteen years of marriage, my husband's sudden death left me a single parent—not exactly what I had signed up for. Somehow I managed to keep things going and send three children to college. I had no choice.

When my son David died at twenty-nine years old of an allergic reaction to an insect bite, I hit a stone wall. My story was over and the ending was not happy. I was headed downhill unless I completely reevaluated my life and beliefs. During the resulting struggle, with all its twists and turns, I eventually started on a new path. Gradually I saw that my story had not ended. I was still breathing and had other worlds to discover.

I have recorded much of my journey in the chapters that follow. I did not even know I was moving in the beginning; I was just trying to survive. I certainly did not set out to write a book, but the path led me to the writing as I explored why stories encourage healing following a significant loss. Stories have been and continue to be a vitally important part of my healing process, and I have seen the positive influences and results they have for others.

As part of my search, I realized I needed a goal to work toward and a focus for some of my creative energy, which led me to enroll in the storytelling master's degree program at East Tennessee State University. The courses, instructors, people, and opportunities presented challenges, enriched my life, and introduced new possibilities. As part of the requirements, I wrote the research prospectus for my thesis on "How and Why Stories Heal," which can be found in the appendix. My advisor, Dr. Flora Joy, encouraged me to write a book because she believed the subject had value for storytellers and those in healing professions, as well as anyone struggling to heal from loss.

I agreed to consider the possibility of a book as I started my research. I mentally decided to stay open to everything and everybody that I encountered along the way. I started reading everything I could find related to my subject and finally thought *maybe I can be the vessel through which something could be learned and passed on.*

Thinking about writing a book on how stories heal overwhelmed me at first. With so much material and so many ideas, how could I possibly collect and organize everything? A friend suggested that I start by just writing *about* the book. I had great encouragement from my friend and storytelling coach, John McLaughlin. One day he asked, "When are you going to realize that this book needs to be written? You are just the vehicle, so get out of the way." I knew the time to start had arrived. I began a working list of ideas to write about, and then wrote every day.

Once I set out on the mission of writing the book, I was amazed by the people and resources appearing in my path. Since I believe that things happen for a reason, I did not dare ignore anyone or anything, wondering if that person, connection, book, article, or insight just might contain the key to my whole topic—the mystery of why and how stories heal.

I found help, answers, and support from the people I met at meetings of the The Compassionate Friends, an international organization with local support groups for bereaved parents and siblings. These people spoke from their hearts and always were willing to hear my stories and ideas about healing.

Of all the people I knew, storytellers as a group seemed to have a unique ability to process and heal from loss. They seemed more willing to share their experiences—perhaps their craft is conducive to doing that. Many of them had experienced significant loss. In fact, I knew twelve storytellers who had lost children—far more than the non-storytellers I knew. This observation filled my mind with questions to explore. *Was there a cause-and-effect or just a coincidence? Did loss lead people toward an interest in stories? Did the interest occur before or after the loss? What exactly was the connection?*

The search for answers in my grief process has been a healing journey. While I had to initiate the quest myself, many people have shared their stories, their knowledge, and their insights with me along the way. The journey was not one I wanted to make or would have chosen willingly, but I know it will continue for the rest of my life. Of course I would give up all I have learned to have David back. Since that is not possible, I have learned to cherish all the people and experiences in my life. Each one entered at just the right time to give me what I needed. The old saying, "When the student is ready, the teacher will appear," has never been more fitting.

Throughout this book I have tried to convey the struggles of my exploration and the sense of wonder at what I have learned. I hope readers will be caught up in the excitement of my adventure. All of the stories herein have been part of my healing process—some of them are personal and some have come from other sources. I could not begin to include them all, but selected ones that illustrated points being made in each chapter. Stories referred to in the book can be found on the healing story list in Appendix 2, along with stories recommended by others. Reading these stories will provide additional insights and understanding.

As part of my research, I interviewed twenty-seven storytellers and writers who had used stories as part of their healing process following a significant loss. Many of them said that exploring their thoughts to answer my questions helped to firm up their own beliefs, which led them to further healing. Many thanked me for the opportunity to be a part of the exploration of the healing power of stories and storytelling. I am deeply indebted to all of them, as well as many others who contributed insights and stories. The value of stories becomes more real to me every day as I continue on the biggest learning experience of my life.

What have I learned from David's death and my journey thus far?

- ⋘ to express love often and openly to my friends and family
- ⋘ to treasure every detail of life
- ⋘ to take nothing for granted
- ⋘ to see how emptiness and fullness can live in the same hurt
- ⋘ to realize how many people have experienced loss
- ⋘ to help people to grieve and grow
- ⋘ to choose to live each day with joy
- ⋘ to believe memories and stories can heal

The research and writing revealed specific reasons why stories heal. I considered dividing the explanations into two sections—one for stories told to an individual person, therapist, or small group, and the other for stories told in a performance setting—but the reasons for both sections were the same. Therefore, I organized the information by allowing each reason to become a chapter. Unavoidably, some overlap between chapters occurred, but I see each chapter as a separate confirmation of the transforming power of stories, regardless of the setting or situation. I hope the results will encourage *everyone* to use stories, whether they are professionals seeking to help or individuals struggling to heal. The value for me has been in the journey. Everything I have learned affirms my resolve to tell the stories we all need to hear to move toward healing, growth, and wholeness.

Stories open hearts and teach us to grieve 1

Breaking emotional barriers

In the weeks following the death of my son David, my twenty-two-year-old daughter refused to talk about her brother. Wendy quickly left the room if anyone mentioned his name and would not speak of him or acknowledge his death at all. We gently tried to encourage her, but she showed no interest. After several months, she began to have "blackouts," which caused her to seek medical help. Fortunately an old friend and family counselor helped her realize what was happening. She acknowledged that she could not allow herself to even think about David because she feared losing control of her emotions. She was afraid if she started to cry, she would never be able to stop.

Gradually the counselor helped Wendy to allow David back into her life by showing her ways to grieve without losing control. He told her to set a clock—then think, talk, or write about David for thirty minutes. When the alarm went off, she must stop and begin another preplanned activity—take a walk, make a phone call, fix a cup of tea, or meet a friend.

The next Mother's Day, she and her older sister planned an overnight trip for the three of us. On the way Wendy announced she wanted us to discuss David and his death later, but only for thirty minutes. So for thirty minutes we talked about him—shared memories and stories and cried a lot. Then we honored her request, stopped our conversation, and went out to eat. Her block was dissolving. The process was slow, but gradually brought a new closeness between us.

Now she frequently includes David in thoughts and conversations, recalling memories of growing up with him as her big brother. She even has discussions with him in her mind and feels very close to him at times. Stories encouraged this miraculous change in her. Instead of avoiding situations that might make her cry, she learned to embrace her memories for the healing they impart.

Acknowledging emotions as a listener

Good stories, particularly ones that deal with loss and healing, can act as vehicles for people to grieve. Stories allow us to acknowledge deep emotions as we become immersed in the story and feel the pain, sadness, despair, and all the other feelings that result from loss. Then healing can begin.

Stories facilitate our feeling a wide range of emotions, a necessary task if we are to be more than robots. I witnessed just how important our emotions are as I observed a friend of mine who receives treatment for manic-depression. After her son was killed, Mollie frequently quit taking the prescription that kept her stable. Without medication, her tremendous mood swings led to numerous problems for her and her family.

Despite her suffering, Mollie reaches out to others because of her loving, caring nature. She helped me understand the necessity for all human beings to express and explore feelings. Knowing she had to cope, she followed her doctor's recommendations most of the time. Suppressing the anger she felt towards her son's killer led to an even greater depression than the one her medication was supposed to treat. One day I asked why she *ever* stopped taking her prescription and subjected herself to such pain and turmoil. With tears streaming down her face, she

> "I hope you never allow anybody to give you Valium at the time of such a crisis, as it will cheat you out of the chance to experience all your feelings, cry out all your pain, shed all your tears, so that you can live again, not only for your own sake, but for the sake of your family and all others whose lives you can touch!"
> Elisabeth Kubler-Ross
> *On Children and Death*
>
> ⇒≫

replied, "Because I need to feel something. After all, I've just lost my son and I have to grieve for him." At times the pain of *not feeling* was unbearable, and she longed to feel something—anything. Feeling pain was better than feeling nothing, for it assured her she was alive.

Mollie always encourages my storytelling—especially stories dealing with loss. She reminds me that people need opportunities to feel deeply in order to transform their pain. We spend much of our life hiding our feelings so that we do not appear weak or unstable. We fail to recognize the basic conditions that make us human and provide stability in the long run. Stories connect us to our emotions and show us how to process them.

Avoiding premature acceptance

Grief is the natural response to the pain of losing something you value. Organized religious groups often fail to recognize the need to grieve following loss. Statements about acceptance such as "it is God's will, trust all things to work together for good, God never gives you more than you can handle, consider it a learning experience, we all have our crosses to bear," and many others are *not* comforting, even thought they may be true. Such comments imply that if your faith is strong, you can deal with whatever happens. Simple answers and trite responses generate unnecessary guilt for those experiencing loss. The bereaved need consolation, not explanation.

Outsiders often impose their guidelines for grieving on others. "It's been a year now, so it's time to get on with your life" is commonly heard from someone who has never suffered a serious loss. I am constantly amazed at the statements well-meaning people make to bereaved parents. Following my loss, I spent the first year in shock, wondering how I might survive. Many attempts to comfort me were simply irritating. *Who put them in charge of the universe and the cosmic timetable and gave them all the answers?* As time passed, I missed David more and more. Increasingly stories, memories, and dreams provided an escape from clueless people and their expectations.

In an effort to help, people often strive to short circuit or shut down the grief process rather than facilitate it. The Compassionate Friends organization says that the only way to it (healing) is through it (grief).

Attempts to accept loss too quickly can lead to mental or emotional breakdowns or actual physical problems. I have seen people "fake it," usually because of pressure from friends and family to move on, only to fall apart later.

The community often views individual losses as events that can be moved beyond. But in fact, a significant loss forever colors the way we view the world. We become different people because of what we have experienced. Our self-image and former personality change, forcing us to redefine our world and ourselves.

> "Failure to mourn impairs a life. Most people's problems with mourning are not caused by compounded losses; their problems are caused by other people's desires to get mourning over with. Family, friends, and medical staff want accommodation of the loss as quickly as possible. Only through mourning can we find a life on the other side of loss. We need to grieve losses and find people who will accept that grieving. To grieve well is to value what you have lost."
>
> Arthur Frank
> *At the Will of the Body*
>
> ≈≫

Supplying individual needs

Following David's death, many of my storyteller friends sent me comforting stories that dealt with loss, grief, and healing in many different ways. Every story spoke to me and seemed to contain just what I needed at the time. Some of the stories were personal, others were literary, and many were traditional folktales.

Rabbi Fred Davidow sent me a book by Sue Alexander entitled *Nadia the Willful*, which I found especially helpful. In the story, a young girl's older brother dies in the desert, and her father forbids anyone to mention the boy's name. Nadia becomes angry and frustrated, forcing her to talk to others about her beloved brother. Only then does she find relief from her pain. Eventually she confronts her father and helps him understand that sharing memories can diminish his grief and keep his son alive. This story showed me that talking about David and sharing memories of him would preserve him forever in the hearts of those who loved him.

Nadia the Willful is a powerful story that deals directly with loss and healing. Being deeply touched by the story, I wanted to share it with others. When I contacted Sue Alexander to seek her permission, she explained that she had expressed her own grief and frustration by writing this story. Following the death of her twenty-nine-year-old brother, her father had refused to talk of his son.

The first time I told the story of Nadia to my older daughter, I sobbed uncontrollably through the entire story. Kathi said, "Mom, I think you need a little more work on this one." I read and told it to myself many, many times. Each time I grew a little stronger. I had to do a lot of processing before I was ready to involve others.

Now when I tell *Nadia the Willful* to an audience, listeners make connections to losses in their own lives, even though the story is written about a Bedouin tribe in the desert. Listeners substitute many different details for the ones in the book, enabling the story to speak to the areas where they need healing—from a loss or a communication failure or a missed opportunity. If that's not power, I don't know what is!

> "The mind-shift between pain and possibility depends on your willingness to feel, to become vulnerable." Rico believes this is done "by focusing on whatever you are feeling here and now, this very moment, and giving it your words on a page." Telling a story about these feelings takes the process one step further and allows even more healing to take place.
>
> Gabriele Rico
> *Pain and Possibility*
>
> ≪≈

Expressing emotions openly

During a discussion with friends about various ways of expressing emotions, the conversation eventually focused on how men and women communicate differently. Someone said men communicate to report and women communicate for rapport. Another added that women tend to have close friends with whom they share their feelings, while men have few close friends and mainly talk about sports and business. One man said that if sports didn't exist, most men wouldn't talk. He had noticed that the men in his family always reverted to talking about sports to avoid dealing with their feelings or any emotional situation.

Such descriptions of men and women are stereotypes, and certainly exceptions exist on both sides. Interestingly, almost *all* the storytellers I know, both male and female, are comfortable expressing feelings and use stories to explore inner emotions. Most of us have learned how valuable stories are when discovering who we are and how we want to live.

Empowering characters

Author and poet Louise Colln said stories helped her to heal following the death of her son from colon cancer and her husband from a malignant brain tumor. She described her healing process as "the telling (on paper) of stories, which gives some of my emotions to a fictional character and, as much as possible, works them out through the story." The ability to heal from stories "may be only true for those of us who tend to turn any emotion, happy or sad, into a creative structure," Colln added. Perhaps we should promote creative activity in others by encouraging them to tell their stories.

In beginning storytelling classes, workshops, and books, the first suggestion for telling a story is to know your characters. Actors do the same thing to make their roles come alive and be believable. Background information explains the emotions exhibited during the story, and we plug in our knowledge of those emotions to know how the individual feels and reacts in the situation being described. In order to tell a story well, a teller or writer must become all of the major characters by exploring their backgrounds, traits, feelings, and attitudes. Imagination plays a big part in the creative process since many necessary details are often missing. Good tellers try to stay true to the characters and meaning of a story but are always influenced by their own life experiences and individual interpretations.

Understanding the feelings of others enables us to transform losses in our own lives in healthy, productive ways as we see ourselves more clearly. Remembering how we *felt* in a given situation may be easier and more useful than knowing exactly what happened. Strong sentiments surrounding an event often indicate its significance to us and the importance of finding ways to cope.

In a speech to the Radio and Television correspondents, Garrison Keillor said that a good storyteller has to be able to feel everything that the major characters in the story feel. And not only do storytellers feel, they are willing to experience and share those feelings with others. I know now how blessed I was to be part of a community that knew the power of stories and was willing to share them openly with me.

Allowing vicarious expression

Gail Rosen tells healing stories in her bereavement programs, stressing their importance in grief work. She believes our culture ignores or minimizes any validation for intense pain as a reaction to loss. She told of a mall in Baltimore that, following Princess Diana's death in 1997, set up a microphone in the mall to allow people to talk about how her death affected them personally. Gail was amazed at the intensity of feelings many women expressed as they talked about Diana, some weeping openly for a woman they did not even know. Gail explained, "We don't know how to grieve our own losses, and Diana gave us a place to take care of our own needs vicariously through her. Somehow we recognized and acknowledged our pain through her death." Diana's story provided a focal point for personal grief, which is precisely what all stories of loss can do.

Similarly, following the bombing of the government building in Oklahoma City in April 1995, a storyteller told a gripping story on National Public Radio. Her story described the senseless killing of so many people and conveyed an overwhelming sense of loss and sadness. The story expressed many of the same feelings I was having. The devastating images created by her story were clearer than ones supplied by the news reports filled with gruesome pictures. While reporters' words told facts and details of the situation, the storyteller's pain poured forth as she reflected the suffering and loss of everyone in the community. I hoped that people were listening to and telling stories all over Oklahoma City to help connect to others and sort out what had happened, as they tried to make sense out of something that made no sense.

Much of the violence and unrest in America today may be connected to a general lack of emotional expression. A great need exists for us to tell and hear more stories—not only for healing after violent acts occur, but also to defuse the violence before it erupts. Just as stories open paths to healing after any loss, they can provide preventative maintenance, possibly avoiding conflict altogether. Listening to and telling stories present opportunities for recognizing and expressing feelings. As storyteller Dan Keding says at the end of one of his stories, "You can't hate someone when you've shared his stories."

Recovering events from memory

Emotions convey stronger messages than do facts. Many researchers believe that events are stored and tagged in the brain based on the *feeling* associated with the event. Therefore, to recover a story or event from our memory, we must first remember the associated feeling, which often can be triggered by another's story. Simply hearing a story sometimes leads to remembering our own stories.

Often writers and storytellers work through their losses by creating stories that openly deal with how they felt. Everyone I interviewed for this book felt stories had been valuable in healing from their own loss. Several also cited evidence of the power of stories to help and heal others. Many gained understanding by creating allegories or personal stories, or by finding stories relevant to their circumstances.

Stories from literature and folklore offer wisdom. Finding these stories and adapting them to our own situations can bring comfort

> "Stories have been healing to me because they have helped me to truly feel my grief without wallowing in it. At family gatherings, or just between my brother and me, I've always tried to encourage the telling of stories about people in the family who've died and whom we miss. There always is a mixture of sadness and joy in the telling. But the stories allow our sadness to be expressed, rather than repressed, and they open the door for other people to share their grief and their stories."
>
> Michael Parent
> National storyteller
>
> ➾

and healing. In addition, we can begin to see our own lives as stories while sharing stories with others. The use of stories to engender healing and growth is available to everyone. Once familiar with the power of stories, we recognize quickly how they provide new insights.

Of course, stories are not the only way to achieve healing in the aftermath of loss. Listening to music, spending time outdoors, getting physical exercise, helping others, seeking ways to be creative, and doing numerous other activities contribute to many healing journeys. I have found help and opportunities for growth in many pursuits, but stories afforded me the best results—immediate comfort and long-term growth. The process of composing and telling stories stimulates our imagination and encourages others, which promotes further resolution.

Living with loss

Everyone wants life to be happy and wonderful and beautiful, and stories to have happy endings. Unless they have experienced a significant loss themselves, even close friends do not know how to respond to our grief and the resulting sadness. Society seems to demand that we put on a happy face. As a result, when suffering a loss we clam up and bury our feelings deep within ourselves. Losing the capacity for emotional response may work for a while, but only until another crisis occurs.

We experience loss in all areas of our lives and find many ways to handle our feelings. A correct way for everyone to grieve does not exist, but often we look for quick, easy solutions for grief because of pressures from others and ourselves.

"All of us face hardship in our lives, but most of us are in fast retreat from the pain and suffering connected to it. We believe that we should be able to rid ourselves of pain. We think that suffering is a waste of time....we forget that suffering is an essential part of the human condition, one of the engines of human development."
    Polly Young-Eisendrath
    The Gifts of Suffering

    ⋘

Sometimes the pain is so intense that any remedy seems worth trying. When the pain from the death of my son was the most severe,

I was exhausted from coping with my emotions. I prayed that I would feel nothing. In my rush to stop the pain, I was seeking ways to turn off my feelings.False solutions such as silence, drugs, alcohol, meaningless activity, and overwork only prolong the healing process and can cause other problems to emerge. Instant cures may seem to deaden our awareness of pain, but the cause is still underneath.

Hearing another person's story can help us come to grips with our own lives. After hearing my story about David, an elderly woman told me that she thought she had fully grieved the death of her partner. She recognized unresolved issues that had prevented her from moving forward with her life. She grew hopeful as she saw new ways to deal with her loss.

Responding to grief

A significant loss and the resulting grief cause many different reactions in individuals experiencing loss. Books on grief therapy list the stages of grief with the emotions that accompany them. In reality, the bereaved experience all of these stages over and over during their grief process. You cannot just check one off the list and move to the next, since they resurface many times. Further, we often deny the emotions that accompany each stage.

The anger we feel after significant loss consumes a lot of energy and often is hard to recognize, particularly when there is nothing to focus the anger on. One of my son's best friends told me that when he heard about David's death, he destroyed everything in his office. I remember having a similar urge when we got that terrible phone call. I was in the dining room and had to restrain myself from smashing everything in sight. Reflecting on my response, I was shocked because I am *not* a violent person. Strong emotions had made me want to react and strike out at something—anything—without regard to the destruction that would result.

In the following months, I heard other parents relate stories of loss at meetings of The Compassionate Friends and saw anger consuming some of them. I knew anger was also still operating within me. *Maybe I should have broken all the dishes that night and relieved the immediate pressure.* Later, to release my anger, I went to the beach, screamed at the top of my lungs, and threw shells and driftwood into the ocean. Fortunately the pounding surf usually drowned out my noise and swept away my missiles, so that I was not locked up for being crazy. I wrote David's name in the sand in huge letters and watched the waves wash it away.

A year after David's death my mother observed that I still seemed angry. When she asked at whom was I angry, I replied, "The whole world. The whole world kept rocking along as usual when David was taken from me." She tried to talk me out of my anger, but I would not give it up. I know now that the anger I felt was sapping most of my energy, leaving little available for anything constructive. Even knowing that anger was one of the stages of grief and a natural response to loss did not make coping any easier.

Eventually my anger helped me heal, once I recognized it. One day I was so angry and missed David so much I could hardly stand it. Shouting at the ocean was not working. But all that energy had to go somewhere. I realized I hated David's death too much to let it have victory over me. Letting it take control by causing me to spend the rest of my life grieving was giving death too much power over me. I was determined not to be destroyed too. My anger slowly transformed into a new commitment and determination to do something positive with my life. Refocusing my anger freed up energy for use on creative solutions to change my outlook.

Rebuilding the lost self

After the initial shock of David's death had worn off, I felt like such a loser. In addition to losing my son, I lost my will to live and any self-confidence I might have had. Several years before, as an instructor for a computer software company, I had traveled alone all over the world to teach classes. Following David's death, I could barely make it to the grocery store. I no longer *believed* I could do anything. A severe, unexpected loss smashes your psyche, making you feel worthless and incompetent. I was no longer the fun-loving, light-hearted, capable person I once was. I felt and behaved like *a loser.*

As I listened to the stories of others, I began to regain my confidence. I did not perceive those who shared their stories with me

> "Stories allow us to see something familiar through new eyes. We become in that moment a guest in someone else's life, and together with them sit at the feet of their teacher. The meaning we may draw from someone's story may be different from the meaning they themselves have drawn. No matter. Facts bring us to knowledge, but stories lead to wisdom."
>
> Rachel Naomi Remen, M.D.
> *Kitchen Table Wisdom*
>
>

in a negative way. In fact, I admired their courage to talk openly about their losses and struggles. Gradually I was able to tell my story to individuals and small groups. Later I created a story about my son's life and death to share with larger audiences. ("Infinite Resource and Sagacity" can be found in Chapter 7.) The process took a long time, and I realize now that my damaged self was being repaired as I crept along. My self-confidence slowly returned, though I continue to struggle with it today. I am always amazed when listeners tell me how much my stories have helped them. The possibility that the power of story somehow works through me leaves me with a feeling of awe. Responses from audiences have helped tremendously to restore my positive feelings and have contributed to my healing. Feedback must be part of why we tell stories—some of us just need more than others.

Dealing with shame and guilt

Feelings of shame can be triggered by a loss, but rarely are connected to the loss experience itself. Shame can be left over from childhood when others used it as a way to control our behavior. I can still hear my mother saying, "You ought to be ashamed of yourself" or "Shame on you" when she caught me in the violation du jour. Since we rarely resolve shame issues, the feelings can control and inhibit us at times when we are vulnerable. In addition, the circumstances surrounding a loss can compound guilt and shame in a way that can be disabling since these feelings are seldom rational.

Guilt and the results that inevitably follow are natural in the wake of loss. Even when real reasons to feel guilty do not exist, we create them. We beat ourselves up with things we should have or could have done differently. Every sentence seems to begin with "If only...." Sensible explanations do not help at all. Nobody wants to be confused with reason when overpowering emotions are at work. Explanations based on guilt are often the only way to impose a sense of order on something that defies rational thinking.

I was convinced that my son's death must have resulted from something I did or failed to do since no other acceptable cause existed. *How could there be? Children don't die before their parents. Mothers are supposed to take care of their children. If something happens to a child, it must be the mother's fault.* To say *it just happened* admits no control—everything happens randomly. Life is a crapshoot, arbitrary, and on and on. And that is too frightening to consider.

So, I embraced the easiest explanation—*his death was my fault. If only we had not moved to Florida, we would not have given David the tree-pruning tool. He would not have been using it and been where an insect could sting him.* My husband's reply that if David wanted to prune that tree, he would have come to our house and gotten the pruning tool just like he had with every other piece of equipment we owned was way too logical. *I should have insisted that David pursue finding a treatment for the histamine disorder that his doctor had diagnosed.* The response that David was not a kid—he was twenty-nine years old and did as he pleased— was not satisfying. *If only we had still lived two miles away instead of four hundred, I might have stopped by when he started having trouble and been able to get him to the emergency room.* My mind churned through all the things that could have been different.

None of my imaginary scenarios seemed absurd as I sank deeper and deeper in my guilt and depression. As I listened to the guilt trips of other bereaved parents, I could not believe how far-fetched some of their explanations were—yet I knew the parents earnestly believed them. The faulty logic of their stories got through to me when reasoning could not. Slowly I realized my own answers made little sense, and I finally was able to let go of the grip guilt had on me.

In order to heal from a loss, we must examine our feelings of guilt. An important part of resolution is believing we have had a chance to tell our story, and people have listened and *heard* it. In telling about the experience, we begin to understand that our guilt is unfounded and can start to release it.

Allowing feelings to return

Many people are unable to heal following a loss because they do not know how to grieve. John McLaughlin said he failed to acknowledge and grieve the losses in his life for years, and added, "If you can help people learn to grieve, you're giving them a tremendous gift. Few places allow people that opportunity."

A friend said the loss of her son changed the way she related to others. Because of her own experience, she is a more caring, compassionate person who knew that listening to the stories of others makes a difference in their lives. In her work with senior citizens living in a nursing home, she noticed that residents who had lost children sixty or seventy years earlier still cried when asked about their families and wanted to tell their stories. They taught her that healing from a significant loss is never finished, but rather is an ongoing process that lasts a lifetime. One resident had never talked about her loss to anyone. Back when her child died, people weren't supposed to mention such thing, and nobody had ever asked.

> "Representing our world to others through story in innately human, as crucial to our soul's survival as breathing is to the survival of our body. Short-circuit this natural process and you will witness all forms of disease. It may show up as a physical symptom or as mental distress. More likely, it will appear under the guise of a nameless anxiety, or a general depression that we can't seem to attribute to anything in particular. These are the symptoms of an un-storied life."
>
> Richard Stone
> *The Healing Art of Story*
>
> ⇉

Stories enable us to discover more about ourselves as we recognize and express feelings, and therefore help us find meaning in our lives. Psychologist and storyteller Jim Granade said, "Humans are meaning makers." Life without feeling is empty and meaningless. When we feel deeply, we truly experience life and gain the understanding we seek. We think the opposite of joy is sorrow and of love hate. In reality, the opposite of all powerful feelings is the absence of feelings. One evening after David's death, I was watching the Van Cliburn piano contest and was suddenly overcome with emotion. As I sat there weeping, I tried to understand why I was so touched by the passion of these young gifted pianists. Watching them pour their hearts and souls into their performances was a beautiful thing to see. I recognized how much I missed my passions while attempting to avoid pain. I remembered David's passion for life and everything he did, and realized that feeling and expressing passion is what gives life meaning.

Learning from stories

Stories provide a way to thoroughly observe the behavior of another person. Recognizing another's problem is always easier than seeing your own. In many stories, the character's emotions, feelings, attitudes, and characteristics are blatantly obvious. Characters often suffer the consequences of their exaggerated actions, especially in folktales. For example, in "The Magic Pot" a woodsman finds a magic pot that doubles whatever he puts into the pot. He and his wife experiment with food and gold, and their greed grows out of control. During an argument over the use of their new wealth, his wife falls into the pot and suddenly the woodsman has two wives. This simple story provides a clear picture of the consequences of greed.

Likewise, in "The Magic Mustard Seed," a woman whose only son has died is completely consumed with her grief. The wise man in her village promises to make a healing potion for her if she can bring him a mustard seed from a home that knows no sorrow. Her obsession to obtain such a seed leads her to find healing as she helps others along the way. Her exaggerated behavior turns out to be her salvation.

In many of the traditional Jack tales, such as "Jack and the Beanstalk" and "Lazy Jack," Jack represents every man and woman struggling to make his or her way in the world. His exaggerated actions give clues about the folly of being trapped by foolish behavior. A story can create vivid pictures with very few words, connecting to things we already know. Seeing something clearly in a story leads us to recognize similarities in our real life situations. Watching Jack make mistakes and ultimately succeed encourages us to seek creative solutions to our problems.

In the midst of my struggle to find direction and purpose after David's death, I heard a story told by author Sophie Burnham at a conference. She heard it from a Buddhist monk, who encouraged everyone to tell the story. Her sentiment was the same when I asked her permission to tell it. The story showed me how difficult real and imaginary barriers are to break. I also saw how rage and anger could lead to further destruction, sadness, and loss. I do not remember the title and have never seen it in print, but I have included an abbreviated version here.

The Soldier

A Vietnamese soldier returned home from war to his wife and a young son that he had never seen. The child was three years old and was very suspicious of this stranger who had suddenly appeared. The wife cried for joy when her husband returned and felt that her prayers had been answered. She wanted to spend every waking moment with her husband, but when she saw how the child avoided his father, she knew it would be necessary for the father and son to spend some time by themselves.

And so the wise mother went into town for a while to give them a chance to be together and get to know each other. While she was away the soldier played with his child and tried everything he could think of to get the boy to call him "Daddy." No matter how hard the man tried, the boy would not even say the word. The young boy finally said, "No, I will not do it because you are not my daddy. Before you came here, a man came every night to be with my mother. She said he was so gentle and kind— I could see them from my bed. He always stood up and walked around when she stood and walked around the room, and always sat down when she sat. My mother talked to him late into the night, telling him how much she loved him and missed him and how being with him was all she ever wanted. When I asked her who she was talking to, she said it was my daddy."

The soldier was horrified, humiliated, and filled with rage that his wife had another man in his house while he was away. When his wife returned home, he refused to talk to her. Instead, he stomped out of the house and headed for the nearest bar, where he got very drunk. The next morning he returned in a drunken stupor and demanded his breakfast. After preparing the food, the wife asked her husband what was wrong, but his sense of pride made him storm out the door again and stay gone all day long. The same pattern continued for several days, and they did not talk to each other—one out of pride and the other out of fear.

Finally the wife could stand it no longer. How could it be that this man whom she loved with all her heart was so cold and harsh to her? What had the war done to him? Believing in his love had given her hope for the future, and now the love and the hope had vanished. In her despair she was so distraught that she went down to the river, threw herself into it, and drowned.

When her husband heard the news, he could not believe it and ran home to see for himself. Finding that it was indeed true, he picked up his son and wept bitterly. Friends and neighbors, who had stopped by to express their sympathy and concern, surrounded them. But late in the day, after everyone had gone home, the soldier found himself alone once again with the small boy.

As it began to grow dark, he put the young child to bed. Then he walked across the room to light the lamp. While the father was returning to his chair, the boy happened to glance up and saw his father's shadow on the opposite wall. The boy pointed to the shadow and cried out, "There, there is my father." And so it was.   .... And so it is.

I heard the message loud and clear. David's life had been about getting the most from every moment and I vowed to do the same. I knew what David wanted me to do. I certainly was not honoring him and his life by letting anger and despair ruin me, so I decided to *live* for both of us.

All of the stories I read and heard helped me look within to see what was keeping me in a state of emotional depression. Wounds must be exposed to light and air to heal. Other activities merely added band-aids without treating the cause. Stories went to the source and brought the problems into the open where understanding could flourish.

Opposite from quick fixes that only bring temporary relief, stories contribute to long-term healing by struggling with pain and meaning, emerging with hope for a new future based on what has been learned. Many people are not willing to put forth the time, hard work, and energy, but I knew the easy way out would not work for me. I had to plunge into the depths in search of answers in order to survive.

Recapturing life's joy

Stories helped reacquaint me with positive feelings—stories about David from others and from my own memory, as well as personal stories about overcoming loss. Because I was a storyteller and avid reader, I naturally searched for books and stories that offered comfort and understanding. Slowly the joy and passion started to return—in very small doses at first.

> "Joy has the power to open our hearts, remove fear, instill hope, and foster healing. Joy leads us to wisdom because it connects us to all we are—our mind, heart, power, and spirit. One of the most magical aspects of human existence is that grieving, or weeping for a loss, eases pain and opens the way to reconnect with joy."
>
> Charlotte Davis Kasl, Ph.D.
> *Finding Joy*
>
> ⇛

Before class one day, my yoga instructor read from the book *Finding Joy* by Charlotte Davis Kasl. According to Kasl, one of the barriers to joy is pent-up grief, sorrow, or anger. If we inhibit one feeling, we inhibit them all. Until we allow ourselves to fully experience all of the feelings within, joy will also be repressed.

Listening to Kasl's words I realized that joy had been missing from my life since David's death. After the initial mourning period, I could function in a way that probably seemed normal to an outsider. I exhibited all the appropriate behaviors and even laughed and smiled at times, but my life contained little joy. All feelings of genuine happiness disappeared the moment I heard of his death, and I doubted they could ever return. I did not understand what was going on, but looking back I can see that the pain and sorrow of losing him temporarily outweighed the joy of having him in my life for twenty-nine years.

I know I shut down emotionally because I was so tired of feeling pain and sadness. Stories have the potential to encourage joy as we let ourselves be part of the story and experience diverse emotions—from despair to ecstasy and everything in between. As I acknowledged feelings, even though vicariously through characters, I felt them myself. The door cracked open just a little. Jogging my memory made me realize that the capacity to experience joy was still within me. Along with that realization came the hope that I might be able to live fully and find happiness again.

Welcoming tears

Certainly good stories can move listeners by tapping in to their inner emotions. Tears result from joy, tenderness, compassion, and fear, as well as sadness. When we cry, we release tension and stress, opening the door that enables healing. I have seen hundreds of people experience the healing effects of a well-told story at the National Storytelling Festival in Jonesborough, Tennessee. Given our society's attitude toward expressing emotion in public, that is powerful medicine.

> "To be alive is to feel pain and to hide from pain is to make yourself less alive. We diminish our souls if we try to avoid, deny or hide from pain. We often turn to painkilling medications, which diminish our ability to feel anything at all....[Some people] have never learned to let themselves feel...are too inarticulate in the language of grief to know what is happening. Putting on the armor keeps us from being hurt, but it also keeps us from growing. The danger is that we will become so good at not feeling pain that we will learn not to feel anything—not joy, not love, not hope, not awe. We will become emotionally anesthetized."
>
> Rabbi Harold Kushner
> *When All You've Ever Wanted Isn't Enough*
>
> ❧

In the book *When All You've Ever Wanted Isn't Enough*, Rabbi Harold Kushner told of a widow whose husband died from tragic circumstances. Friends, psychiatrists, and clergy, all trying to say just the right words to make her feel better, surrounded her. She found no comfort until an uneducated, old man entered the room, walked over to her, and began crying with her. He was the only one who connected with her and really *shared* her pain.

I will never forget a man with whom I worked coming up to me at the funeral home following my son's death. Tears were streaming down his face as he looked at me and shook his head. Pain and sorrow filled him. He hugged me and said he was so sorry about David, then apologized for his tears and said something about wishing he could be more comforting. A lot of people were present that night—most of whom I cannot recall—but I remember Tom clearly. He shared my loss and grief at a time when I did not need people to be strong and stoic. I needed to know they understood the depth of my feelings of loss.

Continuing the healing

Even though I have dealt with David's death at a deep, personal level, I revert to avoidance mode at times. When I fail to pay attention to my grief, something occurs when I least expect it and fills me with pain and despair. Everything stays on track when I stay in tune with my loss and what it means in my life.

I continuously seek inspirational stories that offer encouragement when I need it. Many periodicals, such as *Reader's Digest,* contain heartwarming stories, and sometimes even the daily news can be uplifting. Rereading or telling stories about David reaffirms my beliefs and turns negative thoughts around. Once my attitude changes, I am more aware of the positive things happening in the world around me. When I reach out, something or someone responds to boost me on my upward climb once more.

While writing this book, I entered a slump where I could *not* force myself to write. Depression played a part, but I could not understand my complete lack of motivation since I strongly believed in the importance of what I was trying to do. Self-doubting questions abounded. *How can you possibly write a book about how stories heal when you need healing yourself? Do you think you are an expert on grief, healing, or anything? Why would anyone want to read anything you have written?* On and on... Thoughts filled with the deep sadness and cruel irony of David's death swirled in my mind. The pieces did not fit into a story, but I could not dismiss the images.

Because I was attending a memoir class and needed to write something for an assignment, I created "Oktoberfest"—the story of the circumstances leading up to David's death. The details seemed too painful to put into words, and yet I knew I had to do something to move past the events that were dominating my thinking. I sobbed the whole time I was writing, as I searched to recapture the feelings and find the words to describe them. As always, the story did its work. I have included it here as an example of how getting in touch with feelings and emotions through story can be a powerful healing agent.

Oktoberfest

David never did anything halfway—anything he was interested in, that is. So when he decided to have an Oktoberfest, we all knew it would be spectacular. The first thing he did was brew a special Oktoberfest beer for the occasion. His interest in brewing beer was his current obsession, and he did brew good beer. He acquired and made tons of brewing equipment and even tried growing his own hops. He joined a local home-brew club and was studying to become a tasting judge. He worked with the state legislature to legalize brewing beer at home, which opened the way for the many brewpubs that later appeared in the Atlanta area. When the bill finally passed, he had his picture taken with the governor.

While the beer fermented in jugs in his basement, he made other preparations for the party. He designed elaborate invitations on his computer and mailed them to all of his friends weeks in advance of the party. He wanted them to anticipate it as much as he did. He recorded all of the German drinking songs and related music he could buy or borrow. He found recipes for dark German bread and began baking loaves to store in the freezer. He called almost daily for other recipes, things like German potato salad and sauerkraut. He drove to Helen, a touristy, alpine village in the north Georgia mountains, to purchase an Oktoberfest flag to fly at the party, and while there bought a complete lederhosen outfit to wear, including the hat with a feather. All sorts of bratwurst and other sausages were ordered.

His excitement increased as the party grew nearer. One of the things nobody knew was that he intended to announce at the party that he and his wife, Jennie, were expecting a baby, making them the first of their many friends to become parents. Even Jennie did not know how he would break the news, which had been a recent shock to both of them. Having recovered and adjusted, she knew he would do something crazy and spectacular to fit the news and the occasion.

But then four days before the party while working in the yard, he was stung or bitten by a bee or insect. When Jennie came home from work, she found him lying face down on the kitchen floor. He held the cordless phone in his hand and it was turned on, but he never made a call. Jennie dialed 911, but it was too late. An allergic reaction had caused his heart to stop.

*From the hospital, my daughter called us in St. Augustine and said, "David's gone." **Gone where?** She became hysterical and handed the phone to her sister. The details followed and the nightmare started. I screamed until my voice was gone, and I wanted to break everything in sight. Trying to get things ready—trying to pack to go to my son's funeral—trying to hold it together to get to my daughters and Jennie—even trying to think—was impossible. It could not be true. Not David—he was too full of life—only 29 years old. I had talked with him the night before. My mother had just said she had never known anybody who loved life as David did. There had to be some mistake.*

Finally, we started the long drive to Atlanta and arrived at four in the morning. Jennie told us that she was two months pregnant. It seemed like some cruel joke filled with tears and despair. All of the arrangements, the phone calls, the decisions... Each new voice and face that appeared intensified the pain and grief. We all headed down into a deep, dark chasm that had no end.

And so on October 2, 1993, everyone who knew and loved David gathered to be with him. Everyone was there—they had all been invited. But instead of partying at the Oktoberfest as planned, they attended his funeral. Two close friends asked to play music at the service and poured out their souls on the violin and oboe in a heart-rending tribute to him. Instead of joking and laughter, there was cry-

ing and pain. Instead of carrying on with their foolishness, his six best friends carried his body down the aisle of the church. They were just kids—too young to be carrying a coffin. At the cemetery, a large black crow in a tree overhead screamed during the entire burial service. The harsh noise demanded everyone's attention and we somehow felt it was David, telling us not to be sad. Although free of his body, his spirit was still with us.

Everyone went back to the house where the Oktoberfest flag was flapping in the breeze on that warm fall afternoon. So many people and so much food… After we ate, some of David's friends said they were going to the basement to tap the keg—they knew that's what he wanted. We all went down and sat around on the floor of that damp space where he worked his magic with grain and hops and yeast. In the midst of our tears and grief, we shared our crazy stories and memories about David and everyone agreed the beer was his best by far. Wherever he was, he must have been smiling.

Then we lifted our glasses and gave a silent toast to his life.

-»)«-

When I finished writing, my tremendous burden had vanished. Struggling with my inner emotions in the story had freed me to get beyond them. The overwhelming feelings of sadness and lethargy floated away, and I was able to continue with my research and writing with renewed commitment. I even had the feeling that David was playing an active role in my growth. Reliving the events was painful, but I also found comfort in the memory of the closeness we all felt sharing stories that day down in the basement.

When I finished writing, I went for a long walk and felt new energy and motivation flowing into me. I was more convinced than ever that stories *can* and *do* heal. I had experienced first-hand how powerful they can be, though the healing process was not complete. As everything in life continues to change, the need for stories never ends.

Stories render meaning from chaos 2

Asking the right questions

Finding answers to unanswerable questions is not easy and requires a lot of internal struggle as we seek to redefine our world following a significant loss. Firming up beliefs enough to write or tell a story about them strengthens the beliefs even more. Comprehending our thoughts sufficiently to communicate them to someone else takes the understanding to an even deeper level. In addition, the process validates and gives credibility to our struggle, and the results can help others cope with their own situations.

Following a loss, especially the loss of a child, nothing makes sense or can be understood—except perhaps a story. For weeks after David's death, doubts and questions swirled in my head. *Why did this happen? Why did it happen to David? Why to me?* The explanations I sought were evasive, and the existing facts were meaningless. I continued asking over and over as if finding the right answers would make everything okay. *If I could discover the precise question and stumble on the answer, surely I would understand.* Finally my daughter said to me, "Mom, you are driving yourself crazy with those *why* questions. There are no answers and you have got to stop. Start asking questions that do have answers."

Gradually I realized she was right. No healing could take place as long as I was hung up on knowing *why*. Even if I had gotten the answers to all of my questions, David was gone and that was my real problem. All the explanations in the world would not bring him back.

> "There is enormous satisfaction, even joy, in giving shape to feelings by framing them in language. And framing allows us to reframe—reorganize—and see things from a different perspective. Discovering your own meanings in your own words transforms potentially self-destructive feelings into creative acts, lets you become a do-er, instead of a passive victim. Your pain becomes manageable, explorable, transformable into unexpected patterns of meaning."
>
> Gabrielle Rico
> *Pain and Possibility*

Only when I quit asking *why* did I open myself to the possibility of healing. Then my mind turned to other issues. *How can I go on living in spite of what has happened? What was David's life and death all about? What can I learn from the experience? How can I share what I have learned with others? What can I do to honor his memory and show others how important he was to me?* Making these discoveries required major soul searching, but I knew I could find them if I searched diligently. I realized the process would require work and investigation into areas I had never explored. I also knew resolving the issues was imperative for me to live in a meaningful way. I was open and ready to experience the power of stories.

Learning from others

The discovery progressed slowly, painfully, and not always in a forward direction. The stories of others who had experienced loss penetrated my shell and allowed me to see that I was not alone. These people and their stories offered solutions that started my renewed interest in life. They helped me understand and grow in ways I did not know were possible.

The Compassionate Friends played a tremendous part as I attended meetings and listened to the stories of others in various stages of grief. So many people had experienced loss and understood my feelings. That knowledge sustained me and gave me hope that I might survive. As I observed other bereaved parents talking, laughing, and experiencing life and love and friendship, I thought *maybe, just maybe, I'll be like that again.*

I also read everything I could find about loss, death, and grief. Clinically written books bored me with facts and figures and stages and lists. While they furnished useful information, the words sounded academic unless the author had personally experienced loss. I sought wisdom from people's hearts, not their intellect. My sensitivity was so heightened that it was easy to recognize those who really spoke from experience. An interesting example is the book, *The Problem of Pain*, by C. S. Lewis. The description on the cover says, "The intellectual problem raised by human suffering, examined with sympathy and realism." This book contrasts sharply to his later book, *A Grief Observed*, which Lewis wrote following his wife's illness and death. The first book he wrote from his mind, and the second poured from his heart.

The books written by parents who lost a child were the most helpful, especially at first. I read at least twenty-five books written by survivors of loss and learned something from each one. Clearly each writer learned and grew as he or she wrestled with the same issues I had. Through their struggles they strengthened their understanding about life and death enough to share them with others.

Several authors confessed that they had created their stories for their own growth and development without any intention of making them public. Yet the refining process that took place enabled new insights and understanding. As long as thoughts are nebulous, grasping and making sense of them is impossible. The struggle to create the story boils all the issues down to their essence, their truth. The refining process goes even further when those truths are shared with other people. Rev. John Claypool said, "The truth never lies in any one person, but among all those who truly seek it." The healing power of shared stories provides a perfect example.

Parents who write books seem driven to tell the whole story— background information about their lives and the lives of their children, events leading to the death, the emotional turmoil and grief that followed, and finally the outcome of living with the loss. The resolution usually becomes the focus of the book, and includes their struggle with despair, what they learned, how they coped and reached the decision to carry on with life, and what enabled them to find hope.

Most authors express the importance of hearing the stories of others to feel understood and connected. They mention the value of writing their story down and/or telling it to others. Many authors also include a list of organizations, books, tapes, and techniques for finding help. Each story is the author's attempt to make sense of the tragedy of loss.

Adjusting our vision

Trying to impose meaning and structure on an incident that makes no sense is a difficult task. The process of rendering all the conflicting events down to an acceptable essence that offers hope for the future enables tremendous growth and healing. Ignoring this process often results in getting stuck in the grief process. The bereft *must* complete this necessary work in order to return to a fulfilling life.

Coping with loss of any kind is frustrating, inconvenient, and time consuming. Having something we value suddenly snatched away seems unfair and unjustified, but happens frequently as part of our life process from birth to death. A friend recently shared with me how much memory loss he had suffered following major surgery. The loss has made it difficult for him to work as he once did. Prior to the operation he was able to write a twenty-five page technical document without looking up facts and specifications. He was frustrated and depressed with his diminished abilities since immediate recall had always been such an important part of his life and work. I told him he had just experienced the memory loss all at once that most people deal with gradually as they age. He maintained his loss had nothing to do with age, but rather was caused by oxygen deprivation during the surgery. He had enjoyed the gift of an incredible memory longer than most people ever do.

All significant losses disrupt our lives, and therein lies the rub. Our conversation reminded me of an incident that happened to me years ago, which I later shared with my friend. Many times we take for granted the gifts in our lives and do not even recognize them as gifts until they are gone. Only then do we comprehend their value.

Perfect Vision

I always had perfect vision and never wore glasses except for a brief time in high school when I conned my parents into getting glasses for me even though the eye doctor said the minor correction was not really necessary. I just thought wearing glasses was cool at the time. I wore them for a few weeks and then lost them, and that was the end of that. I had incredible vision—I could read street signs a long way off and never had problems reading even the smallest print.

As my friends turned forty, I laughed while watching them struggle to read the newspaper and kidded them about getting old when they all started wearing glasses. I thought, "That will never happen to me. My perfect vision will never change." And then I turned forty-four. Almost overnight I could not read the phone book or the newspaper without holding it at arms' length. Even reading the cooking directions on a package was aggravating. Finally I went to the doctor and had to get reading glasses, which I constantly misplaced. I grumbled and complained a lot when I could not see something I needed to read and even more when I had to get stronger glasses.

My daughter Kathi heard me one day and said, "Mom, I don't have one bit of sympathy for you. I have worn glasses since I was four years old. At least you can still see, and you don't even have to wear your glasses most of the time. You just need to get a grip." She was right, of course, but I still hated it. Having had such good vision, I did not want to give it up. It was a pain not to be able to see everything with ease as I once had. And then I remembered about Kathi's eyes.

When Kathi was four, I noticed her eyes crossing as she watched television one day. I thought she was doing it on purpose and said, "Stop that, Kathi." She laughed and refocused her eyes as she looked up at me, but soon they were crossed again as she looked at the TV. Again I told her to stop, but when the same thing happened several more times, I decided to call the pediatrician. He told me that four-year-olds do not have the muscle coordination to cross their eyes intentionally and said for me to get her into his office immediately. He said one of three things could cause it—a brain tumor, something equally bad that I cannot remember, or extreme farsightedness.

Fortunately it was the latter. We took her to an eye clinic where she was diagnosed with amblyopia, known as lazy eye, and hyperopia. It took a lot of therapy, filters, and glasses to get her vision corrected. I was so upset at first that my precious little girl with her big blue eyes and long eyelashes had to wear glasses—after all, I never had. But when I stopped to think what it could have been, I was relieved that her problem could be corrected. She has worn glasses or contacts ever since and still sees poorly without them. Playing sports was a problem for her, and there were many trips to get her glasses repaired and adjusted. Her younger sister accidentally knocked them out the window of the car one day, and Kathi could barely see until we got another pair. So it is no wonder she had little patience with me.

After a while I adjusted to my reading glasses. Now I am grateful my vision is still as good as it is. A lot of people who cannot see at all would give anything to have my eyes and my vision for one hour. Knowing that helps me to look at my long-time perfect vision as a gift and makes me realize that sometimes even perfect vision needs correcting.

Reviewing the details

Some ways of dealing with loss bring growth and make us better people, while others bring more pain, suffering, and bitterness. An adjustment period is necessary and rarely happens immediately. Reliving the experience in a story can be helpful to gain perspective and understanding. Perhaps those who are familiar with putting events in a story format have an advantage. Storytellers and writers are accustomed to recording events and using a structure that eventually promotes understanding. In the struggle to get ideas and thoughts together and to record them in a meaningful way for future use, a refining process takes place.

I had been a storyteller and lover of stories even before David's death. After he died I looked at stories I already knew—even ones I had told—from a different point of view. Many of them contained insights I had never noticed. As I looked at these familiar stories in a new way, I started to look at my life in a new way too—*a re-viewing or re-visioning.* I considered the possibility of using parts of my old life to create a new one based on what I had experienced. Although I would never be exactly the same, perhaps I could be better.

We need to distinguish between *healing* and *curing.* According to *Webster's New World College Dictionary,* cure specifically suggests "the elimination of disease, distress, evil, etc." and healing is "the making or becoming whole." Curing implies that some things cannot be cured when evidence of the previous problem still exists. Healing, on the other hand, is always possible as long as we are alive and have opportunities to learn and grow. The pain of losing my son will never be cured, but I have learned things along the way that allowed me to move toward wholeness. Ironically, the suffering that resulted from loss became the very thing that caused the growth.

As Dean Ornish wrote in his book *Love and Survival,* "Healing may occur even when curing is not possible." Ornish wrote about Victor Frankl, the physician and psychiatrist imprisoned at Aushwitz, and said Frankl observed that the concentration camp survivors were able "to find a sense of meaning in the midst of the horrible experience." The survivors could never be cured of the damage done to them in prison, but found healing by looking at life in a new way. If nothing is learned, then all of the pain and suffering is for naught. If something is learned, that knowledge must be shared to be fully realized.

Finding new insights

Sustaining a significant loss almost always forces us to reexamine what is important and ultimately leads to the age-old question, *what is the meaning of life?* Many of the oldest stories explore mankind's greatest questions, and certainly stories today continue to struggle to make sense of what happens in the world. An anonymous quote provides a clue. "Is life worth living? It depends on the liver."

People ask questions about the meaning of life even when they have not experienced loss. However, following a loss, particularly the death of a loved one, finding answers becomes necessary for surviving and continuing to live in a meaningful way. Without the answers that only come through soul searching, the desire to continue living is gone. Mary Semel in the book *A Broken Heart Still Beats* said that following

> "The thing that helped me was telling the story of what happened—absolutely a crucial part of any kind of healing from grief. Telling the story of what happened helps you to make sense of it. When something this tragic happens—something that causes this much grief—you have to re-sort your life out in order to make sense of it again."
>
> David Holt
> Musician and storyteller

the death of her son, any feeling of a sense of order was destroyed and led her to the question, "What kind of universe is this anyway?"

Following David's death, my life was so dramatically changed that I no longer wanted to live in the world without him. I knew I could never take my own life because of the pain my death would cause those who loved me, people who had suffered greatly because of David's death. I simply had no desire to get up in the morning or face life without David. Fortunately, I slept a lot, which offered the only peace and escape I found, and afforded my subconscious the chance to begin healing without my awareness. I dreamed a lot and remembered the dreams vividly when I awoke in the morning. I did not need to be a rocket scientist or Carl Jung to know what was going on. My whole being was trying to extract meaning from all the chaos I felt. A few months following David's death, I had the following dream.

My husband and I went to eat in a large building containing many restaurants. We were seated in one restaurant, which was not where we wanted to be, when we noticed another restaurant had opened. We asked a waiter if we could change and he said that would be fine because they were all really connected. In the process of moving we met up with old friends and they asked us to join them for dinner. Two long tables ran the entire length of the room with some small tables around the edge. We tried to find a place for four, but every table we went to was unsuitable—not enough chairs, too small, already occupied or something. We scurried around for quite a while before leaving, but were never able to find a spot that would work. Finally we left without eating at all.

Not being able to find something that fits describes the way I felt after David's death. Everything that once made up my belief system and my world changed with his death, and the feeling of confusion reflected in my dreams. These types of dreams continued for months, but gradually changed as the next dream illustrates.

I was in a large room getting ready to tell stories. All of a sudden David came into the room. I ran over to him, grabbed and hugged him, and said, "Oh David, I have missed you so much." He hugged me back for a long time and said, "I've missed you too, Mom." I could feel the warmth of his arms around me. I did not think he was dead, only that he had been away and we had not seen each other for a long time. I told him I was sorry, but that I had to do the program and asked him to wait. He said that was fine. I got ready to start and noticed that everyone in the room had faced his or her chair toward the large window at the back of the room and was not looking at me at all. I thought, "Oh well, I'll just start anyway." But just as I began I noticed a large tornado headed toward our building, and I yelled for everyone to get away from the window and get on the floor. The tornado circled the building—round and round until finally the roof lifted off and the rain started pouring in—and then left. As David walked toward me I said, "Well, what did you think of that?" He replied, "Pretty wild." Then we started laughing and I said, "We might as well go since the roof is gone and we're getting soaked." We left together and as I was waking up, I had the very clear, strong impression that David was saying to me, "See, I really do communicate with you in your dreams and stories."

My dream reassured me that he is there. The tornado destroyed the existing scene and seemed to represent his death. Although the approaching storm frightened me, it did not take David away. Everyone was facing the window but did not see the approaching tornado. Only when I warned them did they see the danger and react. *What did all of this mean?*

I often have an increased sense that David is with me when I tell stories, and I frequently ask for his guidance during a program. I believe he can get my attention when I tell stories because I am so tuned in to the moment that my internal filters are diverted. He encourages me to tell stories about his life and death so that people can find ways to accept and acknowledge the value of their losses. We must learn to treasure what we have in life, remembering how quickly it can disappear.

Kahlil Gibran said in *The Prophet,* "And ever has it been that love knows not its own depth until the hour of separation." Gibran expresses so beautifully what many others have felt. When my son was alive, I loved him and appreciated what he added to my life, and I valued the time we spent together. But I never realized how much until he was gone. In reflecting on and sharing the significance of his life with others, I grasp the real value more fully.

Every time I work on another story about some aspect of his life or my relationship to him, I gain new insight into the meaning of life itself. I know I am on a spiritual journey that will continue to the end of my life and beyond.

Sharing the struggle

Many professional storytellers tackle heavy subjects in their stories, but respect the importance of taking care of the listeners. Performances are quite different from sharing a story with a single listener or in a small, intimate group. When telling a story of loss to a large audience, the teller must take the story beyond the actual events to a deeper level of understanding. Sometimes the real truth lies beneath the facts. Sharing what has been learned through the struggle increases the potential of healing for everyone.

Susan Klein is a storyteller, writer, teacher, and coach from Martha's Vineyard. In her workshop "Storytelling from the Inside Out," she said, "Never abandon your listeners in a heavy personal story. If you take them into a bleak situation, you must

> "The task...is to find the theme of our life and the language to hold it, so there can be dialogue between ourselves and our lives.... In order to tell a story, we often bring things in from different places and place them alongside each other so that they and the story are illuminated by their relationship...we see their relationship, and the story is deepened and transformed."
> Deena Metzger, "Stories That House Our Souls"
> *Nourishing the Soul*

bring them back out." This requires the teller to deal with the emotional baggage of the story so it is not dumped on the listener to carry. The audience wants to hear a story, not act as a therapist. The story must contain redemption and hope before being told to an audience. Listeners need to know that survival is possible and life can be meaningful and joyous even on the other side of loss.

"Infinite Resource and Sagacity," my first story about David's death, was definitely not ready to tell to others in the early stages of development. In fact I originally thought the story was only for me and my healing. But with help, encouragement, and a lot of thought and tears, the story began to touch the lives of listeners in a positive way. Some of my stories may never be told to an audience, but creating and writing them helped me focus and redefine my beliefs.

Teaching with stories

Erica Helm Meade is a professional storyteller and therapist who teaches the use of healing stories to other therapists. Her book, *Tell It by Heart - Women and the Healing Power of Story*, shows how storytelling can be used in personal, professional, and therapeutic settings. The book is a collection of case studies in which stories brought about resolution and healing. Most "were inspired by therapeutic work with women of various ages and ethnic backgrounds, each of whom embraced a story as her guide through a process of meaningful change." Almost all of the women had experienced some form of loss and were gently guided to healing through the use of a story. Meade allowed the story to do its work so the women gained the insights they needed.

Throughout the book, the power of stories clearly helped women focus on their lives and discover ways to heal themselves and their relationships. When asked which stories deal with recovery, Meade said, "Out of the fifty or so fairy tales I knew, I couldn't think of one that wasn't about healing from family trauma."

Gail Rosen teaches workshops about storytelling and story listening in grief work. She also works with and tells stories for hospice groups. Many of her stories seemingly have nothing to do with healing or loss, but are powerful agents for healing and growth. As an example, Gail

> "Finding stories that speak to me and telling them to others has definitely been part of my spiritual journey. We all tell the stories we need to hear, and when I tell them, again and again, their wisdom and the comfort they provide have a chance to become a part of my soul and psyche, not just my mind."
>
> Gail Rosen
> Storyteller
>
>

mentioned the Jewish folktale/song of "The Poor Little Tailor." The story tells of a tailor who made a jacket from his worn-out coat, then a vest from the coat, then a cap from the vest, then a button from the cap, until all that was left was a story. As each item wore out, he *made do* by making something else of value. While reflecting on the story, one of Gail's listeners saw the value of being able to "make do or make something out of whatever you have left." This insight provides a creative way to look at handling loss of any kind.

When I told *There's No Such Thing as a Dragon* by Jack Kent in schools, children pointed out to me the reason I have been drawn to this story since I first heard it. In the story a dragon grows larger and larger because nobody will pay attention and believe it is real. When a five-year-old boy acknowledges the dragon's existence by patting it on the head, the dragon shrinks to the size of a kitten and becomes manageable again. The story provides a wonderful analogy for the way most people deal with loss. So often we fail to recognize and deal with our problems while they are still controllable. Several adults have said this story helped them to recognize their *dragon,* which was the first step in taming it.

Redefining life's values

Following my loss, surviving and moving forward required me to reexamine my life and set new priorities. A lot of my previous concerns seemed so insignificant and unimportant. I developed a low tolerance for the trivial issues that consume other people. I had come to realize that in the whole scheme of things, so much really does not matter. We often spend excessive amounts of time, energy, and money as if the outcome is critical.

Figuring out what was important and then concentrating my resources in those areas became crucial. I had to discover who I was at the deepest level and explore areas that supported a new belief system. Many of my old habits made no sense when examined in the face of significant loss. I thought of all the time I had wasted cleaning house, looking for the *right* gift or outfit, trying to get a good tan, and doing other time-consuming activities. Surely life held more meaning than that.

Most of the people I interviewed went through similar processes following loss. Many reported not being able to sit through long meetings or spend time engaged in meaningless dialogue. Most looked within themselves to find out what they valued and then sought or created stories that expressed those values.

In *Composing a Life,* Mary Catherine Bateson spoke of life as "an improvisatory art...the way we combine familiar and unfamiliar components in response to new situations." Not only did she describe life, but she also gave a good explanation of what we have to do after experiencing a significant loss. Bateson said "Self-knowledge is empowering...storytelling is fundamental to the human search for meaning whether we tell tales of the creation of the earth or of our own choices." Self-knowledge is empowering, but some people may not be willing to seek it.

"Story has always been a part of my life—long before it became the basis for my career. Now I tell the stories that touch my soul or rattle my funny bone—both centers of healing—and I teach storytelling and memoir writing because those are two ways that people make sense of their lives. Maybe that's what healing is—re-making sense."

Susan Klein
Storyteller and teacher

≪≪≪

Two types of people live in the world. One group prefers to live life on the surface and seeks books, movies, stories, plays, and interests that are primarily entertaining. The other group digs deeper to search for meaning and understanding and prefers intellectual challenges in order to think, process, and grow. Those who experience a significant loss no longer have the option, as they seek to understand the loss and redefine their life's values.

> "Meaning is at the core of the creative process and of story-telling. It is both the goal and the attribute. When it is our own life story or an incident from our lives we are telling, we become aware that we are not the victims of random and chaotic circum-stances. Despite our grief or feelings of insignificance, we are living meaningfully in a meaningful universe. And, again, the response to our own story, as well as the stories of others, is 'Yes. Yes, I have a story. Yes, I exist.'"
>
> Deena Metzger
> *Writing for Your Life*

I have never accepted anything without asking *why*. Struggling with the question always enables growth. Many stories wrestle with the answers to important questions, which may explain our attraction to certain stories. As Viktor Frankl said in *Man's Search for Meaning*, "Life ultimately means taking the responsibility to find the right answer to its problems and to fulfill the tasks which it constantly sets for each individual." Based on his observations and experiences as a prisoner in the Nazi concentration camps, Frankl realized the meaning of life can never be defined in a general way. Rather, each individual must discover the right action and conduct for his or her life at any given time.

When life has changed, finding new insights and understanding is critical. Stories provide a good source for learning because they often contain more truth than the facts, as we know them. If we look for what they have to teach us, we can gain some of the wisdom that has been a part of storytelling since the beginning of time. The stories that survive through the years are ones people find helpful in under-standing the world

Seeing the whole story

We search for meaning and purpose throughout our lives. Stories help us understand how isolated events fit into our life story. Gail Rosen has always been drawn to stories that deal with the big questions because they offer guidance and "have the power to help people find their way by affirming and normalizing many of the common reactions to grief and by offering a model of wholeness and healing." This guidance emerges as we share our stories and validate each other.

Knowing we still exist and have a meaningful story is vital to survival when faced with significant loss. Our initial reaction to loss makes us believe we live in a random and chaotic world, which is a bleak outlook. Shakespeare provided an example of this despair in Macbeth's response upon being told that the queen was dead.

> *Life's but a walking shadow; a poor player,*
> *That struts and frets his hour upon the stage,*
> *And then is heard no more: it is a tale*
> *Told by an idiot, full of sound and fury,*
> *Signifying nothing.*

Creating the focus

People and stories guide us to meaning in life no matter what has happened in the past. Gradually we see we still have choices to make in the future. In her book *Writing for Your Life*, Deena Metzger explained, "A story is like a lens or a frame: it gives focus, it unifies, and it organizes diverse images into a coherent meaning. Without frame or focus, the events would be random and disconnected. Story provides the relationship, the links, and the connections. One of the reasons we tell stories is that the existence and the nature of relationships becomes clear in the process of telling."

Many find writing poetry helpful to organize thoughts and images, since the process often requires even more condensing of important feelings. Bereavement newsletters are filled with the creative efforts of those struggling to deal with loss through poetry. The poems reflect pain and growth, and help others to recognize their own feelings.

A good friend, Vern Hotchkiss, wrote a book of poetry entitled *Of Death and Recovery* following his wife's death. He said, "In some ways, recovery is the wrong word to use here. You don't ever recover from the loss of a loved one. In another sense, however, there is indeed a recovery that comes from accepting what has happened and proceeding with a decision to continue living, growing and loving."

He found writing poetry extremely therapeutic because of the discipline required to turn his thoughts into a poem, which further helped him refine his ideas.

Vern wrote the following poem for me when David died. His thoughtfulness and caring touched me and let me know that he understood and shared my pain.

WHY

Why must they die so young, Lord
Full in the prime of life
We cannot comprehend what gain
Can come from so much strife

What is beyond the veil, Lord
Which carries them away
Their life's ambitions unfulfilled
Their dream for each new day

Where do we go from here, Lord
This loss has made us numb
With humble, grieving, aching hearts
We seek to overcome

We can but trust in you, Lord
For meaning to it all
Please help us to endure the pain
Which casts such bitter pall

With anguish and despair, Lord
We ask you for your love
There is no way for us to stand
Save help from heav'n above

Creating a story requires the same discipline to consolidate our thoughts—especially when preparing it to share with others. Gathering all the pieces and combining them in a way that makes sense requires concentration. Most losses do not fit with our picture of how the world should be, so imposing order may seem impossible at first. Yet to force structure and a sense of understanding on random events ultimately has value. Looking at all aspects of loss renders what is significant, important, and lasting. Though the creative process may be painful, healing becomes possible as the big picture comes into focus.

Stories penetrate barriers with images 3

Building a relationship

When our world is filled with grief and pain, seeing ourselves clearly is impossible. A fogbank surrounds our mind, closing off the outside to prevent more suffering. Because stories catch us off guard, they penetrate through to our subconscious without our awareness. Stories boost healing because they "act as a kind of 'open sesame' for other therapeutic factors of treatment to enter—factors that develop and reinforce healthy choices and changes," according to clinical social worker Lee Wallas. She uses stories with patients in therapeutic situations and feels "by establishing rapport and lowering resistance, we can open the door for the unconscious to accept the metaphor of a story and to incorporate ideas for new possibilities." Stories provide a safe haven for dealing with intimate subjects in a controlled environment. We trust stories to take care of us. So they are like a soothing balm to a wound, which may be festering down underneath the surface.

> "Stories are metaphors for our own experiences. We can fit them into the framework of our lives, making sense of them as they would apply to us. We are able to accept what the story implies and to incorporate new messages more easily because they are presented as metaphors once removed; suggestions without command. In this way resistance need not be aroused."
>
> Lee Wallas
> *Stories That Heal*
>
>

Two possibilities of why stories encourage healing emerge. First, as Wallas suggested, it is often necessary to build a certain amount of rapport and trust between therapists and clients, tellers and listeners, or writers and readers before a meaningful encounter can take place. This intimacy establishes credibility and tells the receiver, "Hey, this person is like me and might say something worth hearing." Barriers and defense mechanisms relax so something constructive can occur.

Most storytellers attempt to create a relationship with the audience before starting a story so the audience will want to listen. According to Wallas, therapists must do the same thing. After the stage is set, the story itself can create additional rapport and engender feelings of sharing a common bond as the teller shares a story from the heart. Listeners are willing to receive what is being offered as long as they feel the story is genuine and the teller is sincere. Then the story begins to work its magic through the use of images and metaphors. Wallas offered, "the metaphor is powerful because it defuses resistance so that the new possibilities it offers become intriguing suggestions."

The second reason stories encourage healing is because they do not impose judgments or qualifications. Nobody likes to be told what to believe or how to act. A good story does neither—it just *is*. Listeners are free to accept or reject it, and that freedom makes openness and acceptance possible.

Family therapist Wayne Williams said, "Unasked-for advice sounds an awful lot like criticism." I think about his statement on many occasions, especially when I am about to give unwanted advice or when I have just received it. Something about being told what we should do, feel, think, or say makes all of us put up tremendous roadblocks for what follows. Even if the comment was the best piece of advice of all time, heeding its wisdom is difficult because of all the defense mechanisms that pop up.

This common reaction leads to another insight about why good stories work. Rarely do they preach, issue directives, or even tell us the point at the end, unless it is an Aesop's fable with a moral attached. (Most researchers of story believe that the *original* fables did not contain the morals, but clergy who were afraid that people might miss the point added them much later.) If a storyteller tells me how or what

I am supposed to feel at the end of a story, I resent it and assert *I'll figure that out myself, thank you very much.* Most stories, and certainly good storytellers, would not insult the intelligence of the listeners by telling them what to think. Some gifted writers and storytellers offer wonderful interpretations and explorations of stories and their contents, but never cross the boundary and dictate the meaning to others. Because stories *show* us how to think, and don't *tell* us what to think, we are able to listen openly and learn what the story has to say to our hearts.

Interpreting life's lessons

Stories make us think about things that we might otherwise block at a conscious level. For example, someone might say to me, "You really ought to spend more time with your mother. You know she is not going to be around forever. When she is gone, you will be sorry and wish you had done more with her while she was alive." I would agree that the statements are absolutely correct. However, hearing such advice, particularly if my own mother were to say it to me, makes my hackles stand up in resistance. On the other hand, if I heard or read a story like Shel Silverstein's *The Giving Tree,* where the tree continues to give and give of itself without expecting anything in return from the boy, I might think of my mother. I would think about how much she has done for me without any conditions—just because she loved me.

Hearing Susan Klein's story about the Christmas she got a bicycle when her family had very little money moved me to tears. I clearly understood the necessary sacrifices involved and how much Susan's mother loved her. Further, I could see the influence of her German mother's love on Susan's life.

These two stories get the message across in a way that a lecture about mother's love never could. They have the potential to cause the listener to think about and deal with the relationship where unconditional love played a part and perhaps healing is needed—either because the relationship no longer exists and needs to be remembered or the relationship itself has suffered and needs to be nurtured.

John Ward, writer, storyteller, and public relations expert, believes that opportunities for intimacy and friendship have suffered greatly in our fast-moving culture that rarely allows enough time for either. He said, "I think stories stimulate healing at a time of loss because they allow a level of intimacy that is non-threatening. Stories also create an atmosphere of friendship."

Stories have a way of showing and teaching without lecturing or cramming things down our throats. If someone is telling me that he or she has all the answers, I am automatically skeptical and not likely to believe anything said. Good stories are not like that. They meet people where they are and help to move them along their way without using force or threats or intimidation, all of which arouse suspicion and cause barriers to be erected. Stories overcome or avoid these walls altogether because they are merely offered to the listener as a gift.

Entering a closed mind

In the early days following the loss of my son I would not have believed I could survive and be stronger and more whole because of my experience. While struggling to cope with my grief, my mind was not open to new ideas and concepts. My survival instinct erected barriers to anything unfamiliar. Stories with simple visual images gradually allowed me to see new possibilities even while I rejected the facts surrounding David's death.

My mind seemed to revert to my childhood, a time when I was comforted by stories and fantasies. I was out of touch with reality and my brain did not function normally. At times I even pretended David was still alive, although I knew that he was not. Because their concepts are simple and easy to remember, stories were all my thought processes could handle. Oddly enough, a story or part of a story that I had heard in the past would pop into my consciousness and leave me to contemplate its meaning.

Even in the midst of grief when we are not open to anything constructive, stories can get through and do their healing work. They come through the back door without pretense, much like a good neighbor or an old friend. Our resistance is down because they seem familiar. Stories can silently touch our broken hearts and help them open enough for healing to begin.

I read Shel Silverstein's book *The Missing Piece* years ago and found it entertaining and insightful, but discovered new meaning in it following the loss of my son. Then I knew what it meant to have my heart ripped out so that, indeed, a piece of me was missing. In the story, which is described as an adult fairy tale, a circle sets out to find the pie-shaped wedge of itself that is missing. It searches everywhere, finding many pieces, but none of them fit. As it bumps along, the circle realizes it cannot travel as fast as when it was whole, but finds the slower pace allows it to see and enjoy more along the way. After days of searching, the circle finally finds the missing piece and quickly reconnects with it. The fit is perfect, but the circle lets go of the piece once again. The circle realizes that the process of looking for the missing piece brought more growth and wholeness than when it was complete.

> "We are more whole when we are incomplete, when we are missing something. There is a wholeness about the person who can give himself away, who can give his time, his money, his strength, to others and not feel diminished. There is a wholeness about the person who has come to terms with his limitations. There is a wholeness about the man or woman who has learned that he or she is strong enough to go through a tragedy and survive, the person who can lose some-one through death, through divorce, through estrangement, and still feel like a complete person."
>
> Harold Kushner,
> *How Good do We Have to Be*
>
> ⋘

The story opened my mind to the possibility that my life could be more meaningful than it had been—even without David. I did not understand how, but the story planted an idea to explore.

Discovering a new self

Maybe a redefining of self becomes necessary following a loss, even though that process causes additional pain in the beginning. Some times even the words don't fit. We have a word for a child who loses his or her parents—orphan. We have words for people losing their mates—widow and widower. But we have no name for a parent who loses a child. *Is that person still a parent—a mother or father—without a living child?* In *The Missing Piece,* a circle is *not* a circle when it is not complete. Through the metaphor created in this story, the search for that missing piece can help to redefine a new being that is stronger even after a part is missing. What a thought! It makes no sense to our logical minds, and yet through the story we understand. By applying that knowledge to our own lives, we realize that even greater possibilities may await us down the road.

I certainly never dreamed I would be where I am today. What started out as a nightmare has made me more compassionate and in many ways a better person. The simple story of *The Missing Piece* opened my mind to possibilities I never considered. As time passed, I found metaphors that offered inspiration and hope in every story I heard and read.

The Missing Piece and other stories led me to decisions and conclusions I would not have reached without them. Through the use of metaphors, stories have the ability to create simple visual images, like a circle with a piece missing, to explain a paradox or other complex concepts in a way that can be accepted and applied to our lives. The results can be a powerful agent to accept change and healing in our lives.

Getting the message

I asked storytellers if stories that approached loss directly or metaphorically were more helpful to them and other people. Of course, the answer was that both ways could be beneficial depending on the circumstances, the individual, and the story. Some favored personal stories that dealt directly with a specific loss. Others preferred the use of metaphors, which allowed listeners to substitute their own situations and draw individual conclusions. Many tellers said that although stories dealing directly with loss were most helpful at first, they learned more from metaphor after the pain eased a bit. A few thought one might work better than the other for some people, depending on the individual's age, circumstances, and personality type. Jenna Eisenberg said, "Some people miss the point and their attention is lost with metaphor. Some people enjoy the metaphor and may or may not make a connection, but the healing still works. Left-brained people want a direct story in order to feel they've gotten the message."

Journalist and storyteller Audrey Galex focused on the ability of stories to bypass the mind and all its defenses and speak to the heart, the part of a person that grieves and suffers. She added, "Stories have the power to open channels within the psyche and spirit so that words of comfort can take hold and ready a person for healing."

Storytellers, as well as their listeners, find stories filled with metaphors to be helpful in dealing with personal losses. Texas storyteller Elizabeth Ellis said, "Stories that deal with loss through metaphor are always helpful. Just hearing the vocabulary used can give you another whole way of looking at your own experience." John McLaughlin prefers stories dealing with loss through metaphor because they "give the listener more room to interpret and find his or her own story within the story." He added, "folkloric and mythological stories have been best for my healing," but noted that all stories could strike a healing chord.

When we think about a story long after we have heard it, the story can continue to work on us

> "Sacred stories move us; they get us thinking about what is important; they communicate through symbol and metaphor deep truths about the mysteries of life...even if we don't understand the message intellectually, we are aware that some profound lesson has been imparted....As we continue to search for ways to heal ourselves, each other, and the Earth, stories and storytelling will continue to flourish."
> Charles & Anne Simpkinson
> Introduction, *Sacred Stories*
>
> ⋘

and impart additional ways for us to heal. John Ward said, "A story can deal with the loss of anything and still work. From experience, I tend to believe that a story that deals indirectly with loss is better because the person has the opportunity to make connections—it seems to give more power to the listener." Christine Reese believes metaphors would be helpful to someone who *cannot* deal directly with or is fearful of the real story, perhaps because of the intensity of their pain or feelings of guilt. Mary Fears pointed out that stories dealing directly with loss are often too sad to be helpful. Talking about his ten-year-old daughter who died, David Holt said, "As a professional storyteller, I tell a little bit about Sara. I found I don't tell the whole story. Most people are just too blown away by it unless they've dealt with something like this. But they are always quite moved if I mention [Sara's death] at all."

Learning from metaphors

When stories contain metaphors that reflect our situation, we discover new possibilities for using our creativity to find solutions. Stanley Robertson's book, *Nyakim's Windows,* is filled with metaphors that expanded my view of the loss of my son and the resulting separation. Robertson was inspired to write the book by a dream of being lured into a cave to receive the gift of stories. Hearing and reading his stories gave me fresh insights that enabled me to find understanding and acceptance of my loss. One of his stories clearly showed how to use an experience or dream to help others—another key part of my growing understanding.

"Like night dreams, stories often use symbolic language, therefore bypassing the ego and persona, and traveling straight to the spirit and soul who listen for the ancient and universal instruction imbedded there. Because of this process, stories can teach, correct errors, lighten the heart and the darkness, provide psychic shelter, assist transformation and heal wounds."

Clarissa Pinkola Estes
The Gift of Story

Stanley Robertson lives in Aberdeen, Scotland, and is a well-known storyteller of the Scottish Traveller people. The sharing of his beliefs from his traveller tradition showed me that death does not separate our loved ones from us. I can still hear Stanley's lyrical voice saying, "Your laddie's work was done on this earth and he's gone to the place where his work is now." (For more information on Robertson and his traditions, see Appendix 3.)

Tina Alston, a developmental psychologist, professional storyteller, and writer, developed a technique she calls *storyimaging.* When Alston listened again to the Nigerian Cinderella story "The Secret Son," she was "inspired to try out a dream technique of imaging the story. I took parts of the story, and said to myself, 'I am the king disguised as a beggar, I feel _____. I am the banished wife in rags, I feel _____.' The story was a catalyst in letting go of a former relationship and finding a lost voice in myself."

The exercise led to her book, *Storyimaging: a way of accessing feelings, images and points of view,* in which she showed how to use folk tales to discover images that can lead to recovery from many types of loss. She said that stories full of transforming images can become life changing and "are most powerful when they are told aloud. Even if a person has to read a story aloud to a favorite pet or picture on the wall, the story has potential for changing that person's point of view." Alston successfully used this technique in "working with groups of homeless Vietnam veterans who had experienced death so many times, that they sought protection in drugs and alcohol." She also successfully used *storyimaging* with dislocated plant workers, drug abusers, and others who have suffered losses.

> "Young children 'think' in pictures more than words during preschool years...developing extraordinary powers of forming pictures. Metaphors are word pictures...stories strong in metaphor touch that inner core that was so vivid in a three-year-old's mind. Stories rich in metaphor do not need a tag at the end to teach a lesson. The lesson lies in the word pictures, which can act on individuals in unique ways."
> Tina Alston
> Psychologist and storyteller
>
> ⋘

The importance of stories becomes clear when we realize how many images in today's world provide inappropriate solutions and behaviors for dealing with feelings and emotions of any kind. In a discussion on the importance of metaphors, Brody and Punzak in the introduction to *Spinning Tales, Weaving Hope* said, "We want to provide our children with metaphors they can trust and grow with, helping them lead lives that are more caring, loving, and thoughtful." Their method of providing children with those positive images is to tell them stories. Children and adults need the images to find constructive ways to cope with their daily problems.

Expressing feelings

Gabriele Rico in *Pain and Possibility* said, "The language of the emotions is elusive, fragile, multifaceted, because our emotional being is profoundly involved in the formative, in the logically undefinable. Forms of feeling emerge through the evocative language of images and metaphors. We need open-ended tools to tap this language." Stories are full of evocative language that can lead us to our feelings and on to healing.

Writers and storytellers create metaphorical stories to deal with their own healing processes. The stories are often allegories where the characters, objects, and happenings have symbolic meaning. A wonderful example is *The Mythical City of Beaversbark,* a book created by Ginny Conrad, a storyteller and retired Montessori teacher. She acknowledged "the story of the book's preparation and the creation of the little animals that inhabit their homes in the Mythical City is the story of years of healing." The animals were kind, caring creatures that taught love by example. They grew into a society and then a city. Conrad created comfortable homes for her characters to inhabit at a time when she was losing her home and family because of a painful divorce. What began as doodles developed into hundreds of stories, and as Ginny said, "Beaversbark stories in my head, out of my mouth, and from my fingers helped me heal."

The following story has appeared in many newsletters of The Compassionate Friends. Author Jeanette Isley and her husband Webb cofounded the Topeka, Kansas chapter of The Compassionate Friends over thirty years ago following the death of their son Steve. Isley used the metaphor of a broken vase to show how the death of a child affected her entire family.

A Fable

There once lived a family who felt that they had been especially blessed by God. They had health and felt secure in their love of God and their love for each other. On the mantel of their fireplace stood a vase. It was a strong, sturdy vase—attractive but not extravagant. It had been a wedding gift, and to them it symbolized their family. It had withstood the bumps of moving and toddlers' antics as the family had withstood the buffets and ordeals of life. The scars and chips could be detected only on very close scrutiny.

The day the oldest son in the family died, the vase was found on the mantel, shattered into many pieces. No one bothered to gather up the pieces. It was left for some time in its broken condition on the mantel.

After some time had passed, thought was given to putting the vase back together. Little enthusiasm was generated but eventually the task was begun. The family worked together, each adding a piece or a suggestion about getting it mended. Each one of the family members got discouraged and, more than once, one of them was heard to say, "It can't be done."

Finally after many months, the vase was back in its normal place on the mantle. To the casual observer it looked strong and sturdy, and no one would guess it was less than perfect. But on closer examination, it obviously had been shattered and put back together, and on turning it around, one could see that one large piece was permanently missing. It had never been found and served to remind the family that although their hearts could mend and heal, their lives would never be the same.

Michael Parent wrote a metaphorical, fictional story entitled "Mary's Song," which was based on his friend Joanne's loss of her son. He said, "I think the attempt to capture what it was she went through and continues to go through, was a way of expressing, rather than burying, my own grief." This story has touched many listeners and helped them to understand their own grief as well as the grief of a close friend or relative.

Parent explained, "If we think of the loss as the wound, and the stories as the balm or salve that helps heal the wound, I suppose we could consider various kinds of stories (direct, metaphorical) as different kinds of balms. There are times when direct repetition of a tragic loss is what's needed. That is what she [his friend Joanne] did for months. When I wrote the fictional story based on her experience, it took a few months before she was ready to listen to it...she seemed to know instinctively what kind of balm she needed, and when."

Acknowledging images

Good stories, both written and oral, are filled with visual images. These powerful connectors provide numerous opportunities to take back some control of our lives and destinies as we see our situations more clearly. Jeannine Auth, writer and storyteller, said, "The use of metaphor is always effective to speak to the reader or listener. It has been said that metaphoric images are our first unlearned language."

> "We don't know quite when, where, and why stories heal, but they flat out do. Perhaps it's as simple as the concept that stories—though seemingly language-based (and therefore an intellectual pursuit)—are actually image-based and so are a function of the collective unconscious where so much of the intangible yet meaningful parts of our lives take place."
> Susan Klein
> National storyteller
>
> ⋙

Because healing is a continuing process, a particular story may affect us in many different ways, depending on where we are in that process. Stories work on us long after we first hear them. A good story might exert influence on us over a lifetime, continuing to speak to our conscious, as well as our subconscious minds, since we can never completely turn off our brains.

Susan Klein used the following example when asked how she had used stories to help others.

A friend and former boyfriend called me in the middle of the night many years ago to say goodbye. He'd had a long run of bad luck and was suicidal. I'd never dealt with that before and when I ran out of things to talk about to try to keep him on the phone (he refused to disclose his whereabouts) I felt compelled to tell him a story. He agreed to listen to it and I told the story of the emir's son who flees the fighting of the lion (to attain his rightful throne) and no matter where he finds himself, there's a lion to fight. The story ends with the boy finally facing his fear and thus disempowering it. At the end of the story, my friend hung up. I was awake all night wondering. Next day, I received a call that he had decided to go on living. I can't prove it was the metaphor of the story that made meaning for him in that darkest of hours—but I'd bet the farm on it.

Stories furnish necessary links to the healing processes that lie within all of us. The human spirit is resilient and longs to be free and whole if we will allow it to find a way. Appalachian storyteller, Mary Hamilton, said in her story "Sailing the Flying Ship" that she realized her stories provided charts and guides for her to navigate her life. Recognizing these insights is sometimes difficult as many things divert our attention. The diversions, too, can be opportunities for growth and healing if we tune into them.

Psychologists tell us that true learning occurs when a person takes something he or she has heard or read and, through either inductive or deductive reasoning, comes up with a new discovery, application, or conclusion. During this internal processing, we acquire new knowledge. Stories supply the best opportunities for learning, healing, and growth, since they encourage us to make these new discoveries and connections. Good teachers and speakers tell stories, knowing that the created images are easier to remember than a list of facts or a structured outline. When the stories are filled with metaphors, the listeners can make creative links to their own memory bank.

> "It is easy to forget how mysterious and mighty stories are. They do their work in silence, invisibly. They work with all the internal materials of the mind and self. They become part of you while changing you. Beware the stories you read or tell: subtly, at night, beneath the waters of consciousness, they are altering your world."
> Ben Okri
> *Birds of Heaven*

Marion Woodman wrote a chapter in *Nourishing the Soul* entitled "Sitting by the Well." In it she said, "Metaphor is the literal language of the soul." She believes our culture is out of control, "in part because we have lost our sense of metaphor—our sense of how one thing is parallel to or like another, our sense of the connections between different realms of experience." Ms. Woodman continued, "Like Carl Jung, I believe that metaphor is a healer. Because we cannot pin down a metaphor, cannot define it precisely, it holds an element of mystery. That mystery requires that we contemplate metaphor with our whole being, not simply our intellect. As we ponder, very often there is a flash of insight—a moment in which everything comes into focus, in which we say, 'Yes, that's it.' For a moment, we are whole: emotion, imagination, and intelligence. In the contemplation of a metaphor, soul, body, mind, and spirit are working together. Such a moment reminds us what wellness is."

Stories preserve and perpetuate memories 4

Explaining loss

Medical science can never adequately explain the death of a loved one, so we must turn to stories. Even if someone could demonstrate to me in scientific terms with charts, graphs, and logical descriptions why my son died so that I could completely understand, I would still be left with the fact that David no longer walks upon this earth. Therein lies my pain. I can no longer pick up the phone and talk to him and hear his laughter. He is always painfully absent at family gatherings. We never can have another water gun battle or play practical jokes on each other. The joy and fun that he brought to my life cannot be there again—except in the stories that I tell and am told about him. But the good news is—I have learned to keep him present in my life through stories.

Finding ways to remember

People who have lost a loved one search for ways to remember the deceased and maintain his or her presence in their present lives. The need seems extra strong on special days, like birthdays and holidays, since we normally spend those occasions with people we love and give them special gifts. Bereaved parents often establish memorial scholarships or other special funds to perpetuate the memory of their child by benefiting others. In David's memory, I contribute to an Empty Stocking Fund each Christmas and purchased an American flag that hangs from the Bridge of Lions in St. Augustine on national holidays. I especially like the image of the flag flying free in the breeze—imagining David's spirit also soaring in time and space. A brick in the wall surrounding the St. Augustine Lighthouse, one of David's favorite spots, displays his name and the dates of his birth and death. Others pay tribute to the memory of their loved ones, attempting to remember them in meaningful, creative ways.

But I have come to realize that the character, spirit, and energy that was and is David can best be revealed in a story—certainly not in facts, statistics, and descriptions alone. Even pictures fall short because they only capture a moment in time unless they tell or prompt a story. David Holt created and printed a beautiful picture book entitled "Sara Jane" to share with those who knew and loved his daughter, who died at age ten. This treasure is a tribute to the relationship they shared and lost. Each picture brings a story to mind and all combine to tell the story of his daughter's short life.

Connecting to memories

One of the goals of a good story is to create a series of pictures in the receiver's mind so that he or she can actually watch the story unfold. The process stimulates the brain to make connections to other stored memories and experiences. Herein lies another key to how stories impart power for healing and why they are easy to remember. Because the images produced are the receiver's own images, they are forever captured in his or her brain and can be revisited whenever the need exists. Pictures that are provided externally can quickly pass through consciousness without an internal connection. If images do not stimulate the brain to do what it is designed to do—store and retrieve information—they have little long-term effect on learning. In addition, the temporary images of movies and television can even interfere with the healing process by successfully blocking out mental stimulation necessary for grief resolution and healing.

Meinrad Craighead, in her chapter "Drawing Your Own Story," found in the book *Sacred Stories,* told one of her favorite stories about memory and said, "Remembering binds us together." In the story from Germanic mythology, Odin and his two pet ravens, Thought and Memory, reveal the vital importance of memory to give life meaning.

Each morning at dawn Odin sends forth his ravens to go down, circle the Earth, and find out what has been going on. Each evening, they come back to roost, and all through the night, they tell Odin all that they've seen and heard. In this way Odin stays in touch with his universe. One dawn, having sent forth his ravens, he begins to think, "What would happen if one of the ravens should fail to return? What would I do? How could I live without both ravens?" He ponders this. In his pondering, he comes to understand that he can live without Thought but he cannot live without Memory.

Remembering the stories

Sharing stories provides an avenue for remembering the loved ones we have lost. North Carolina storyteller and teacher Donald Davis said stories have the power to heal individuals following a significant loss because they "enable us to keep alive, honor, and bless people who are no longer with us. The story enables others to meet someone whom they will never actually meet in their lives. The story helps us process and understand our relationship with the person whom we have lost."

Florida storyteller Carrie Wharton described a poster she once envisioned that said, "We do not remember days, we remember stories." She said she grew to know the truth of that statement through her losses— her childhood experience of losing her mother and, later in life, her husband. In helping her three children deal with the death of their father, Carrie affirmed, "I believe the most significant power in healing from loss comes from

> "Stories have been a great big part of my healing because it is the only way Melanie [her daughter] can continue. After losing a child, the sense of the legacy is lost. I wanted people to know her and feel she lives on with us all. The stories of her life helped me keep her around and helped me help her friends. They would, and still do, come by to sit and talk about their friendship. Opening my house and heart to hear their stories helped them continue their growth process."
> Myra Davis
> Florida storyteller

remembering. And I believe stories have great power to help us remember, perhaps more than any other medium. Stories can be our own pure memory or can grow out of our memory. And the stories of others can nudge or reflect our own memory."

Carrie Wharton has found stories from her own memory to be the most beneficial in her healing process. As a child of twelve she lost her mother, and when she was thirty-eight she lost her husband—both to cancer. Carrie's experiences showed her the importance of sharing stories about those we lose. Carrie explained, "Stories that are pure memory may be painful during early grieving, but when revisited often become a source of comfort, and later can even bring us security. We welcome them and hold on to them like precious treasures." What a strong testimony to the healing power of stories!

Carrie learned how vital those stories were, because without them the memory of her mother faded over the years. She said, "As a child it became harder and harder to see my mother—to remember her voice and her smell

> "Knowing all of that [the importance of sharing stories] now has helped tremendously in guiding my children through their grief and healing in the loss of their father. We remember openly and naturally and without hesitation. We have favorite 'Daddy Stories' that we love to tell over and over among ourselves and sometimes share with friends. After the sharing, we are always left feeling empty, but full. There is always joy in the memory. Revisiting those stories often and at significant and appropriate times has helped all of us ride the waves of grief as the tides of life ebb and flow."
> Carrie Wharton
> Florida storyteller
>
> ⇛

and her person. In time she was reduced to a three by five photograph that sat on a shelf in my room. We didn't do nearly enough sharing of memory stories in my family. But we didn't know how important it was to do that—none of us had experienced loss before. As adults, we have tried to resurrect her memory by sharing stories as our memories allow, but it is labored and difficult because there are so many holes."

Struggling to survive

When my husband died suddenly at age forty-one of a heart attack, I felt pressure to be strong and make everything seem as normal as possible for my three children, aged nine, thirteen, and sixteen. I was attending graduate school and returned to class the week following my husband's death. Someone told me that was the best thing I could do for my children and myself to prove that we could survive and life would go on. But our lives were no longer *normal,* and I chose to avoid the issues by staying busy. I talked to the children very little about their dad—partly because they seemed to get upset if I cried in front of them and partly because his death was so difficult for *me* to accept, much less explain to them. So I stopped trying, waiting until I was alone to confront my loss. I did not say much about my pain and concerns, nor did I ask them about theirs. Looking back, I am sure the outside world thought we were doing great. In fact, people frequently told me how brave I was and how well I was handling the massive disruption in our lives.

My younger daughter, Wendy, was only nine when her father died. She recently told me that she had very few memories of him and felt a void in her life because of this lack of connection to him. Because I had not learned the importance of keeping those we have lost in our lives, we did not tell many stories or share our memories of her dad. Eventually we grew accustomed to his absence and avoided mentioning his name.

I wish I had known about stories then—the healing power of sharing stories and memories—because I know it would have helped all of us. We had boxes filled with family movies and pictures, but did not look at them for a long time for fear the memories would cause pain. Years passed before we talked openly about the experiences shared with their dad and our feelings of missing him. By then, many of our memories had diminished and were difficult to recover.

Fortunately the childhood love of stories reentered my life while listening to Betty Ann Wylie tell stories to adults one evening in Atlanta. Betty Ann gave me such a gift as I saw the possibilities stories offered. I got involved with a local storytelling group and immediately felt the excitement of listening to and sharing stories. At the first National Storytelling Festival I attended, I heard the African tale, "The Cow-Tail Switch," which resounded within me. I do not remember the teller, but I will never forget the message I heard—*those we love are never lost as long as they are remembered.* When introducing the story to the audience, the teller explained how the word "re-member" originally meant to bring back together the separated parts of a body, a concept powerfully illustrated in the story.

In "The Cow-Tail Switch," which can be found in a book with the same name by Harold Courlander, a hunter went into the forest, but did not return. His wife and sons wondered what could have detained him, but after a while did not mention him or his disappearance. When the youngest son began to talk, his first words were "Where is my father?" While trying to explain their father's absence to the young boy, the older brothers began to ask questions and search for him. Eventually they found the remains of their father, who had been killed by a wild animal. Each son had a special power that was needed to bring the hunter back to life. At a celebration feast, the father awarded a decorated cow's tail to the son who was most responsible for his return. Each older brother thought he should receive the reward, but the hunter awarded the treasure to his youngest son since he was the one who asked, "Where is my father?" Asking the question caused the "re-membering" and reminded everyone of the saying, "a man is not really dead until he is forgotten.

The strong visual image created by "re-membering" has never left me, and continues to provide guidance and insight into handling grief from loss in more constructive ways than my previous attempts. Without my knowledge, those insights prepared me to better handle the death of my father and later the greatest loss of my life, the death of my son—although no amount of preparation could have been sufficient.

Filling the holes

Since my renewed interest in storytelling started several years before David's death, I was able to encourage the sharing of David stories with family and friends. My family and I know the valuable role stories played in helping us heal from the huge hole his death left in our lives. Sadly, I will always regret that I did not comprehend the healing value of stories when my husband died, because memories do fade with time if they are not written down, told frequently, or simply remembered. The connections must be made to cement them in our minds.

When I am with both daughters now, I try to remember and share stories they might not know about their dad. Sometimes remembering the same incident jogs their memory and enables them to retrieve the same incident or perhaps another one altogether. I recently told them about the time we got two rabbits for Easter. Their dad felt sorry for the rabbits because they had to stay in a cage most of the time since we did not have a fenced yard. He bought a small leash so he could take the rabbits for a walk to get some exercise. He quickly learned that rabbits do not hop along on a leash like a dog would walk. In fact, the only way he could get them to move at all was to get behind them, stomp his feet, and scare the stew out of them. Then they took off like a shot, which did not make for an enjoyable, leisurely walk. The stroll was so sporadic, no one knew who was walking whom. The first time he put one of the rabbits on the leash, I laughed so hard I was sick, and later all of the neighbors came to watch whenever he walked the rabbits. My older daughter Kathi remembered the episode and added her comments as well, enabling us to share a wonderful memory and a lot of laughter.

Wendy has gotten excited about these remembrances and looks forward to learning more about her father. Coming up with a new story each time we are together stretches my memory, but has helped Wendy "re-member" him. She has even started taking violin lessons so she can touch and play the same instrument that her father held in his hands years ago. The sense of touch has been helpful to her in making a connection with him and shows the importance of using all of our senses to recapture our memories.

Collecting family stories

Family stories are wonderful to collect, tell, and record. After my father was diagnosed with bladder cancer, he and my mother had to stay at home a lot. I asked them to write down some memories from their earlier years for their grandchildren to enjoy. My dad said he could not think of anything to write, and he was sure that nothing he did back then was worth remembering anyway.

But my mother, who has always enjoyed writing, became excited about gathering our family stories. After writing some of her memories, she read them to my dad. He immediately thought of incidents from his childhood, and she recorded his stories as he shared them with her. The natural response to a story is always another story. Once a week I visited them to collect all Mother had written. Reading through the stories as I typed them on my computer generated a lot of questions, which I asked the next time I went to see them. Their answers produced more stories, and the cycle continued until we had quite a collection. They enjoyed the process of uncovering the memories, collecting the stories, and rediscovering people and places from their past. I loved learning more about my parents and other relatives, and often weave their experiences into my stories. For example, my mother's experience with a peddler at her grandmother's house helps me tell "The Peddler's Dream," a story about a peddler who found a treasure when he paid attention to his dream. Introducing a myth or folktale with an incident from my family's history connects the story to me in a meaningful way.

The following year my father died. I was grateful for all the stories he shared with us. Many of the stories would have been lost since he was the last of his generation in his family. Thank goodness we got them in time! Those treasures are part of our family history, which is preserved now for generations to come.

Mary Fears gathered stories from her relatives and wrote a book about her family history entitled *The Jackson-Moore Family History and Genealogy*. Talking about the experience Mary said, "Writing about close family members helped [me] to relive happy as well as sad times in the family. Family stories served as a comfort to me and caused me to smile as I remembered incidents about my mom, dad, aunts, and uncles."

Uncovering all the parts

Rabbi Kushner points out the importance of acknowledging all the memories, both good and bad. All parts must be remembered to see a real, living human being instead of a saint or a villain. We must create the complete person with all the bumps and warts for the character from our memory to be believable.

Donald Davis is especially skillful at bringing characters to life in the minds of listeners as he paints pictures of the people in his stories. Carrie Wharton said that Davis's stories "Listening for the Crack of Dawn" and "Mrs. Rosemary's Kindergarten" were particularly helpful to her in dealing with the loss of her husband. She said, "These stories helped me to see that it is okay and also important to remember even the quirky imperfections of a person who is gone. It helped me not to be afraid to be honest in my memory. Sometimes in loss we tend to be afraid to admit that our loved one was less than perfect, but in fact, I don't believe our healing can be complete until we are honest in our memory."

> "Only human beings can defeat death by summoning the memory of someone they loved and lost, and feeling that person close to them as they do so.... Memory can be painful, as everything that makes a human being more than an animal can be painful. Good memories deepen the poignancy of what we have lost. Bad memories keep the resentment alive when the occasion is long past. But memory is what ultimately gives us power over death, by keeping the person alive in our hearts. Memory is what gives us power over time by keeping the past present so it cannot fade and rob us of what we once held precious...we have all the yesterdays we are capable of remembering and all the tomorrows we can envision."
>
> Rabbi Harold Kushner
> *How Good Do We Have to Be?*

Early in the grief process, memories may be too painful to remember completely, but at some point we feel a strong urge to cling to those memories lest they slip away and the important details about the life of our loved one be forgotten. Shortly after David's death I felt extremely anxious, thinking I would not be able to hold on to everything I wanted to remember about him. I wanted to keep the memories for my own comfort, but also to share with his son, who would never know David except though stories from those who knew and loved him. (When David died, his wife was expecting their first child—a miracle child named David Michael.) Others' memories would be my grandson's main connection to his father, so recording them seemed important and urgent. *One day he will want to know all the details—good, bad, humorous, touching, and exasperating—and I may not be around to tell him.* I had to overcome the tendency to dwell only on the good things so I could accurately portray David. Remembering the real person was important, even through David was no saint.

Finally I made a list entitled "Things I want to remember about David." Whenever the panic of forgetting washed over me or memories flooded my head, I recorded my thoughts. Sometimes in the middle of the night when I could not sleep, I added things to the list or began to elaborate and fill in the details of items already there. Many of these fragments later became stories and, in the process, long forgotten memories resurfaced. Often tears splattered on the keyboard as I wrote, but I always felt better by the time I stopped. At least I knew the stories about David were preserved and perpetuated. I was mining for gold—the more I dug into my thoughts, the more I uncovered and rediscovered.

Over time, the act of reminiscing about my son's life calmed me and made me feel close to him and others I have lost. I relaxed when I realized the storehouse of memories was inside me and only needed to be tapped. Dreams, too,

> "Reminiscing—recalling events, conversations, occurrences from the past—is one of the important ways we mourn. And paradoxically enough, reminiscing is a way of thinking that can result in getting free from our depression and sadness...The figures of the past are not just 'memories' or mere abstractions but are still present and available to us in certain ways: as sources of awareness, learning, and wisdom; as reminders of goals and ideals; as part of the context we have for making decisions in the present."
>
> Elizabeth Harper Neeld
> *Seven Choices*

turned out to be a rich source of memories and feelings available for exploration. I recorded my dreams for a while and later reflected on what each one might mean. I had the strong feeling that David somehow guided my dreams, memories, and thoughts—helping me remember and convey the important things to his son and others. I gradually came to know that our loved ones are never gone as long as we remember them in our hearts and stories. Stories, such as *Nadia the Willful* and *The Cow Tail Switch*, offer the insight, but discovering and absorbing its truth gave all of those stories new significance and meaning. The stories had always offered hope and comfort, but now I actually felt their message.

Building on the past

The process of remembering became a powerful source of healing for me and gradually led me to create "Infinite Resource and Sagacity," my first organized story about my struggle with the meaning of David's life and death. I realized that he could be with me still, anytime I quieted my mind and allowed his spirit to enter my awareness. He is so close at times that I feel I can almost touch him, and in my dreams I actually do. Often I even sense his frustration if I am too busy or distracted to allow him to get through to me. When my mind is filled with other things, those wonderful memories and insights are blocked. Therefore, having a quiet time each day for a dose of healing is important for me and for him.

When I went to bed in the evening after writing the above section, I had an amazing dream. I have included it here just to show the power of being tuned in to our innermost selves.

I was attending a school. Dinner was served only between 6:30 and 7:30 PM and I missed it because I was looking for something I could not find. I was walking along a sidewalk feeling rather upset. All of a sudden David came running out of a building wearing his tuxedo, and he had two earrings in his left ear—one was a fairly large diamond one. His hairstyle looked like the old fashioned flat top. He had a huge smile on his face, which exuded happiness. I was so excited to see him and screamed as I said, "Weeelllll, don't you look cute!" He laughed and replied, "I just love looking this way, and I love wearing this wig. It is so much fun." I said, "Are you wearing *a wig—I didn't know that was a wig." It really did not look like one—just a different hairstyle for him. He laughed again and said "yes" as he snatched it off his head, but his own hair looked exactly the same. I then gave him a hug and thought in my dream, **I really can feel him—just like I wrote in my book.** I held on to him for a long time while tears poured from my eyes and my body shook. I felt so much grief and joy—grief at first because I knew that he was really gone from this world, but joy because he was still part of my life.*

Feelings like the ones I had in that dream are undeniably real and help me continue living the joy I experienced. David is certainly in a position to help me more than anyone in this world since he is connected to a higher power symbolized in the dream by the energy center in the top of his head, which he exposed by taking off the wig. He clearly helps me whenever I let him, and the tremendous gift always arrives just when I need it most.

Living in an unchanged world

Preserving our memories in stories—to be told, written, or read—helps give them the significance we think they deserve. When we have been shattered by the death of a loved one, it is hard to understand how the world can continue as if nothing happened. We want everyone to acknowledge, and therefore validate, the significance of our life-changing event. In reality only a limited number of people are affected by any single event. We wonder... *Since the earth keeps turning in its orbit, and people keep getting up in the morning and going on with their normal lives, how can we show them the significance of our loss? How can we communicate the extent to which our life has been impacted and changed?*

People find a variety of creative ways to keep lost loved ones alive in their lives. When telling many of her stories, Ginny Conrad uses puppets named after significant people in her life. Talking about the loss of her mother, she said, "Telling personal stories about her, naming a puppet after her, and using it in stories keeps her with me. This is probably one of the most healthy, comforting things I do."

The authors of *A Broken Heart Still Beats* quoted William Maxwell, a former fiction editor for *The New Yorker.* Maxwell said writing enabled him to "tap into the healing power of memory to cope with the most shattering event of his life: the death of his beloved mother when he was ten."

Longing for acknowledgement

The outward expression of our grief may be apparent to others, but no one comprehends what goes on behind closed doors when we are alone with our thoughts and lost dreams. Most people who lose a child long to talk about their child. Just hearing their children's names acknowledges their existence. Unfortunately friends and family often shy away from mentioning a child who has died, as if speaking of the loss or the deceased might make them more vulnerable. I have heard people say they do not want to remind the bereaved of their loss by mentioning it—as if *not remembering* was even a possibility. The following poem, "There's an Elephant in the Room," by Terry Kettering accurately expresses our longing.

> *There's an elephant in the room.*
> *It is large and squatting, so it is hard to get around it.*
> *Yet we squeeze by with 'How are you?' and 'I'm fine'...*
> *And a thousand other forms of trivial chatter.*
> *We talk about the weather.*
> *We talk about work.*
> *We talk about everything else—except the elephant in the room.*
> *There's an elephant in the room.*
> *We all know it is there.*
> *We are thinking about the elephant as we talk together.*
> *It is constantly on our minds.*
> *For, you see, it is a very big elephant.*
> *It has hurt us all.*
> *But we do not talk about the elephant in the room.*
> *Oh, please, say her name.*
> *Oh, please, say 'Barbara' again.*
> *Oh, please, let's talk about the elephant in the room.*
> *For if we talk about her death,*
> *Perhaps we can talk about her life.*
> *Can I say 'Barbara' to you and not have you look away?*
> *For if I cannot, then you are leaving me*
> *Alone...In a room...*
> *With an elephant.*

⇒⟫⟩✕⟨⟪⇐

As we attempt to cope with our grief, we become desperate to say *it was important—something happened that changed my life completely, and I will never be the same.* People are often uncomfortable if I say David's name in normal conversation or mention something he once did. Yet recollections become increasingly precious to me with every passing day. My existing memories of him are the only ones I will ever have— *there are no new memories.* Old bittersweet ones cry out to be told and heard, causing people to say *what a terrible loss!* Admitting that he died acknowledges that he lived.

Unfortunately, some people get stuck in a suffering mindset— continuing to relive their grief over and over like an actor rehearsing his lines. In fact, some bereaved assume a permanent role of a wounded individual, the grieving mother, the violated body, the rejected spouse, the broken person, or the victim. When such a routine becomes fixed, they give up on any healing process that could make them whole again. As long as someone feels and acts like a victim, he or she is held captive by their own negative thoughts. Comments like *this is who I am and where I get my identity, woe is me,* and *nothing can make things better or different or worthwhile for me again* perpetuate the inaccurate impressions. New ways to look at the past are necessary for healing and growth to begin, and stories offer the best opportunity to break the cycle.

Accepting gifts

The most helpful gesture anyone made toward me after David's death was to talk about him and share a memory with me. In those moments, I often learned something I did not know about my son. Sometimes I had forgotten the incident and the process of remembering always warmed my heart. One of his elementary school teachers told me she would never forget the look on his face and the delight in his eyes when the pinhole camera he had made by himself actually worked. Her story made me smile, as I remembered seeing his look of accomplishment on many occasions. A friend of David's told me about their trip to the beach in David's old MG. They traveled six hundred miles round trip, and the car used fourteen quarts of oil— almost more oil than gas. Listening to the description of their adventure was hilarious. When others reached out to share memories, my spirits lifted as I visualized David in the story. Their experiences created new memories for me!

Later stories I created from my memories had the same effect. When my thoughts and stories triggered vivid images of David, I felt like a breath of fresh air had entered a room full of pollution. Those pictures helped take away the pain and brought my *living* son back to me.

Friends who did listen when I needed to talk gave and continue to give me something I treasure. Unfortunately most people who have not experienced loss are too uncomfortable to discuss David's life or death. I have seen embarrassed looks on faces and heard rapid attempts to change the subject to something less threatening. Even now I sense some people are uneasy when I talk about my son, but when I tell a story they are drawn to listen. Listeners know the story is true, but the truth told in the form of a story is less threatening in some way. People often tell me they are deeply affected when they hear intimate feelings shared. Listening to a story does not require a response or reply, perhaps making internal processing easier.

Treasuring memories

Facing loss of any kind, and certainly loss due to death, makes us look at our lives, appreciate what we have left, and treasure our memories. We no longer take our health, our lives, or our loved ones for granted, knowing how quickly everything can change. Certainly my family and I have had numerous opportunities to reevaluate our lives. After my husband's death, my three children and I knew what it was like to lose someone we loved. We grew close to each other and valued our relationship, which added to the crushing blow my daughters and I felt when David died.

In many ways, David was a father and friend, as well as a brother, to his two younger sisters. I, too, thought of him as a friend—we had such fun together and were always playing tricks on each other. He was one of my best storytelling supporters, encouraging me by giving me books and coming to listen when I told stories. Anytime David heard a good story or joke, he called to share it with me, and I could not wait to tell him ones I had heard. I loved to watch the twinkle in his eyes as he approached a punch line or see his reaction as I pulled off a surprise ending on him. Sharing stories with those we love enables us to convey things we think are important and allows us to laugh together.

A month before David died, the two of us drove to a British pub in Atlanta one evening to hear some storytellers and have a pint. We loved the stories, laughing and talking about them all the way home. After dropping him off, I remember thinking how lucky I was to have a son his age to laugh and share things with, and one who wanted to spend an entire evening with his mother. We both knew how lucky we were that night, and I will treasure the memory forever.

Stories validate listeners as individuals

Filling individual needs

We all need to be heard and understood, especially following a loss. In order for this need to be satisfied, someone must listen to what we have to say. I always feel supported and validated when someone really listens with full attention. Listening to someone else and being listened to offer great potential for healing.

In *Healing and the Mind,* Bill Moyers commented, "Sharing sorrow makes us 'wounded healers,' as Carl Jung described people whose knowledge of inner healing came from experience with their own wounds." When this wisdom is shared in the form of a story, both the teller and the listener can find healing through the strong bond they share. Sometimes when we cannot think clearly, listening to others helps us to see our own situation more accurately.

"What we begin with is the first and most powerful technique of healing, which is simply listening, just listening. One of the greatest gifts you can give another person is your attention...We are all healers of each other...the reality is that healing happens between people. The wound in me evokes the healer in you, and the wound in you evokes the healer in me, and then the two healers can collaborate."

Rachel Naomi Remen, M.D. from Bill Moyers' interview in *Healing and the Mind*

Telling what needs to be heard

A good story meets the teller and the listeners where they are. Each person in a diverse audience can hear the same story, but get something different from the telling. Native American storytellers tell their traditional stories to everyone in the tribe, regardless of age. Each one responds at his or her own level, but even young listeners begin to learn the values and truths of the group at a basic level when they first hear the stories. The story's meaning continues to reveal itself as the listener ages and grows in wisdom and understanding.

When I tell a story, I am always amazed at the different responses I get from listeners. After hearing a story about the loss of my son, listeners often tell me their own stories of loss. Some see my story as a struggle to survive; others see creative ways of coping; others see the joy I experienced with David as a child; others see sadness and despair; and others find hope that they might survive such a loss if one occurred. *How can that be?* The story is the same, and yet one story fits all.

Of course, the answer is each person brings his or her own situation, needs, and attitudes to the hearing, and a good story touches them all—at many different levels. We are in a different state of mind each time we tell or hear a story since daily events and thoughts are constantly changing. We are able to hear, think about, and learn something new from a story, provided we quiet our minds and listen receptively. Even though I have listened to some stories many times, I still learn something new from hearing them. Maybe I just cannot grasp everything they have to say to me at once, or perhaps I am a different person each time I listen. Many tellers say they continue to *tell* a story as long as the story contains things they need to hear and learn.

> "In the right place and time, the genre [of healing stories] is not important. When someone tells my story, it hits home. I have found myself telling a story that I'd told many times before and suddenly—because of who I'd become—the story did new work inside me."
>
> Susan Klein
> National storyteller
>
> ⇒⟩⟩

If I ask listeners what they think a story is about, I get many different responses. I have been in a workshop, listened to a story, and felt confident I knew what the story was saying—at least to me. But in the discussion that followed, no one else heard what I did. Sharing our individual insights enriched us all and offered additional opportunities for learning and growth, provided the meaning is *discussed,* not *dictated.*

Through personal interpretation, each one can take from the story exactly what he or she needs to hear and learn—*if* the teller does not prescribe what listeners are supposed to get from the story. As soon as a teller editorializes about the significance or meaning of a story, he or she robs listeners of the opportunity to have a story do its potentially healing work. Browne and King in *Self-Editing for Fiction Writers* caution us to remember RUE—resist the urge to explain.

Hearing what needs to be told

In her article "The Healing Power of Story Listening," which appeared in *Storytelling World* magazine, Oceanna said she "had often used stories and songs to ease the transition between life and death" in her work with hospice. She learned from an old man the importance of listening to the stories of people who are sick and dying and explained, "I see storytelling and transitional story listening as important aspects of the dying process." Oceanna's article reminded me of some of the people I met through my volunteer work with hospice patients. These experiences proved to me how valuable listening can be.

Jean

When I first met Jean, she had frequent anxiety attacks and was terrified of her lung cancer and impending death. One day while visiting her, I asked about her earlier life. She started telling me fascinating stories, which she verified with numerous newspaper clippings, about her modeling career as a Gibson girl in New York. She also told me about becoming the personal assistant for Gloria Swanson at the time Ms. Swanson was romantically involved with Joseph P. Kennedy—with more clippings. Jean breathed heavily each time she got out of bed to get the box where she kept the memoirs of her life. She told me about her career in broadcasting and about her deep regrets that she had spent so much time away from her two young daughters. As a single parent, Jean was forced to let her mother raise the girls so she could earn a living for all of them.

After listening for a while, I asked if her family knew all the stories she had told me. She said they weren't interested. I suggested she might consider taping or writing about her experiences to preserve the stories so her grandchildren could know them some day. I shared a memory of my grandmother sitting on the porch in her old rocking chair, relating family stories from her life. Nobody ever thought of recording them and now it was too late. I told her I could not remember all that my grandmother said and would give anything to hear those stories again. Jean perked up at the idea and seemed excited over the possibilities. She said, "Maybe I could get my daughter to find my old typewriter."

*The next time I arrived at her daughter's house, Jean was out of bed and in her clothes, dragging the long cord attached to her oxygen tank all over the house. Her eyes twinkled as she showed me what she had typed on her **manual** typewriter. She exuded more energy than I had ever seen from her, and her labored breathing and anxiety attacks were barely noticeable.*

Jean's transformation occurred because I had listened to her and been interested in what she had to say. Jean was able to write many things she had never been able to say to her family. When she died, Jean left her family a treasure and validated her own life story as she reevaluated its importance.

Nora

Immediately following the death of one of my male patients, his frightened wife called and asked me to come to their home. I found Nora sitting on the porch and held her shaking hands while we waited for the hospice nurse to arrive. She sobbed as the memories flooded out about her marriage and life, both of which had been filled with sorrow and disappointment because of her husband's alcoholism. His condition had caused him to mentally and physically abuse her and completely dominate her life. Nora insisted their life had been good in the beginning, but gradually all of her hopes and dreams dwindled away. They had moved far away from home to make a new beginning, but things only got worse. They had no friends and she felt like a prisoner in her own home, especially after he was diagnosed with lung cancer.

Nora's husband died like he had lived—violently. In the midst of a thunderstorm, he screamed and drew his last breath as a tremendous bolt of lightening struck nearby and the resulting thunder roared. She wept bitterly for a long time and finally said, "I'm not crying because he's gone, I'm crying for all that might have been."

*Nora slowly recovered her self-esteem and began to make a new life for herself. She often told me how much it had helped to be able to pour out the whole story the night her husband died. As I sat listening to her, we both found healing. She made me realize how utterly sad it was to get to the end of your life and cry for all that was missed. Her poignant statement delivered a powerful message—**live life so there are no regrets at the end, no tears for what might have been.***

I was still struggling with my son's death and trying to find direction in my life. Nora's story contained a reminder that I needed to hear. My listening enabled her to release the things in her heart. Paying attention to her story had been healing for both of us, and I told her so. As we talked over the months that followed, she realized that, although she had lost her husband and part of her life, she still had time left to live and wanted to avoid another story of missed opportunities. Watching Nora come out of her shell was a beautiful, rewarding experience, and I know listening helped.

Nora's story and life proved the power of listening to another person's story, helping me to clarify my own thoughts and feelings. Sometimes focusing enough attention to really hear what someone else has to say is difficult. All too often we are too tied up in our own story and too busy trying to tell it to listen to others. Many times we are not open, thinking *what could that person possibly have to say that would interest me,* and we miss opportunities to grow.

Careful listening has great healing potential for listeners and speakers. Listeners can gain insight into their own situations, thereby helping resolution. When speakers know they are being heard, they feel validated and understood. Receiving insight and being heard are precious gifts listeners and speakers exchange.

People desperately need someone to hear their stories when their lives are coming to an end, for they are losing control of everything. They need to know that their lives were worth living. Extensive evidence shows the importance of reminiscence in helping bring closure to a life. But successful reminiscence requires someone to listen—really listen—not with the television on, not while knitting, and not checking the time every few seconds. Looking directly into the speaker's eyes and listening with your heart convey that he or she is important. Confirmation that someone lived a life that mattered eases the difficulty of accepting death.

Alice

The hospice volunteer coordinator said Alice wanted someone to help write her memoirs. I called and scheduled a visit right away since both of us were excited about the project and felt an urgency to get it done. She had selected old photographs representing her life and wanted to tell the story behind each picture. At our first meeting, she showed me how she wanted to format what she had written about her mother, grandmother, and great-grandmother. They all shared the name Alice, the name of her book.

I offered to record her voice, but she refused because of the difficulty she had speaking and breathing. Alice wanted to tell me about each picture, and then have me ask questions and write the story. We met several times, and between meetings I copied the pictures to include on the pages and typed her stories. Her strength diminished rapidly, but she dictated enthusiastically about her early life. Once when we met, she seemed weak and agitated and said she didn't feel like working, asking me to come back later. I had a couple of questions and as she answered them, her anxiety subsided and she decided we could work for a while. She relaxed as the stories began to flow again.

When I arrived the following week Alice announced that she had completed everything by dictating to the people who were staying with her around the clock. She slept as I read through all the bits and pieces, making notes and a list of questions for her to answer. I shared her growing realization that she was very close to death. She needed constant care by this time and had been told by her hospice nurse that it was a matter of weeks now, instead of months.

I completed the rough draft late one evening and took it to her home the following morning. She slept most of the time, but I managed to tell her that the work was done and showed the pages to her when she roused slightly. As I described the different sections, she reached out to touch them and said she wished she could see better. Barely able to speak, Alice whispered that she wanted three copies printed and bound. I followed her instructions, including her selected dedication:

> *To Alice-*
>
> *Be good sweet maid, and let who will be clever;*
> *Do noble things, not dream them, all day long;*
> *And so make Life, and Death, and that For Ever*
> *One grand sweet song.*
>
> *"A Farewell" by Charles Kingsley*

That evening her closest friends gathered to sing songs, read scripture, and pray with her. Early the next morning, exactly one month after our first meeting, Alice's spirit became free to travel through time and space, continuing to touch the lives of all who encountered her.

Alice was obsessed with leaving her legacy to her two nieces, also named Alice, and she stayed alive until the project was complete. She and I were the same age, and many of her pictures, memories, and stories were similar to mine. The entire experience reminded me once more of the importance of telling and recording stories to help bring closure at the end of life. Alice will never die as long as she is remembered in the minds and hearts of those who loved her, and gathering her memoirs gave her the comfort and assurance to die in peace.

The strength and insight of the dying people I have encountered through hospice fill me with awe. Losing a friend is always sad, but they have taught me so much about living and dying. Some of them maintain a sense of humor even near the end of their lives. One day I visited a patient who was very close to death. I asked how she was feeling and if she was in pain. She replied, "I seem to be sleeping more and more these days. But then I guess that's what I'm supposed to do now. Of course I don't really know for sure because I've never died before, you know." We laughed together.

One of the questions I asked in my interviews for this book was *what type of stories have you found healing?* Texas storyteller Elizabeth Ellis responded, "as a teller, my personal stories have had the greatest role in my healing process. But mythology and folktales can be healing too." Other tellers preferred personal stories, children's books, and stories from Jewish folklore. Several of those interviewed mentioned that poetry, or a specific poem, provided the turning point in their healing process. But all spoke of the importance of *listening*— to our own stories and those of others. Their insistence on listening in an active way reminds me that *you must be present to win!*

Remembering what is needed

Receiving individual insights from a story substantiates the mind's ability to know what it needs to bring healing and wholeness at any given time. Dr. Herbert Benson dealt with this concept in a scientific and scholarly way in his book *Timeless Healing.* He described a phenomenon called "remembered wellness," which enables a person to determine and seek out what must be done to restore the mind and body to a state of wholeness and wellness. The ability to find what is needed seems to be a genetic predisposition having to do with survival of the species and as such, is a function that is wired into our brains. Because stories define life and powerfully invoke memories and images, they can aid the brain in remembering a healthy state.

Dr. Benson's hypothesis was that all human bodies foster an internal healing power. He said, "Our senses are obviously responsible for recording many of the details of an incident that go into the files our memories maintain." Good stories tap into all of the senses—

sight, smell, taste, sound, and touch—to create images and sensations that listeners see in their own minds. Storytellers know that the senses are the direct channels for accessing all of the memories, thoughts, and emotions stored in the brain. Getting in touch with these memories seems to be a prerequisite for healing to take place.

> "[Emotions are the] dispatches of the brain as it interprets the body's experience in everyday life, both the challenges of the physical environment and the values, concerns, and stories that enrich our encounters. They play a far more crucial role in our physiology than most of us realize. [Our impressions are] easily manipulated and cultivated in storytelling."
> Dr. Herbert Benson
> *Timeless Healing*

Recalling positive memories

Because stories can gently guide our feelings, they seem to be especially comforting to listeners when used in eulogies. In fact, most often a eulogy is a story about the person who has died, recalled to comfort the mourners. Positive memories help the survivors to think back and focus on a time of wholeness and joy. In addition, eulogies can have a tremendous affirming and healing effect for the person telling the story.

My friend Avis Fox has been an actress and storyteller for many years. A couple of years after David's death, her husband Lowell died after a struggle with colon cancer. My husband and I felt close to Avis and Lowell because we had shared many fun times together, and his death touched us deeply. I agreed to give one of the eulogies at his funeral, and then thought I must have lost my mind as I was still struggling to heal from the death of my son. *What could I possibly say to offer comfort to anyone else?* But as I began to gather my thoughts and focus on a story about Lowell that would bring healing to those who loved him, I found myself affirming life, which had a powerful healing effect on me.

Much later when I asked Avis how stories helped her heal, she answered, "When I lost my husband of more than thirty years to colon cancer, at first I felt vacant, unsure, angry, lonely, and deeply depressed. I had never experienced depression before in my life. When

Diane eulogized at my husband's funeral, she told vivid stories with fun-loving examples of his love of live—and that is when my heart began to heal. Others eulogized also about how he had lived his life so fully—was positive and loving in all phases of his life, and a true inspiration to others. Specific stories were told about how he had encouraged each person in different ways. Because of these healing stories I came away from the funeral at peace, knowing that there were so many others who truly loved and admired my husband, and that I was not alone in feeling the loss or the impact he had on others."

Audrey Galex said although her interests in storytelling began years ago, "My recent losses only deepened my interest in storytelling and reaffirmed the critical role it plays in my life and the life of my family." Hers is another powerful testimony to the healing effect stories have for tellers as well as listeners. She continued, "I pride myself in listening to those who need healing as they tell the stories of their loved ones." Even though listening takes time and energy, the rewards are worth the effort.

> "When my paternal grandmother passed away, the honor of writing her story, as part of her eulogy, and then delivering it, were powerful story sharing opportunities that have helped me cope with her loss. Only a few months before she was diagnosed with pancreatic cancer, I wrote and performed the story of her and her mother's immigrant experience, which I adapted from listening to her oral history. I sent her a copy of the performance and she sobbed as she told me that I'd 'gotten it right and we were cut from the same cloth—you and I.' So when Sugie [Audrey's grandmother] was diagnosed with cancer and then died two week later, there was a part of me that knew her story will live on."
>
> Audrey Galex
> Storyteller and journalist
>
> ⇛

Refocusing the mind

Stories can slow down the mind and calm the spirit so that healing becomes possible. Author Louise Colln said she had trouble sleeping at night after her husband's death because she had been up frequently with him during the final months of his life. She said, "Shortly after he died, as I was trying to learn to sleep through the night again, I stumbled onto the use of story tapes to stop the useless noise in my mind and let me drift off to sleep."

Storytelling's calming effect on listeners may be a carry over from childhood. When I hear the words *Once upon a time,* I relax and anticipate something magical about to begin. Focusing on the story and the storyteller's voice causes my mind and body to relax and be receptive. Buddhists often talk about *monkey mind,* the condition where numerous random thoughts bombard the mind and prevent clear thinking. Calming the mind is necessary to focus and be receptive without constant chatter interfering. Getting rid of *monkey mind* ties into the importance of activating the "relaxation response" to achieve healing.

> "No matter what methods individuals use to elicit the [relaxation] response, the physiologic changes are the same. We know that the experience seems to clean the slate of the mind, making it more receptive and creative. When you let yourself focus, and get your harried mind out of the way of your body's natural healing ability, calling on the beliefs that mean the most to you in life, a peace that defies description may be possible."
> Dr. Herbert Benson
> *Timeless Healing*
>
> ⋘

Much has been written in recent years about the mind/body connection and little doubt of its reality remains. Since stories access the mind in a calming and natural way, their ability to facilitate healing in the mind, the body, and the spirit seem obvious.

Penetrating the grief

Of course negative thoughts and beliefs can block the body's instinctive progress toward wholeness. In the midst of my grief after my son's death, I reached out to find anything that would help make sense and ease the pain of my loss. Certainly the grief was too intense in the beginning for me to be open, but even then, a few things got through. On the night David died, I remembered something he told me when he was sixteen years old, just after my husband, his father, died suddenly of a heart attack. He said, "Mom, I don't want you to be like Jeff's mom. After Jeff's father died, Mrs. Brown was so bitter and miserable that she made Jeff and everyone else around her miserable too. Please don't ever be like Mrs. Brown. That would be such a waste."

Another thought penetrated my fog bank—something I had heard years before when three teen-aged boys in our area had been killed in a car accident. At a community Thanksgiving service, a local minister said that the incident showed us we can never control the things that come into our lives. The only thing we can control is our reaction to those events and what we become because of them.

I do not know how those thoughts got through to me on that terrible night, but they did. With the passage of time, I grew more receptive, especially to stories about David and about others who had experienced loss and *survived*.

Understanding sacred stories

In his chapter entitled "Exploring Your Personal Myth," found in the book *Sacred Stories,* James Carse explained why it is important to develop the skill of listening to the wisdom contained in myths. Carse said, "First, it brings into clearer focus the fact that our life is indeed an unfolding story and therefore helps us to understand where we are in that story. Second, it exposes the great range of possible paths lying ahead of us. Third, because there is no story with just one character, there is no way we can reach greater self-understanding without achieving greater intimacy with others. Fourth, by exposing ourselves to the boundless power of myth to transform the meaning of our lives to give us an intimate place in the larger community, we open ourselves to the divine. In addition, the active study of myth can reveal how intimately connected we are to both the living and the dead."

As my understanding of the power of stories has increased, I have realized that all sacred stories impart the wisdom about which Carse wrote. Sacred stories change the way we view the world and our role in it. Perhaps the classic myths better define and distinguish the distinct stages of life's journey, but as Carse said, "Myths, after all, are stories that we tell over and over again and cannot forget...pay attention to the stories that most frequently appear in your recollection or imagination. Their persistence means they have something to tell you." Developing the skill of listening that Carse endorsed is another thing that deserves our attention. Without opening our hearts and minds and souls, we cannot possibly acquire all the wisdom we need to lead us to healing and wholeness.

Learning to listen

Most story *tellers* are also incredible story *listeners*. The craft requires it. The ability to tell our stories is enhanced by our willingness to pay attention to others and ourselves. Observing and analyzing the development of another person's story teaches us to tell our own stories better. Because storytellers have developed the skill of listening, they open themselves to the power within all stories.

Many people do not listen well, thereby depriving themselves of available wisdom. You cannot *listen* and talk at the same time. You cannot *listen* while planning what you are going to say next, as many people try to do. No wonder we often fail to remember what has been said and to find the possibilities of healing in the stories of others.

"Listening to the stories of others is healing in another way. The stories of others, be they personal stories, folk tales, myths, or legends, can mirror our own experiences and memories and trigger the continuation of the healing process. Sometimes it can be a seemingly small insignificant part of a story that reaches in and touches that part of us that needs to be healed at that moment. We take from a story what we need. Like ET's finger, the story helps move us toward wholeness."

Carrie Wharton
Florida storyteller

⋘

At a workshop at the Conyers, Georgia monastery, Clyde Annandale told a story which illustrated to me the value of listening to what another person needs to say. The following is my version of the story.

J. D. Dupree

J. D. Dupree lived to be 98 years old. He owned a large furniture company in North Carolina and his millwright had been with him since the company started. When his valued employee died suddenly, J. D. rushed to the funeral home to pay his respects to the widow, but he could not think of what to say to show her how sorry he was. He was filled with sadness over losing, not only a close friend, but also a vital worker at his factory.

The next day at the funeral, J. D. went up to the widow, but still could not think of what to say. At the burial, he wanted to say the right thing, but he could not think of what it was. Later that day, many friends and family members gathered at the widow's home to bring food and be with her and J.D. was there, but still could not think what he wanted to say. He stayed until everyone else had left, still trying to think of the words of comfort he should say to this woman, but he could not think of a thing.

When they were alone, the millwright's widow asked J. D. if he would listen to something, and he said he would be glad to. She disappeared into her bedroom and returned with a box overflowing with papers. She selected a few and began reading aloud the most beautiful, heartfelt poetry that he had ever heard. After an hour or more had passed, she stopped reading and thanked him for listening. That night as he walked home, J. D. Dupree realized that he was not supposed to say anything—only to listen. He also wondered about all those wonderful poems written by a man he thought he had known, and realized he did not know him at all. He wondered if his friend was a millwright who happened to pen poetry or if he was a poet who just happened to be a millwright.

-»><«-

Like so many people, J. D. Dupree felt he had to say something and that it needed to be just the right words—as if there were words to make everything okay. *Why do people think such words exist?* The truth is words cannot make pain and sadness go away. Comfort comes from someone really listening, sharing a memory or story, and offering a sincere expression of sorrow and caring.

The story of J.D. Dupree also points out to me how unconnected we often are with the people we see every day. We honor people by recognizing who they *really* are and taking time to listen. Such affirmation opens doors leading to new insights, healing, and growth. To be really *heard* is a gift—one that heals because our need to be loved and understood is met.

Exchanging healing

After the death of his daughter, David Holt said he found it helpful to hear about the incident from others who had been involved—all the ones who helped him and his family get through the crisis. Hearing the story from their perspectives helped him understand what actually happened, while helping to deprogram those friends. David stressed the importance of being a good listener and said he was "a much more sensitive person because I've been through a huge loss and I'm not afraid to hear about other people's losses...that's helpful to them and to me."

> "Healing from a story is a mutual happening. It takes a teller and a listener. It takes trust on both sides. Sharing a loss with others willing to listen helps put the situation in a more understandable perspective. Sometimes a story needs to be heard or told numerous times before it can serve its healing purpose."
> John Ward
> Writer and consultant

Most storytellers I interviewed confirmed that both listening to others and being heard contributed to their healing. Michael Parent said, "Solitary grief seems like a story longing to be told that isn't. Shared grief is a story told *and* a story well listened to, in a situation where the teller and listener get to switch roles. Each person has the unique privilege of really listening and of being really heard." Parent recalled how listening over and over to a friend's story of the loss of her son was healing for him, whereas the telling and re-telling of the events of her son's dying and the stories of his living were healing for her. Parent's role as a listener surely encouraged her healing process.

Writer and storyteller Jeannine Auth said that stories are like connective tissue. She explained that listeners heal because "we hear and see ourselves reflected in the stories of others, for we are truly bound together in the human experience. No matter the circumstances of our lives, if we love, we will at some point experience the pain of loss. By listening to the stories of others who have had the courage to resist the darkness, we can bring our own story out of the shadows and begin to examine it in a new light."

We can and do! AMEN!

Stories connect us to the universe

Making a universal connection

Even when loss isolates us from everyone, stories bring us back and make us part of the world again. Every time I hear another tragic story on the news, I am reminded how universal loss is. People everywhere suffer losses of all kinds. Yet I immediately remember how alone I felt in my grief following David's death. Most people initially believe no one else has ever experienced the grief and pain they are feeling. Each situation is unique, with matchless circumstances and pain. Only when we see loss occurring all around us can we begin to sense a connection.

Establishing a bond with others who have survived loss is vital, especially to those who became better, and not bitter, following what seemed to be an insurmountable loss. Stories from the past link us to our roots and culture, while stories from the present show us how people are putting joy back into their daily lives to continue living in the future.

The connection to others through their stories provides a structure by which we see can our own story. Fully grasping our story leads to an acceptance of our loss, a necessary step for moving through the grief process and finding ways to live and heal on the other side of loss.

Hearing stories of loss encourages healing because we gradually realize loss is universal and we are not alone. In the interviews I conducted for my research, I heard this sentiment expressed over and over in answer to the question *how have stories healed you?* Most believed a spoken story traveled directly from the teller's heart to touch the hearts of listeners. The personal contact of hearing someone describe the intimate details of his or her loss and the struggle to survive allows the listener to observe the sincere expression of emotions.

Undeniably many have found help through reading stories too. Printed stories are sometimes more accessible and easier to find than another person willing to share a story. I have read many insightful personal stories that were written for a reader, not a listener. Authors often feel a greater freedom to release their deepest grief, since they never encounter a live audience. All stories, spoken or written, have the potential to create a bridge of understanding from one person to another.

In his book *Love and Survival*, Dean Ornish wrote, "When we gather together to tell and listen to each other's stories, the sense of community and the recognition of shared experiences can be profoundly healing." He believes that love and intimacy are at the core of suffering and healing and provides numerous examples and studies to support his beliefs. Since stories offer opportunities to share love and intimacy in a non-threatening way, they can initiate and encourage the healing process. Ornish continued, "Anything that promotes a sense of love and intimacy, connection and community, is healing." Nothing promotes such bonding more than a story shared from the heart. Even those unaccustomed to communicating in an open manner can be touched by a story and may be more comfortable telling a story than discussing their feelings.

Experiencing the side effects of loss

Loss compounds loss. Following a loss, the bereaved must deal not only with overwhelming grief from the loss itself, but also with all the side effects related to the loss. The ripple effect is like throwing a pebble in a pond and watching the waves go on forever. Legal, financial, and health problems can cause additional emotional ambushes. Each time I have experienced loss, the person I used to be changed drastically. Others affected by loss voiced similar feelings. In fact, my daughter Kathi expressed the loss of her former self this way, "It's not only the person [that is lost] – everything is reordered. Your existence is mapped on a new timeline that includes events that occurred *before* or *after* [the loss.] The world is completely different, and all relevant things that happened exist in terms of their *pre* or *post* significance."

A friend who lost her son commented, "One of the things I miss most is myself. I used to be light-hearted and fun loving, and now I'm not. Everything makes me sad and I seem to cry all the time. My husband must feel like he lost his wife as well as his son." In addition, her daughter developed serious emotional and health problems resulting from the loss of her brother. My friend's marriage fell apart, a frequent result from losing a child.

Being supportive to a spouse is extremely difficult when consumed by personal emotional needs. Very little energy remains with which to comfort others. Children feel emotionally abandoned, believe they have little value to their parents, and often feel guilty that they are still alive. Many friends and relatives keep their distance, failing to respond in helpful ways. Loneliness intensifies as relationships collapse out of fear, lack of understanding, and communication breakdowns. The entire family structure goes into a downward spiral, decreasing feelings of control while increasing isolation from the world. No wonder hopelessness and despair often result.

Following a loss of any kind, people feel isolated and alone, believing they are the only ones to go through such a painful of experience. Part of the pain stems from the resulting loneliness combined with the assumption that nobody comprehends the significance

> When losses are "socially unspeakable ... members of the social system cannot be of any assistance to the bereaved. They tend to shy away out of ignorance of what to say or moral repugnance. Examples include death by murder, suicide, or an overdose of narcotics. Frequently, the death of a child is a socially unspeakable loss because of its anxiety provoking nature."
> Therese Rando
> *Parental Loss of a Child*
> ⋘

of their loss or the intensity of their grief. They are disappointed by those who cannot understand, and often surprised by those who do.

Enduring isolation

Immediately following David's death, people surrounded my family and me, meeting our physical needs and trying to help. I cannot imagine surviving without them, and yet I felt completely isolated and alone in the magnitude of my grief. I *knew* I was the only one who had ever experienced grief as gripping and deep as mine. As days passed some people I considered friends seemed to avoid me—maybe they could not deal with events too painful to imagine. I was a constant reminder of how fragile life can be. At times I felt like I had the plague, as people I had known for years turned to go another direction in the grocery store to avoid making contact. If we spoke, the light, trivial small talk often made me want to scream.

I probably avoided others, knowing they could not understand. The lack of contact with others increased my feelings of sadness and depression. Feeling a tremendous need to communicate, I did not know how to start or have the energy to try.

Fortunately there were exceptions. Some people listened and shared my pain and genuinely wanted to know how I was doing, even if it meant hearing painful experiences. A few asked questions and encouraged me to talk about David's death, knowing that was what I needed to do. But at the end of the day, they all went back to their normal lives, leaving me all alone with my loss.

Finding a connection

One day, someone I had never met called. She had lost her son and wanted to visit me. We shared our stories, talking about our sons and their deaths. A tremendous relief swept over me as I talked freely about David. I could say *anything* and she understood. We cried and laughed and felt each other's pain and grief. We felt an immediate bond and for the first time I thought *maybe I'm not completely alone.*

With the passage of time, I started to realize how *many* others had experienced the loss of a child. All of a sudden stories were everywhere. Everyone I met had lost a child or knew someone who had. I received many books written by people who had lost children. Every magazine I picked up contained an article about how a bereaved parent survived the loss of his or her child. Hearing all these stories forced me to accept that I was not alone in my grief.

When I listened to stories of others who had experienced similar losses, I felt instant connections. Hearing their stories of pain lifted me out of my isolation. People who have experienced loss reach out to the newly bereaved because they understand and can truly share the pain and despair. They remember how it felt to have their hopes and dreams for the future suddenly smashed.

Then I started thinking about wars and natural disasters and accidents—so many world events have claimed huge numbers of people. Tragedies like the Oklahoma City bombing and school shootings cause our entire nation to grieve. As I looked outside myself I found loss everywhere and seemed to take on everyone else's pain even as I felt my own. The feelings overwhelmed me at times.

Intellectually I understood the universality of loss, but comprehending it with my whole being was a new concept for me. As I absorbed the magnitude of loss and the resulting grief and pain, I felt more a part of the human race than I ever had. I grew more in touch with the world's pain and losses, not just my own. At this depth of feeling and understanding, I found a sense of hope and encouragement. Somehow my load got lighter as I knew I *wanted* to survive and give back to the world some of what I was learning. I saw and felt evidence of survival all around me, and that boost started me on an upward path. As stories helped me accept loss and suffering as the human condition, I found my reason to get up in the morning.

I felt a greater sense of understanding and connection with absolute strangers than I did with people I had known for years. People who had taken the time to explore their losses through writing or telling stories were more in touch with their real feelings and emotions than those who offered trite suggestions or quick solutions. Their stories wrestled with the same issues I was facing, and arrived at answers that were worthy of the struggle.

Arthur Frank in *At the Will of the Body* says, "Human suffering becomes bearable when we share it. When we know someone recognizes our pain we can let go of it." Not all at once of course, but if I recognize the pain of others, surely they must recognize mine too.

Many of those I interviewed shared the connections they found in the stories of others. Susan Klein said, "I reconciled myself to certain parts of my life or felt an affinity to others who shared similar life events in their stories." Tennessee storyteller Christyna Jensen believes the greatest power for stories to heal comes from sharing the human experience and condition. She remarked, "It may be related to the fact that humans need human contact. Remember that babies decline if they are not cuddled. Stories may be the adult equivalent."

Audrey Galex shared an example of how stories connect by saying, "Stories can forge links between people and take people out of the isolation that often accompanies loss." In addition to loss through death, Audrey mentioned that the loss of her youth—turning forty— had been an interesting opportunity for friends and acquaintances to share their stories of coming to terms with aging. She added, "It's been a great way to connect with other women, as fellow travelers and wisdom seekers."

Jeannine Auth said, "When I was still deep in grief months after my grandmother's death—she was my best friend—it was a simple little story told to me by a friend at work about her relationship with her grandmother that led to my healing. The similarities in our relationships, and the knowledge that my friend Martha had finally been able to accept her grandmother's death, for some reason touched a spark in me and made me come to terms with my loss." Having someone share a story that connects to our situation proves that we are not alone in our feelings of loss. Hearing how he or she dealt with the loss and started to live again offers hope that we can not only survive, but also know joy in our lives.

Releasing pain through stories

One of the people I interviewed for this book was Sarah Swanson, a teen-aged girl from Illinois. While driving with her two best friends, she swerved to miss a dog that ran in front of her. The car hit a tree and both girls were killed. Sarah found it helpful to write out the story of her accident and tell it at school and later at a storytelling event.

She said, "When I told the story about my accident it was like finally I could have people listen and I could get it off my chest."

Sarah reads a lot about people who have experienced similar accidents. Those stories "heal because your heart goes out to others who have had similar situations, and you know you aren't alone. I listen to stories and always relate them to my life. When I read a powerful story, it makes me cry and release some of my inner emotions."

Few things help deal with emotions like a story. A friend said hearing Sarah share her experience was one of the most powerful and memorable stories she had ever heard. This brave teen-ager has touched the lives of all those who have heard her story, which connected them together and furthered her own healing in the process.

Margaret Lawrence said that nothing helped at first after her ten-year-old son died of polio while her family was living in India. She just kept going because she had three younger children to care for and had no choice. She was isolated from her entire support system—friends, extended family, and culture. Personal stories gradually began her healing process. She wrote a lot and realized she was not alone in experiencing loss when she "learned that one of my cousins had backed his truck over his two-year-old son and killed him. Later, another cousin killed a child who ran out in front of her car. I began to see that there were people hurting even more than I was."

David Holt said he was so grief-stricken and depressed after his daughter died that every morning he made a list of reasons to stay alive that day.

"After my initial grief, it helped to hear other people's stories. When you lose a child you think nothing could be worse, absolutely nothing. And then you hear about someone who lost two children or three children murdered—there's always something worse than what happened to you. I even started collecting a book of stories called 'It Could be Worse.' I never finished it, but have a file of those I personally interviewed, heard on TV, or read about in the newspaper. Knowing it could be worse was healing."

David Holt
Musician and storyteller

≪≪

These lists helped him get through those early times and included things like "seeing the first daffodil in the spring, walking in the woods of North Carolina, hearing the hoot of an owl at night, touching a baby's hand, and listening to the sound of a national steel guitar." He felt the beautiful tone of that musical instrument expressed a crying feeling that was as healing to him as the stories.

I had a similar experience at one of the first Compassionate Friends meetings I attended. I met a woman who lost all four of her children in a house fire. Another woman lost two daughters and her mother-in-law in a commercial airline crash. Later I met a woman who lost both of her sons and her husband in a boating accident—her entire family wiped out instantly. I could not begin to comprehend their pain, but thought, *if they can survive, surely I can.* I had lost a lot, but I had not lost everything. I still had a lot of people in my life to love and many friends and family who loved me.

Building a foundation

In the face of such overwhelming loss, what factors enable people to survive? In the November 1979 issue of *Parabola,* James Hillman's article, "A Note on Story," discussed the value of hearing stories during childhood. Hillman wrote, "From my perspective as a depth psychologist, I see that those who have a connection with story are in better shape and have a better prognosis than those to whom story must be introduced." Early exposure to stories helps establish a certain perspective on life itself and teaches the brain to create images for internal processing.

Hillman continued, "One integrates life as story because one has stories in the back of the

> "This connection between our own life stories and the stories of the great myths leads to another connection. When we come to know the stories of our lives, we come to know the meaning of our lives as well; stories shape the way we see ourselves. Because the active study of myth has the power to change the way we tell our life stories, it can also transform the very meaning of our lives."
>
> James Carse
> "Exploring Your Personal Myth," *Sacred Stories*
>
> ⇛

mind (unconscious) as containers for organizing events into meaningful experiences. The stories are means of finding oneself in events that might not otherwise make psychological sense at all." Finding oneself in a story enables a person who has experienced loss or other traumatic events to work through the pain by creating a new story that is meaningful and acceptable. Hillman asserted that this ability might be the essence of healing. Further he stated that the traditional stories of our culture, "Greek, Roman, Celtic, and Nordic myths; the Bible; legends and folktales," expand our consciousness of the world. Such traditional stories are "the fundamentals of our Western culture and they work in our psyche whether we like it or not."

Many of those interviewed said stories about real people work best to promote healing, but even stories about imaginary characters can heal. If such characters are believable, they were probably based on real people or were condensed from many different characters to represent people who actually lived. Fictional characters can impart their truths with as much impact as real people. Many stories containing such truths have been preserved and passed down through the centuries. Because fiction often renders the essence of feelings, attitudes, and truths, it is sometimes more powerful than a true story.

Learning from history

Mythology, legends, and folktales have survived for hundreds of years because of the value they impart to readers and listeners. Although personal stories always affect and inspire me, I have gained the most long-lasting insights from the stories found in literature of the past. This ancient wisdom eventually led to acceptance and a new resolve by forcing me to look at my loss from a global point of view. Transcending the personal realm to the universal was mind expanding and contributed greatly to my healing process.

John McLaughlin went on a Storyfest Journey to Arthurian England led by Kelly and Robert Bela Wilhelm following a divorce after twenty years of marriage. John said, "It was a very healing experience as stories helped me to see that life went on, and that men and women have struggled with relationships from the beginning of time. I think stories heal by giving us another way to see our situation. They help us to put a different spin on the story of loss." Old stories from another era can provide a connection to people, imaginary and real, who have walked before us.

> "Story organizes the events of our personal lives into meaning, and myth builds upon this, fusing the individual story with the collective one. Through the smaller stories, we weave together the diverse aspects of our lives, plumb the depths of our psyches, and place ourselves in society. But through myth we come to understand the greater meanings that play upon us and connect us to the universe itself."
> Deena Metzger
> *Writing for Your Life*

People who suffered great loss and continued to live lives of value to themselves and others inspire us. Robert Frost, for example, lost four children and endured to write some of his most heart-felt poetry. Perhaps feeling the pain of his loss allowed him to write with even more intensity.

Abraham Lincoln suffered from depression most of his life due to his mother's death when he was only nine. He was elected president after losing a son, and another son died during his presidency. Lincoln was known to be a great storyteller and it was said that he used stories "to whistle away his grief." His funny stories kept his depression away and deepened his bond with other people. He used language to comfort himself, as he pondered the meaning of life and the bitterness of death. Despite numerous personal losses and the overwhelming sadness he felt during the Civil War, Lincoln was a leader of great strength and compassion.

Lincoln's wife, Mary Todd Lincoln, was never able to successfully deal with her losses. To sooth her deep depression, Mary tried to find comfort in possessions. After losing a third son following Lincoln's assassination, she succumbed to her grief and tried to kill herself. Her remaining son committed her to an asylum. History is filled with examples of those who became stronger following significant loss and others who were unable to cope.

Stories from history show us how real people survived loss in the past in spite of tremendous difficulties. I have portrayed three historical women through story in recent years. Looking back, I wondered what drew me to them. All three women suffered great loss and not only survived, but embraced life on the other side of loss. All three never gave up and represent an affirmation of the human spirit's capacity to process grief. Research in history books and old records reveals the strength of their legacies.

My first character, Clarissa Anderson, came to St. Augustine from Boston in 1837 after her first husband died. She arrived to care for the children of a family friend, who had just lost his wife. She married the widower and gave birth to a son. After only a year, her new husband died of yellow fever, leaving her in a strange place while caring for several young children. She worked hard to survive and prosper, becoming a prominent businesswoman and member of the community.

The second character I portray is Maria Andreu, the first woman light keeper at the St. Augustine Lighthouse. She became the head keeper in 1859 after witnessing her husband fall to his death from the tower while whitewashing it. According to census records, she also lost at least one child, yet took care of her family and ran the lighthouse until the beginning of the Civil War.

I also developed a first person story about Betsy Ross, America's flag maker. Her story of convincing George Washington to have five-pointed stars on our country's flag fascinated me. Washington argued that six-pointed stars would be faster to make, but Betsy Ross demonstrated to him that she could cut five pointed ones with a single snip of the scissors. While researching her life for the story, I discovered that her family disowned her because she married outside the Quaker faith. Later she buried three husbands, but continued her life as a seamstress, mother, and outstanding citizen for years.

All of the research and character development for the stories of these three women allowed me to interject my emotions as I portrayed the way they chose to live in the world. When I put on the period dress of each woman, she lives through me. Their stories of survival offer hope and strength to listeners and to me.

Preparing for the future

We find healing in creating stories, in sharing them with others, and in listening to the stories of others. Whether an allegorical story or a personal experience or a tale from folklore, mythology, or contemporary literature, all stories contain the potential to heal. When a story resonates within us, something in our life is connecting to that story. We may not always consciously know the reason for the connection—but for some reason, the story attracts our attention. A story can even prepare us for something that has not yet happened.

Ada Forney said, "We are sometimes sent stories and do not understand what binds us to that particular tale until the time when we need it and its power to heal." She told of hearing "The Dark Candle" at a story camp and feeling the story spoke to her heart. The story was about a man whose wife died as she gave birth to their only child—a daughter. As the girl grew, the father loved the child with all his heart. When the girl was only eight years old, she suffered an illness and died. The father's grief and sorrow deepened as each day passed. One night he had a vision of his daughter at the end of a great procession of angels, all carrying brightly glowing candles. His small daughter was quiet and sad as she carried her candle, dark and unlit. In his dream, the father embraced her and asked, "Why are you so sad child? Why is your candle dark?" When she told him that his tears of grief put out her light each day, he gave up his grief. The vision filled his heart with love

> "Stories reach in and touch the wounds we cannot name and sometimes do not even know exist within us. Stories do heal after tragic loss in incredible ways we often do not understand completely. I know because of personal experience with 'The Dark Candle.' It helped my entire family through one of the greatest tragedies anyone can ever experience, the loss of a child. Hearing the story helped me to learn to share the glorious memories of my granddaughter and find joy to replace my sorrow. Telling the story allowed me to touch and heal my grieving family."
>
> Ada Forney
> Florida storyteller

once more and he spread the warmth of his memories throughout his village.

Forney said, "Six weeks after hearing this story, the phone rang and brought tragedy into our lives. Our seven-year-old granddaughter Angela had been killed by a hit and run driver. At that moment I knew why the story had been given to me. I was the one who would need it more than anyone else. I told it as her eulogy with her standing beside me. I will also tell you that I was a skeptic and had not believed in visions or angels until that day. She took my hand and we told her story. Then, we lit a single candle and began to tell memories of her time with us. Sharing these precious memories of her specialness brought joy and light to all of us."

Ada has never been able to find a copy of the story in a book, nor was she able to find the woman who told it at the Florida camp, but thinks it is a European folktale. She believes the story was a gift and freely shares it with others. When she posted the story on a public discussion forum for storytellers on the Internet, Ada received thank-you notes from many people, including storytellers in Oklahoma City who were affected by the bombing of the Federal office building. She felt a strong connection to those who shared their experiences as they responded to her story.

> "Underlying many stories, even very humorous ones, is the message: you are not alone; someone, somewhere has had the same feelings that you have. And it is that underlying message that has the power to heal. When you know that you are not alone in what you are feeling, it makes it easier to cope."
> Sue Alexander
> Author

Teacher and storyteller Ginny Conrad said, "It helps to know we are not alone...and to see how others deal with and triumph over loss." Jenna Eisenberg added, "More than anything we don't want to be alone in our suffering or grief or pain. A story can let us know that others, real or imaginary, have gone through a similar situation or circumstance. And the stories that show that the person has gotten through it, has triumphed, has been healed, has moved to another phase in his/her life, those are the stories that can heal."

Relating to others

After David's death, I made an appointment with my physician of over twenty-five years to tell him what was going on in my life, knowing my health could be affected. His response was, "I know how you must feel. I just lost my dog that I've had for many years and it almost killed me." I was angry and disappointed. His statement was not comforting at all, although looking back now, I am sure he thought it was in some way. *But he was a doctor, for crying out loud!* In his career dedicated to human life, surely he understood that pets, even greatly loved pets, are not children. Inappropriate statements like his caused me to feel even lonelier and more convinced that no one really did understand.

A child dying before a parent is not the natural order of things. Such an untimely death causes a grieving parent to withdraw from the world. Even when surrounded by people who care, bereaved parents feel isolated. Friends mean well when they say *I know exactly how you feel,* but their statements increased feelings of separation. Their lives are still intact, while a parent whose child has died has no life.

At a Compassionate Friends meeting, someone told me, "My son died twelve years ago and I still miss him. My heart breaks for you as I remember my pain in those early days. I wish I could make the pain go away, but nothing can. I can promise you that it will get better, but it takes a long time to figure out how to live with that pain." She told me about her son, his death, and things she had done to survive. She listened and *did know exactly how I felt,* although she never said the words. We became friends because of our bond.

One of the benefits of support groups is taking turns telling and hearing stories and finding help from both the telling and the listening. Further healing takes place when you see your story helping someone else's understanding, just as their story helps you to recognize your situation. No single story supplies all the answers, but the combined stories have tremendous power as each one adds bits of wisdom and insight. The process of gathering the pieces builds a strong foundation, one brick at a time. Healing was not an *aha* experience for me, but rather a gradual growing of understanding, acceptance, and encouragement. Support groups and twelve-step programs work because they are based on the benefits of shared stories. Individuals feel completely understood in those groups, as they link with others who have walked the same path.

When asked who helped them most in their darkest moments, people who have suffered loss almost always respond *a person who had experienced a similar loss.* Genuinely feeling a newly bereaved person's pain and reflecting compassion comes from direct experience. The success and popularity of support groups proves the validity of this statement. Although feelings of loss are common, people who have not suffered *a similar loss* can never comprehend the event or its consequences. Suggesting otherwise is a slap in the face to someone in the midst of grief following a loss. A shared story says more than all the well-meaning comments often expressed to those in the grief process. Stories can convey that someone, somewhere, understood. When the story is from the teller's own experience, the potential for connecting and healing is strong.

No one wants to be a member of a group like The Compassionate Friends. However, once the reason to become a member occurs, a connection exists to other members of the group. The credo of the organization affirms

> *We need not walk alone.*
> *We are The Compassionate Friends.*
> *We reach out to each other with understanding and hope.*

Everyone in the group knows what it means to lose a child and feels linked to every member, regardless of sex, race, or religion. The bond is immediate, but the closeness develops slowly as stories are shared. The candlelight service held during the Christmas holidays each year is a vivid reminder of the healing power of being connected to others. As each person lights a candle for his or her child who has died, the dark room fills with light and symbolizes the power and strength the group has together. The feeling of being linked to others is therapeutic for everyone.

All support groups for people who have experienced loss know that no experts exist in dealing with grief except the ones who have been through it themselves. Since most counselors and psychologists agree that the death of a child is the most difficult loss to accept, anyone who has experienced and survived this trauma *is* an expert. Most assert *there are no right or wrong ways to grieve—do what works best for you.* Certainly no one can tell another how to deal with loss. I am only an expert in knowing how I handled my situation and would never attempt to tell others what they should be doing.

Dealing with internal grief

Florida storyteller Annette Bruce tells the following story, which illustrates how often the outside world misunderstands the necessity of dealing with grief in an appropriate way for the individual involved. Annette created this story from a short article she once saw in a newspaper.

Greevin'

A Florida backcountry woman was hoeing out beside her weather-beaten house. A neighbor stopped by and leaned on the fence. "Effie Mae," she said, "you know it ain't fittin' for you to be hoein' out here today when the whole town knows that you just had a letter from the government sayin' that your Jim is layin' out in one of them furrin heathen lands, dead! It just ain't fittin.' Why you oughtta be dressed in your funeral clothes and actin' more respectful."

Effie Mae rested on her hoe and looked at her neighbor with level eyes, bloodshot from staying awake all night. "Friend," she said, "I know you mean well, but you just don't understand. This is Jim's land, and it rejoiced his heart to see green things growin' because it meant that the young'uns and me would be eatin' and cared for. This is his hoe, and when I'm hoein, I can feel his big strong hands on mine and hear his voice sayin', "That's good, Maw. That's real good!" I can't even afford a stone monument for Jim. Workin' not weepin' is the only headstone I can give him. So if you don't mind, neighbor—if it's all the same to you, I'll do my greevin' in my own way."

Sharing with others

In *At the Will of the Body,* author Arthur Frank wrote, "Talk is not the only way to elevate illness beyond pain and loss, but for most people it may be the most reliable way." Although he is referring to physical illness, the depressed state of mind following a severe loss can certainly be viewed as an illness and often causes physical symptoms. Talk is the most accessible way we have to touch pain or loss, and meaningful talk always leads to telling stories— talk with a purpose.

As we reach out to share our stories and hear the stories of others, we rejoin the world. When I share a personal story, I feel connected to the listeners and they validate me as an individual by their attention. When I hear a heartfelt story, I feel linked to the speaker because he or she cared enough to share something special with me. Sharing personal stories makes us vulnerable, and that very vulnerability opens us to growth and healing—both as speakers and as listeners. Nothing bonds us together more than sharing our stories.

> "The magic of medicine occurs when the healer and healee go on a deep personal journey by sharing stories. Our medical experience at Gesundheit [a home-based medical practice in West Virginia] has shown that real healing can occur when two people genuinely share them-selves....Human beings need a collective that knows and loves their stories."
> Patch Adams
> *Gesundheit!*

Anne McCracken and Mary Semel, authors of *A Broken Heart Still Beats,* said they "have come to believe that comfort, such as it is, derives from recognizing that others before us, many others, have felt this very pain, struggled with the same questions, and reluctantly given up the lives they too had counted on." They both lost children and derived inspiration from courageous individuals who stayed productive in spite of terrible personal losses, concluding, "it's this kind of inspiration—inspiration by example—that proved most healing for us." Sharing this insight after meeting each other led them to write the book together.

Expanding our capacity for life

In the stories of others we find guides for of courage, determination, and hope. Realizing we are not alone in our grief, we begin to accept the events in our own lives. Stories lead us to our inner strengths and point out new solutions that we might not see otherwise. We must make new connections if we are to continue to develop and grow throughout our lives, since old ones (synapses in our brain) often die with age. Telling and listening to stories cause us to think, forcing our brains to construct new relationships in order to make sense of our losses.

Jeannine Auth spoke of her friend who survived a terrible automobile accident but had little memory of her past as a result of brain injuries. Jeannine and others visited their friend every day, sharing stories and memories of former times. After several weeks, the injured woman's brain began to make associations and she gradually regained her entire memory. Some of her recovery was due to reduced swelling in the brain, but the doctors believed that shared stories and memories played a major role, making new connections where old ones were damaged.

> "In my own odyssey, I discovered I was not so alone, so different as I had imagined. I discovered we all have metaphoric cracks in our hearts, sad stories to tell, hurts to heal. It is the human story. Only the particulars differ. The goal is not to banish pain, but to develop tools with which to transform it....Expression empowers us to transform our feelings; it permits us to connect our stories with the stories of others, to bridge the gulf of our essential isolation from one another."
>
> Gabrielle Rico
> *Pain and Possibility*
>
> ⇒⇒

Similarly, a friend of mine suffered a stroke, which resulted in permanent brain injury. She progressed for a while, then hit a plateau and could not improve further. She looked and talked like the same person, but part of her memory was gone. I sent her a tape of my personal stories, some of which she knew. Her husband said the stories enabled her to make connections to incidents in her past like nothing else the therapist had tried. When I was able to visit her, I know she recognized people and events as I continued to tell her all kinds of stories. The potential for accessing stored memories is obvious and exciting—particularly when associated emotions and feelings can be triggered.

As a writer, Gabrielle Rico believes writing helps us to discover our true feelings and leads us to new discoveries. As a storyteller, I know creating and telling stories does the same thing. Both have a way of getting us to our truths.

Encouraging others to grow

When people want to tell a story that was evoked by listening to mine, I am always honored. Sometimes I am amazed at how different the stories are; yet the listener makes a connection. I can feel that bond, too, when I open my heart to listen. Unfortunately there is rarely enough time following a performance to hear all that listeners want to say. I recognize *their* need to be heard by encouraging them to share their stories with each other.

Sometimes listeners report the experience of sharing their story with a friend or family member. Chain reactions often start when listeners are inspired by a story to tell their stories, and on and on— a wonderfully healing ripple effect. Someone has to drop the stone in the pond—somebody has to start the ripple by telling the first story.

> "Many of the most powerful medicines, that is stories, come about as a result of one person's or group's terrible and compelling suffering. For the truth is that much of the story comes from travail; theirs, ours, mine, yours, someone's we know, someone's we do not know far away in time and place. And yet paradoxically, these very stories that rise from deep suffering can provide the most potent remedies for past, present and even future ills."
>
> Clarissa Pinkola Estes
> *The Gift of Story*

My cousin gave his friend Frank a copy of "Infinite Resource and Sagacity," the story about my son. Frank, whose son died in a hiking accident, said he felt very connected to me when he read it, even though we had never met. The story was not his, but my feelings of grief, loss, and love triggered feelings he associated with his loss. Both of us had lost sons, though in very different circumstances. We started a friendship through e-mail because of our common bond, and still have never met.

After corresponding with Frank for several months I asked him to describe the connection he felt and how had it affected him. He replied that the first few paragraphs of my story hooked him because of the amazing similarities in personality between his son and mine as young boys. Things I said about David had prompted memories of his son. He told me a story that illustrated those similarities. In reality, the details about the two young boys were quite different, but the specific details of my story had evoked distinct memories in him.

Frank also related to my pain, sense of loss, and all of the emotions I expressed, having experienced them himself. He said, "It was a great help to know that I wasn't going through this alone and that the feelings I was having weren't weird or abnormal. It was also helpful to have a peephole into the future; to read about some of the things that were coming up for me that you had already experienced. Finally, it was reassuring to know that I wasn't the only one who felt he [his son, Danny] was using my thoughts, ideas, and memories to get through to me—that this wasn't just the delusions of a grief-stricken parent."

He related an experience his daughter had that was therapeutic for both of them. Hearing the story further confirmed his belief that Danny was still around in spirit.

Laura lives in Austin, Texas, where they have had a ton of rain lately—flooding and the works. She tried to phone her mother in Michigan last week and reached her maternal grandmother with whom her mother lives. Her grandmother said "Hello" and Laura replied "Hi, Grandma" but her grandmother couldn't hear her and kept saying "hello, hello, hello." Laura felt there was a problem with either her phone or her grandmother's phone. She hung up and tried from another phone in her house with the same results. She tried again from her husband's business phone and his business fax phone with the same result. She then tried calling her mother's sister who lives near the mother and grandmother and again got the same result. Finally she gave up and sat down on the couch feeling extremely frustrated. That's when she actually heard Danny's laugh and his voice saying, "Now you know how it feels for me!"

Being open to tell stories that others need to hear is important. I do not mean passing judgment about what stories that *I* think they need to hear. Often I feel a strong urge to tell a particular story that I had not planned at a specific performance. Every time I pay attention to my intuition and tell the story, people from the audience thank me afterward, explaining why they needed to hear it. I do not fully understand how this happens, but I know it works when I keep my mind open and my spirit willing.

I was not so flexible when I first started telling stories. I lacked confidence in my stories and myself. Over the years I have observed much evidence of the real power of stories when I take a chance, ask for guidance, and trust the answers. People everywhere need stories, and I must share ones that need to be heard.

Connecting through details

One of the fascinating things about a well-told story is seemingly a paradox—the more specific the details of an event, feeling, or character described by the teller, the more precise the pictures and memories evoked in the listeners. This occurs even when the listener's situation is quite different from that of the teller. It seems that vague descriptions with few definite details would allow listeners to explore memories and fill in the blanks with their own pictures. However, our brains do not work that way. No one can *see* a generic description, so such a picture conveys nothing. Use of specific, vivid images evokes individual images and feelings in the minds of listeners, building bridges to their own stored memories and stories.

For example, if I describe my grandmother's Christmas tree—exactly how it smelled, felt, and looked, you can see a tree, but probably not my grandmother's tree.

At the living room window stood a tall, skinny, cedar tree that smelled like the blankets that came out of the chest in the hall. Gran always said, "Now that's a real Christmas tree—the kind of tree we used to have in the country." The branches felt like strands of silk yarn unless you rubbed them the wrong direction, and then you got stickers in your hand. Colored lights with tubes of bubbling water rising from each bulb, plastic icicles that glowed in the dark, pinecones sprayed gold and sprinkled with glitter, and red and white striped candy canes covered the entire tree. Strings of popcorn and cranberries draped the branches and silver tinsel sparkled in the light. A huge silver star on top made it look like a tree straight from fairyland.

Such a description probably connects to childhood memories, conjuring an image of a Christmas tree that looked very different from my grandmother's tree. Perhaps each detail of my description lets readers either *agree* or *disagree and replace* with their own specific memories. If my details are thorough, the listeners or readers will be able to formulate their own complete internal images.

Healing stories must operate the same way. When others hear the story of my son's death, they substitute personal images, feelings, and emotions as I relate mine. The more specifically I describe details and feelings, the more complete the examination/substitution will be. Healing does not begin until the memories are brought up, touched, and dealt with—no matter how painful. This process evokes strong emotional reactions, spilling tears outwardly and inwardly. But then the listener can say, "Yes, someone else understands how I feel and shares my pain. I am not alone. I am not going crazy after all. What a tremendous relief."

Stories expand imagination and creativity 7

Experiencing change

If we live long enough, we all experience significant loss that forces us to look at life in new ways because the old views no longer fit. We cannot go back to the way life was before the loss. We face difficult choices. The loss and resulting change present an opportunity for us to decide how we will live our lives in light of what has been lost. We must undertake massive reevaluation, leading to new outlooks and insights. Once we recognize that what we have lost was too important to pass unnoticed, the only way to rediscover value in our lives is to embrace living in purposeful way. While grieving our lives come to a standstill. From that point, we can determine our direction instead of being trapped in a life that just evolved.

Loss changes every part of our life. Our sense of self is redefined, changing who we are. Reestablishing our identity in the wake of loss takes a long time. Change is always hard, especially when it is forced upon us. We resist and fight in every possible way when the future is uncertain. *Stick with what you know* is common advice. In reality we deal with minor, gradual change all the time, for nothing stays the same. But we are never prepared for radical change.

After David's death I no longer related to anyone, anything, or myself in the same way. I felt like I was having an out-of-body experience. I looked at the dislocation, not as an opportunity for growth, but as an insurmountable obstacle. Even though many changes *are* positive, few of us seek them. The unknown frightens us.

We fear that we will be like Humpty Dumpty when "all the king's horses and all the king's men couldn't put Humpty together again."

Good stories always include elements of change. Otherwise, no story exists. Storyteller Donald Davis teaches that a good story clearly describes the status quo first so the significance of the subsequent turn of events is understandable. His formula for a good story includes showing what normal life was like before the loss or crisis occurred. He does not think listeners can fully appreciate what happened without knowing what life was like before. Then comes the crisis. *And then one day* signals an alteration in the current situation, and we know nothing will ever be the same again. Life could be better or worse, but will definitely be different. Then the struggle unfolds. Finally a picture of the new life emerges where we discover what has been learned as a result of the loss or change. Davis remarked, "There is mythological power in good personal stories."

Learning through struggle

After much searching and struggling, the main characters usually acquire new insights. They receive help along the way from others, often a wise elder or even an animal, and return to the real world to use what is learned. This is the classic hero's journey, with which mythology is filled.

Jack Tales are examples of stories in which characters change because of a crisis. The main character, Jack, represents every man or woman and is always the hero in traditional folklore. He leaves home and sets out on a journey to accomplish a task. He gets into a predicament, one of his own making or one that he encounters, as he seeks to find his fortune, kill the giant, or sell the cow. Jack struggles, often trying absurd solutions, and finally is triumphant. Whether he receives help or prevails through what seems to be blind luck, he always grows in the process. Jack, like most of us, has a short memory because he soon finds himself in the thick of things again, in another story.

Taking the risk

Traditional fairy tales, like Cinderella, also follow the classic pattern. Life is drab and bad for Cinderella, *and then one day* a fairy godmother appears. We know Cinderella's life will change, bringing new challenges and opportunities. When Cinderella accepts her fairy godmother's offer, new possibilities are available that she can accept or reject. Rejection is the safe choice—nothing changes and no risks occur. But acceptance brings new opportunities she never dreamed possible, including marrying the prince and living happily ever after.

In the real world few princes sweep us off our feet and rescue us. In fact, most of the time we must be our own prince and create our own solutions. Opportunities abound when we are willing to accept the risks inherent in change. Stories show us how change can offer opportunities to reconcile situations, to regain missed opportunities, and/or to move in new, positive directions. The risks often seem great, but the real tragedy is to have the experience and miss the opportunities for understanding, growth, and healing.

Healing a wounded spirit

Loss creates a wounded or incapacitated spirit, resembling physical illness in many ways. In fact the psyche *is* ill and cannot function normally, causing the body to suffer too. The key in the mind-body connection seems to be getting the mind to take the lead in moving toward wholeness or wellness. Bill Moyers, Dr. Herbert Benson, and others have examined the mind-body connection as it relates to physical illness. Their conclusions confirm the problems stemming from loss since both illness and loss cause physical stress to the body's systems.

Gradually I have realized that healing is possible although I will never be cured of the grief resulting from my son's death. Healing from a loss is an ongoing process and means learning how to live in spite of the pain. While the pain never goes away, it becomes more manageable.

> "Healing is different from curing. Healing is a process we're involved in all the time. It's very close to the process of education. 'Educare,' the root word of education means 'Leading forth, wholeness or integrity.' Healing is also the leading forth of wholeness in people."
>
> Rachel Naomi Remen, M.D.
> from Bill Moyers' interview
> in *Healing and the Mind*
>
> ⋘

Robert Bela Wilhelm suffers from Seasonal Affective Disorder, a severe depression that strikes in winter months when the amount of daylight decreases. The disorder affected him for years before he was officially diagnosed with SAD. Following his diagnosis, he decided to try stories as treatment since no known cure for the disorder exists. Medication did not help him because of the side effects. He turned to stories to fill his mind with brightness to help combat his depression. As a storyteller and theologian, he began telling and listening to stories that helped him create visual images of light.

Wilhelm believes that all of life is a spiritual journey, and knows storytelling has played a significant role for him. Much of his telling consists of lengthy, mythical stories, which he tells by first visualizing them completely in his head. His visualization process provided a natural treatment for his disorder. He said, "I deal with the loss of light and the corresponding clinical depression through the creation of images of light in my winter storytelling." It is the only thing that works for him, except heading south as winter approaches, which is not always possible. What a powerful example of using creative images to be agents for healing. (For more information about the disorder and Wilhelm's case, see Norman Rosenthal's book, *Seasons of the Mind.*)

> "In traditional tribal medicine and in Western practice from its beginning in the work of Hippocrates, the need to operate through the patient's mind has always been recognized. Until the nineteenth century, medical writers rarely failed to note the influence of grief, despair, or discouragement on the onset and outcome of illness, nor did they ignore the healing effects of faith, confidence, and peace of mind....Awareness of the mind's powers was lost as medicine cast out all 'soft' data, the information that's not easily quantified or scientific."
>
> Bernie Siegel, M.D.
> *Love, Medicine and Miracles*

Envisioning success

Dr. Bernie Siegel encourages his patients to use positive imaging in their healing processes. His books include exercises to help readers begin to incorporate this technique into their daily lives. Much has been written in recent years about imagining the body free of illness. Cancer treatment often includes guided imagery where the patient visualizes the cancer cells decreasing or being destroyed or eaten— any number of scenarios whereby the disease is stopped. Growing evidence indicates how effective this can be.

Jenna Eisenberg said that every day for three months following her divorce, she listened to a guided visualization tape by Bernie Siegel. She said, "There were four different scenarios that he talked me through while I visualized myself in the story. The words he used had lots of metaphors. I used this to picture myself healing. I was in the healing story."

Businesses offer effectiveness-training classes that show sales people how to make a successful sale by using positive imagery techniques. Many workshops include guided imagery sessions where the participants imagine themselves accomplishing their desired goals. A pediatrician once told me his "wart removal stick" is successful fifty percent of the time. The stick is nothing more than an interesting piece of driftwood he found on the beach. Since people believe it will work, it does.

A friend whose son won two gold medals for swimming at the summer Olympics in Korea talked about how much of his training involved positive imaging. He learned to visualize himself swimming through the water, imagining perfect execution of each stroke and turn, and reaching the finish ahead of other competitors. He always spent time before a meet in this visualization process. He got better and better, both at visualizing his victories and actually accomplishing them.

Activating the imagination

These examples show how tapping into the imagination can be a powerful tool for changing and improving skills and behaviors. The vital element required is an active imagination. Stories enable us to create images of ourselves in new situations, stimulating our imagination in the process. This creative process must be an important key in understanding why stories heal. Stories prompt our imagination, this wonderful gift we always have at our disposal.

> "The body-mind-spirit connection is very real. Each of us has the ability to use the power of the mind to heal our bodies and spirits. But most of us do not have enough imagination to see ourselves healed and whole in the midst of our illness and loss. Stories are an aerobic exercise program for the imagination. Each time we hear stories our imagination is strengthened."
> Elizabeth Ellis
> Storyteller and teacher
>
> ⇛

Stories naturally allow us to see our own situation in a new light that leads us toward wholeness. They can initiate our creativity to deal with events and feelings in new ways. Storyteller Elizabeth Ellis said, "The body, the mind, and the spirit are all intertwined. Any activity that produces 'dis-ease' can be addressed through story. The more 'at ease' we are, the less pain we experience." Her insight into the meaning of the word *disease* reveals important clues about dealing with it in a positive way.

Adults often say they had an active imagination as a child, but outgrew it with age. Creative individuals know our imaginations never disappear and can be tapped into at any time. Everyone still has the ability. Most adults just do not take the time and energy to use it. Too many people and things tell us what to do and how to think, and we get lazy in our thought processes.

Engaging creativity

Unleashing creative energy is a constructive way to access our imagination and empower ourselves. The simple act of doing something creative always has a calming, uplifting effect, which is a positive step. Storytelling has worked for me, but many people find their creative gifts lie in other areas. Channeling creative energy toward healing and growth can come from music, art, time spent in nature, meditation, massage therapy, nutrition, and many other activities. These pursuits offer comfort, encouragement, and hope to the giver and the receiver, proving we can still find joy in our lives.

In *A Broken Heart Still Beats,* Mary Semel wrote that after the death of her son she tried many things to relieve her grief such as, "aerobics, swimming, yoga, tennis, writing and above all good books...which led to my search for literature about the death of children." She did not know the search would end in a published book, and said, "I was simply looking for the solace of contact with other wounded souls." She now believes that "grief often inspires creativity...[it causes] the compelling need to express yourself creatively...that is probably why so much of the world's great literature is about grief and loss."

> We have found stories "empower people to clarify their feeling and values by helping them escape from the narrow viewpoints the world is always trying to thrust upon them....What else can take your mind and heart to places they have never been, let you experience events and emotions far from your daily routine, tailor itself to your own moods and reactions, and leave you with new dreams and insights?"
> Brody and Punzak
> From the introduction to
> *Spinning Tales, Weaving Hope*
>
>

Carrie Wharton said her most significant healing story came a few months after her husband's death. She was inspired to write down a personal remembrance of him for her family to treasure. She said, "It came out in the words of a child remembering. The simple text reflects that remembering is safe and healthy and is the key to staying close to those we love even when they are no longer here. Later I saw that the words might be helpful for other children experiencing loss, and so with encouragement from the children's bereavement counselor at our Hospice, I decided to submit it for publication as a children's picture book." Carrie has signed a contract for the book's publication with a major publisher. The creative activity that helped her will heal others too.

The creator of a story stretches beyond this creative impulse to access the imagination and inner self. During this process, a storyteller first imagines the story in his or her mind, constructing all the images that are part of it. Then those images are converted to words so they can be conveyed to listeners or readers through metaphor and sensory description. The listening process encourages the receivers to create images and open their minds to new possibilities through the resulting connections and insights.

> "The creative impulse is part of being a thinking/feeling creature; it strikes me that the creative impulse is as powerful as the drive to survive...Healing and creativity are two sides of the same coin. Underlying both is the idea of wholeness. The urge to survive and the urge to create are interconnected. Both can harness the enormous energy of the emotions for constructive purposes."
> Gabriele Rico
> *Pain and Possibility*
>
> ⇛

Anne Henry Ehrenpreis wrote in *The Literary Ballad,* "Storytelling is, after all, the oldest preoccupation of literature.... Simplicity and economy of expression, which are preeminent among the ballad's natural virtues, are lessons that every poet must learn. The ballad's way of looking at life is unsentimental, often ironical; it can suggest a whole vision of tragedy in the briefest stroke." Reading or hearing the creative efforts of others to express their grief often sheds light on our own inner struggles. The irony in our own story becomes apparent and more acceptable.

Forging new beliefs

Many of my assumptions and beliefs about life seemed stupid and meaningless after David's death. Experiencing loss felt like having all the doors and windows of my world nailed shut, leaving no way in or out, especially as long as I remained trapped in my old belief system. As I examined ideas and beliefs that previously I would have considered on the edge or too far out, new passages to recovery opened. If I wanted to survive, I had to explore them. Moving toward recovery was necessary because staying in that pain was not an option. I looked everywhere for new insights that might bring comfort and meaning.

Breaking with my established thought patterns was difficult at first. As a female who was raised in the Bible belt, majored in mathematics, and worked in the computer industry for years, I was definitely a left-brained person with a fairly narrow outlook on life. Anything that could not be seen or proven just did not exist, except for religious matters. I had accepted many of the literal doctrines of the church to prevent something bad happening to me. But the worst *had* happened. My old beliefs were no longer sufficient for responding to my loss, so I had to look for answers in other areas.

I began to read books that contained thoughts and ideas I had never been exposed to with my strict religious background—books by George Anderson, Raymond Moody, Brian Weiss, and people who had survived near-death experiences. Some of this information frightened me at first, but gradually opened my mind to different perspectives and freed my thinking in ways I could not believe. I was fascinated as I read about experiences before birth and after death, interactions with the spirit world, spiritual guides, time as a continuum, and meditation to assist in learning and visualization. Many ancient myths and legends confirmed these new ideas and possibilities, making me want to dig deeper. Surprisingly, nothing I learned contradicted my previous religious beliefs, but rather enhanced and expanded them. I began to feel that I was on a renewed spiritual quest, which was both astounding and exciting. I remained extremely skeptical as my logical mind continued to question and evaluate, but felt compelled to learn and explore. I am still amazed when I look back at what was going on. My childhood training triggered guilt feelings, and I frequently thought of the saying, "I don't care what the world thinks, just don't let my mother find out."

A year and half after David died, I attended a "new-age" conference with a friend whose daughter had died from a brain tumor. Many of the authors whose books I had read were presenters at the conference, including George Anderson, who is probably the best known and most publicly tested "psychic medium" in this country. As I listened that weekend, I realized I still had many things to learn and explore and think about. Most importantly, I listened to the stories of the people I met. They were normal people just like me, all struggling to find their way in the world. Many of them had experienced loss. I remember thinking that we were all looking for a new story to accept and embrace.

Moving forward

A few weeks later I attended a storytelling workshop led by Donald Davis where I processed many newly discovered concepts. I felt safe in the presence of other storytellers as Donald guided us in his calm, caring way. Creating "Infinite Resource and Sagacity" allowed me to use the structure of a story to put together for the first time everything I had been learning. I received tremendous support and encouragement from the group and felt I had taken a giant step forward. The positive accomplishment provided the boost of energy I needed. ("Infinite Resource and Sagacity" and my description of creating it follow at the end of this chapter.)

After returning home, I saw an ad for another workshop entitled "Healing the Wounds Within," led by storyteller Susan Klein and therapist and storyteller Annika Hurwitt on Martha's Vineyard. When I called and one opening remained, I knew I was supposed to attend. That four-day experience proved to be another wonderful step propelling me forward in my healing process. My newly discovered feeling of moving ahead out of confusion added to the momentum.

Attendees were supposed to come to the workshop with the *bare bones* of a story that spoke to us of creativity. I searched a lot of books and ultimately found (or maybe it found me!) "The Magic Knot" in *Tales from Silver Lands*, a collection of South American stories compiled by Charles Finger. The story is about a young boy who was able to accomplish great feats when he willingly accepted new possibilities and the guidance of a wise old woman. The story was obviously very old, probably predating European colonization and Christian missionary influence in South America. Processing and learning "The Magic Knot" prompted more growth and insight. The story delivered an important message to me—trust my own creativity and accept the power of things I did not fully understand.

All of the stories told and shared at the workshop reinforced what I was learning, as Susan and Annika helped us explore our creative processes. They used guided imagery exercises, written assignments, and a lot of stories. All of the participants were struggling with growth and development issues as they processed events in their own lives. Sharing our struggles enabled more insight and understanding to emerge.

Following the workshop, my daughter and I decided to start working through Julia Cameron's book, *The Artist's Way*. Both of us had owned the book for months but could never make the commitment required to get started. Setting a day to start and promising to follow the instructions provided the motivation we needed. We supported and encouraged each other, both finding ideas for healing and growth in the procedures and exercises suggested in the book. All of our efforts led us toward freeing our creativity to do its work, thereby enabling us to achieve new goals and dreams.

As a result of the change and growth in my outlook, in the spring of 1996 I enrolled in the Storytelling Master's degree program at East Tennessee State University (ETSU). Slowly I was regaining my confidence. My energy level had soared from those early months of grief and I was excited to get out of bed each morning. The dam had burst. I felt more on track with what I was put on this planet to do than ever before in my life.

Stories spoke to me all along the way. Answers came from many different stories—stories from across the ages and stories from the present, stories from my own culture and stories from other lands. Personal stories, folktales, myths, and legends contributed their wisdom. I found more truth in stories than anything else I knew. Examining a wide variety of stories helped me view my situation as part of the human condition. I connected with cultures other than my own through stories that openly dealt with loss, death, and the spirit world. Some stories even included rituals and customs that helped the survivors to cope. In the United States, such subjects often seem taboo. Our cultural obsession with the search for youth, beauty, and happiness has made us insensitive to those who do not fit that model. Our attempts to harness nature leave little room to discuss things that cannot be controlled, like death, illness, and other losses.

Building bridges

At some point in the creation of my new identity, it occurred to me that I needed a bridge between my world and David's world. I could not accept that the energy and spirit that was my son had been obliterated or ceased to exist because of his death. The scientific principle that energy is neither created nor destroyed reminded me of the vital life force and energy of David's life. *Where was it now?* If his energy had been transformed, I should be able to perceive and interact with it somehow—but first I needed a bridge.

Again I returned to stories—*what stories did I know about bridges?* The first one that came to mind was Pleasant DeSpain's version of the old Appalachian tale, "Old Joe and the Carpenter." In the story a man asked a carpenter to build a wall between his property and his neighbor's. The hired worker built a bridge instead, which broke down the emotional wall that had developed because of the stubbornness and miscommunication of the neighbors. The bridge allowed both men to realize the value of their friendship so that old wounds could heal. I could see how healing in a story could facilitate healing in people. What an interesting concept—a story about building bridges, and the story itself was a bridge. As before, a story opened my mind and showed me the way to new growth.

We often need bridges in our relationships and experiences to lead to new insights and understanding. *Nothing bridges human understanding like a story.* Many times the bridge exists already, but something obstructs the way: an attitude like prejudice; an emotion like fear, anger, or grief; or a condition like poverty or ignorance.

Learning from other cultures

In the midst of my continued struggle and growth, I had the good fortune to attend the University of Edinburgh with an Appalachian Cultural Exchange group from ETSU as part of my storytelling course work. While in Scotland I researched my new ideas about death, which led to a paper entitled "The Scottish View of Death and Dying—It's Reflection in Their Stories and Songs." My experiences in Scotland provided tremendous insights into many of my questions, as I interviewed people in various parts of the country, from Edinburgh to the Outer Hebrides. The answers flowed naturally and openly as I asked about death, dying, and life after death. (Because of its effect on my healing process, the research paper appears in Appendix 3.)

Once again stories brought me to a new level of understanding. In Scotland I found many stories that dealt with death, not as the end of life, but rather a deeper dimension or *extension* of life. Many Scottish stories about experiences with spirits from the other world are told with belief and conviction.

My interest in stories that dealt with the transition from life to death and the connection to the spirit world led me to explore the life of the Scottish travellers. The oral tradition of this group is an important part of their culture, reflecting their values, attitudes, customs, and beliefs. For many years the traveller folk kept to themselves, enabling them to preserve their stories and way of life with little influence from the outside world. Many of their stories reaffirm their spiritual link with the past and their belief in the close association between the world of the living and the dead. (More information on this subject is available in "The Language of Traveller Storytellers" at www.arts.gla.ac.uk/www/english/comet/starn/crit/langtrav.htm)

"From birth to death seems a natural enough sequence of events—at least to the Scot; for, to us, death has never held the fears that it holds for some of the world's peoples. Death has never meant the end. We have always thought of death as another beginning, as a re-birth, and as a re-birth to something better. And this faith we held long before the Christian doctrine of the Immortality of the Soul was brought to us to lighten our Pagan hearts! Indeed, there is much to prove that our distant ancestors held very decided views on spiritual re-birth, and the notion of another and brighter world beyond. From our Celtic forebears there has come the beautiful legend of *Tir-nan-Og*, the Land of Eternal Youth; and other legends, too, of invisible other worlds. There are references to a Celtic other world where the natural and the spiritual dance together in a green harmony."

Ronald MacDonald Douglas
Scottish Lore and Folklore

≪≪≪

In an interview during a ceilidh (a gathering of people sharing music and stories) at the School of Scottish Studies at the University of Edinburgh, the well-known traveller storyteller Stanley Robertson said, "People who have passed are not gone—they are just beyond the veil. Sometimes I feel so close to them I feel as if I could reach through the veil and touch them." When Stanley's aunt Jeannie Robertson died, he accompanied her body to the funeral home. He said, "On the way there, she sang to me and taught me a song I had never heard. I know this song and sing it today." She was considered one of the greatest traveller storytellers and ballad singers of all times.

> "Traveller children were taught to accept death as something natural, not something to fear....The very fact that Stanley [Robertson] has so many stories featuring Death points up how fine a line travellers place between the world of the living and the dead, and how realistically they accept death as the natural extension to the life cycle."
>
> Barbara McDermitt
> From her dissertation at the University of Edinburgh
>
> ⇛

Stanley continued in his lyrical voice, "The American Indian view of death is much like the Scottish. They talk openly about it, but most Americans don't. I think if you've ever lost a loved one, you know they are not really gone. I've actually gone beyond the veil myself—several times— and had the opportunity to look around and see things....I've seen it and you'd be surprised how close your loved ones still are—they are all around you—they touch you and help you more than you can know."

Scottish silkie tales, stories about seals having the supernatural ability to become human, reflect the belief that those who die at sea are not really gone, but rather have gone to live with the seals. Scottish ballads, too, have strong elements of the supernatural. Many of them are about spirits who return to visit and comfort their loved ones. The vivid images created in the ballads reflect the Scots' belief in spirits living on after death. A strong sense of interaction with the deceased is woven throughout much of the literature of Scotland. (Several examples are included in Appendix 3.)

The firm conviction that death is a transition to another state of being that continues to make contact with the living appears in all parts of Scottish life. While studying in Scotland, observing the Scots' view of death and dying as a natural part of life influenced my acceptance of David's death. In fact, the entire experience provided a turning point in my healing process. My belief that stories help transform the pain following a loss was strongly confirmed. All of these insights provided the bridge I needed between the land of the living and the spirit world.

Creating a new story

I did not originally look at the events of David's life as a story, but gradually saw unifying threads running throughout. His ability to always have fun, learn new things, make people laugh, and look for challenges reflected his love of life. Sometimes those pursuits got him into trouble, but his enthusiasm never subsided. I wondered if putting the events of his life together in some sort of sequence might help make sense of his death. I was looking for answers and under-standing, and in the process I *found* healing.

Looking at David's life in a story was like pouring alcohol on an open wound. The task hurt terribly in the beginning, with a lot of tears and pain. But once all the pieces were visible, healing did begin. The following story, which appeared in the Summer 1998 issue of *Storytelling World* magazine, was the result.

Infinite Resource and Sagacity

When David was a little boy, he was the most precocious child you'd ever meet. Now I know everybody thinks their children are the cutest, the sweetest, the smartest—but he really was. He asked more questions—I spent half my life looking up or making up the answers to his questions because 'I don't know' was never acceptable to him. He loved books and stories and words. I always thought it was because when he was two months old, I went back to school and took English literature and so every day for two semesters I read to him from Beowulf, Chaucer, Shakespeare, Wordsworth and Elizabeth Barrett Browning. The words and the sound of my voice charmed him.

As he got older, he continued to love looking at books and being read to, and one of his favorite stories was one by Kipling called 'How the Whale Got His Throat.' This story talked about a man of infinite resource and sagacity and David thought this was the coolest thing he had ever heard. He went around talking about this man of infinite resource and sagacity. The funny thing about it, he was only two years old—imagine a little guy with blond hair, blue eyes, and a big smile talking about a man of infinite resource and sagacity. People were amazed when they heard him and one day someone asked if he knew what that meant. David answered, "Yes, it means that man was really smart."

As he got older, he loved challenges—puzzles, surprises, and tricks. My brother, who wasn't married at the time, loved spending time with my children and one of the things David loved about Uncle Tom was that he could perform magic. One day Uncle Tom was visiting and David begged "Do some magic, do some magic" and so Uncle Tom started with simple tricks like making a quarter disappear and then suddenly pulling it from behind David's ear. After a few more tricks, he said, "David, how would you like me to make you disappear." Well, he wasn't so sure about this — but after thinking a minute he said, "OK, that would be great." So Uncle Tom called out, "Everybody gather around—I'm going to make David disappear. This is going to be tough because I've never done anything quite like this before." He began to rub his hands together and say his magic words and then "Poof—I did it! He's gone. I made David disappear." David looked around—looked at his hands and clothes, touched himself and looked a little concerned. We all started talking as if he weren't there. After a while Uncle Tom asked if we were ready to bring David back and I said, "No. It is really nice and quiet around here. Maybe I'll finally get some rest." David's eyes really got big as he looked around the room from one person to the next. He started to jump around making a little noise, stomping his feet and waving his hands. Then he started yelling, "Hey, it's me, David. I'm here—I'm still here." Finally I said, "You know, even though it is quieter, I really love that little guy and I miss him. Maybe you'd better bring him back." So Uncle Tom said, "I'm going to need everybody's help. This is really going to require some concentration cause I've never done this before and it may be even harder." Everybody got really quiet—including David—and his eyes were so big, they were about to pop out of his head. Uncle Tom began rubbing his hands and saying his magic words again—we all stared at his hands—then "Poof! He's back. David you're back. It's so good to see you."

David continued to love magic tricks for a long time. Uncle Tom gave him tricks every year for Christmas and his birthday and taught him how to perform them. David had me make him a big black cape and he got an old briefcase from his grandfather to carry his tricks around in. He had a tall hat and a magic wand, but he never let Uncle Tom make him disappear again.

As he grew up he always enjoyed challenges—things a little out of the ordinary. When he was in high school, one year at the state Latin convention he gave a speech - in Latin! In college, he and his roommate wrote a computer program for Dungeon and Dragons— before computer games were on the market. They installed it on the Vanderbilt computer system and it worked! He went to work for Kodak as a systems engineer, got married, loved riding his mountain bike, playing the piano, brewing beer, and baking bread—always looking for new and challenging things to learn.

And then one day, when he was 29 years old, he had an allergic reaction to an insect bite and he was gone. It's a parent's worse nightmare. All of a sudden my whole life turned upside down taking with it so many hopes and dreams for the future. His young wife was two months pregnant with their first child. His child would never experience the joy of knowing David.

Struggling with all of this I realized one day that now he was the man of infinite resource and sagacity for he had all the answers, and I had all the questions. As I continued to try to make sense of something that made no sense, I did a lot of reading, writing, screaming, reaching out, thinking, searching—none of the traditional answers fit anymore. It gradually occurred to me that death is not the end, but rather a transition to another state or dimension that we don't fully understand. And the frustrating part is that we don't know how to communicate. I'm convinced that he hears me and knows my feelings—I express them often enough. But I didn't know how to understand him—until I noticed that he was using my thoughts, my memories, my dreams and my stories.

One day while jogging in Anastasia Park near my house, my mind was clear and free. All of a sudden that incident when David was four years old—the day Uncle Tom made him disappear—popped into my head. I had not thought of it in at least 20 years, and it comforted me. Later that day, I was looking for something in my kitchen and saw a small metal box that I hadn't seen for a long time.

Wondering what was inside, I opened it and found a stack of David's business cards. Since he worked for Kodak, the card had his picture on it. As I stood there looking at his face, I suddenly knew what he was trying to tell me. It was loud and clear, "Hello. It's me, David. I'm here. I'm still here."

*Then I saw his gift hanging on my dining room wall. About a year before his death, David was on a business trip and picked up a copy of Robert Fulghum's book, **All I Ever Needed to Know I Learned in Kindergarten.** When he returned home he called and said, "Mom, you really need to read this book. I think you'd really like it. It's full of great stories." So I read it and I did like it. I noticed in the front of the book something Fulghum had written called the Storyteller's Creed. When I returned the book to David, I told him that I wanted to get a copy of that creed. That year for Christmas, he used a fancy font on his computer, printed it on rice paper and framed it for me for Christmas. It was special to me at the time but even more so now. It goes like this:*

> *I believe that imagination is stronger than knowledge,*
> *That myth is more potent than history,*
> *That dreams are more powerful than facts,*
> *That hope always triumphs over experience,*
> *That laughter is the only cure for grief,*
> *And I believe that love is stronger than death.*

⋙⋘

Included in *Storytelling World* was the explanation of how I created the story.

Writing David's Story

Writing this story occurred after struggling with my son's death for two-and-a-half years. I could not have written it sooner, although it seemed a very natural part of my healing process. Stories have been an important part of my life for such a long time and I am more and more convinced of their power to cause healing and growth.

At a workshop with Donald Davis, I began thinking of the events in this story as being connected. Donald asked us to tell a story about someone that would "cause the listener to know us better." The story seemed only for me at first because I found so much healing in it. But as I struggled with it at the workshop that weekend, others encouraged me to tell it.

A friend at the workshop called several weeks later and said she had not been able to stop thinking about my story. She had told someone about it, and that person also had been touched. She closed by saying, "You have to tell that story. It gives me and others hope that we could survive, whatever our loss might be."

Part of my concern about telling the story was not wanting sadness to be the dominant feeling people were left with. I have heard stories of personal events and tragedies and felt the teller should be relating them to a therapist and not an audience. I resent being told stories that are so heavy that I end up feeling down or depressed. A story should not make listeners deal with grief that has not been fully explored and dealt with by the teller.

This is not to say that there should be no emotion in a story. I love stories that make me laugh and cry and feel all sorts of emotions, but I just do not want to be left hanging with a feeling of unresolved sadness or hopelessness. Good stories should elicit feelings, but not more than the audience can handle.

So that was my concern. I did not want my story to make people sad. The story was really about my relationship with David, and I wanted listeners to feel the love and joy in that and not be over-whelmed with the sadness. In addition, I did not want to dissolve into tears when I told it in front of an audience.

But because I felt David's life and the story were gifts, I did not want to keep them to myself if they could be helpful to others. I began by telling it in small family settings. We all cried, but each time I told it I got a little stronger. Then I told it to The Compassionate Friends, a support group for parents who have lost children. Tears are always appropriate there, but I got through without crying, although my voice quivered at one point. The group members encouraged me to keep working on it. They obviously sensed the sadness but had felt hope—for me and also for their situations. That was exactly what I wanted to hear.

The following week I attended the Florida Storyteller's Guild Camp and signed up to tell it Sunday morning during "Stories from the

Heart." Even though I have found storytellers to be supportive and helpful, I almost took my name off the list several times. When Sunday morning came, I told the story to an audience of about 150 tellers.

The response was unbelievable. One lady said she had a situation in her life that she had wanted to tell a story about, but never had been able to do so. She told me a beautiful story about her husband planting some tulips not long before he died. She said her daughter needed to hear the story and I had shown her how she could tell it. Another woman told me she had recently lost her mother with whom she was very close, and my story had given her so much to think about in dealing with her loss. One woman pointed out that we all suffer losses in life, and my story showed how they could be dealt with in creative ways to make us better people.

I have told the story many times since then and know it is powerful. I am mindful to tell it in situations that are appropriate and not just for the effect it has. Many times when I arrive at a performance, for some reason I feel led to share it. And every time that happens, at least one person comes up afterward and tells me that I must have told the story for them because it was exactly what they needed to hear. So I try to be open to telling it when I get that feeling.

One of the most meaningful responses came from a friend who heard it for the first time one evening in a rehearsal for an upcoming group performance. She wrote me the following note.

> *I was so moved by your story tonight that I wanted to let you know. You have truly honored your son in a most beautiful and unusual way. He came alive for me through your eyes, your memories, and most of all—your love. What a special young man!*
>
> *I'm awed by the courage you have in sharing this story with others. We all need this message because we've all experienced loss, and all need to hear again and again that we can never be truly separated from those we love.*
>
> *Your story is beautiful, and I know that Friday night when you tell it, your son will be very proud.*

That was more than I ever dreamed it could do. Let me quickly add that I do not have that kind of ability. Once again, it is the power of story!

How could a story that started out to be just for me trigger so many different responses in listeners? The comments I received encouraged me. "It is a story about your love for your son"—and it was. "It is a story about survival"—and it is. "It offers hope"—and it does.

Stories enable growth and learning 8

Looking inside to grow

Believing that healing *could* occur opens the listener to the positive approaches found in many stories and life experiences. Although roadblocks are bound to arise, fresh insights and situations surround us all the time. Stories have a subtle way of confronting us, making us ready to hear and receive what we need. Then receptive listeners see new possibilities and solutions that lead to growth and constructive action.

In stories we can recognize loss, grief, and death for what they are, even though our society often avoids painful events and feelings. Only after affirming the significance of our loss can we begin to learn and grow as we attempt to find a way to heal. The real question is *can we perpetuate and use what we have learned?* Continuing to tell our stories provides the opportunities we need to reinforce our knowledge and help others in the process.

Therese Rando in her book *Parental Loss of a Child* said, "In order to successfully complete grief work, the bereaved parent needs repeated opportunities to be heard nonjudgmentally, to express the pain of separation, to accept the finality of the loss, to articulate and process the many different feelings about loss and its consequences, and to engage in the recollection and review procedures that will facilitate healthy decathexis [release from the pain of loss]." Rando's comments about bereaved parents really apply to anyone who has experienced a significant loss of any kind. Most personal accounts of

> "Stories are doorways into seeing and experiencing your inner and outer worlds.... As a storyteller and therapist, I know that to hear and tell stories, both personal and traditional, brings profound healing and nourishment."
> Elisa Pearmain
> *Doorways to the Soul*
>
> ⇒≫

loss accomplish, to some extent, all of the goals listed by Rando. Of course, simply telling the story to an individual or a therapist fulfills the speakers' need to be heard. Crafting a story for an audience forces a storyteller to confront the issues at an even deeper level before the story is ready to be told. Grief work may never be completely finished, but opportunities to share the story certainly help to move it along.

Processing feelings

My first experience with loss came at the age of thirty-three, with the death of my grandmother, whom I adored. She was one of the few people in my life that loved me unconditionally and supported me no matter what. I was devastated by her illness and subsequent death as I gradually lost the person she was. I did not mention her in any of my stories for a long time because I felt I could not adequately convey the depth of my feelings toward her. My memories and feelings were too significant to risk not portraying them accurately. Only after painful examination did I realize how much she affected me.

After the death of my son, when I had no choice but to yield to my feelings of grief and pain, stories about my grandmother began to creep out of me. A tragic loss opens up previous wounds due to loss, especially when the losses were never fully resolved. A story still lurks inside me about the confusion and emptiness I felt from losing my number one champion and watching all the indignities she suffered as her beautiful life ended. Eventually I began to acknowledge the influence she had on me, as the following story shows.

Not Presh

A friend once told me that some things in life are worth doing even though you have to suffer the consequences because you can only catch so much hell for any one thing. Well I've got news, my friend was wrong.

Gran loved everybody—especially me. I was her first granddaughter and she always called me "Presh." She would come to my aid in a flash in any situation, including a disagreement with my own mother (her daughter), because in her eyes I could do no wrong. I knew she loved me unconditionally—nothing I could have done would have diminished her love for me. That was such a gift, but something of a burden too because when I did something I was not particularly proud of, I was so afraid Gran would find out. Not that it would have mattered to her—she probably would not have believed it. "Not Presh," she would have said. But I did not want to tarnish the halo she had placed over my head. I wanted to be everything she thought I was.

But it is hard to be perfect, no matter how hard you try. In fact it became increasingly difficult with age, especially with parents that did not understand my true nature as Gran did. Many disagreements erupted as peer pressure exerted influence on my behavior and I got interested in boys.

When I was twelve years old, my friend who lived across the street was having a party one Friday night and I knew my boyfriend was going to be there.

"Mother, can I go to Linda's party Friday night?

"No."

"Why not?"

"Because her parents won't be home."

"Yes they will. I asked Linda and she said they'd be there."

"Well you still can't go."

"Why not?"

"Because I said so."

Now in those days "because I said so" was sufficient to end the conversation. How could you argue with logic like that? When I realized I was getting nowhere, I decided to take change my tactics.

Not going to the party was not an option that I even considered. I just did not mention it for the rest of the week.

After eating dinner on Friday night and watching television for a while with my parents, I announced that I was really tired and thought I'd go to bed. As things in the house settled for the evening, I got back out of bed and dressed again. Then I climbed out of my bedroom window and went to the party. The window was about twelve feet above the ground, so I had to jump to the edge of the front porch from the windowsill. Then balancing carefully, I eased myself down to the water spigot before dropping to the ground below. I couldn't just walk across the porch for fear that I might be seen. Once on the ground I edged along the shrubbery and crossed the street quickly.

The party was fun and he was there, but I could not completely relax and enjoy myself. Absolutely nothing happened, which proved that my parents should have let me go to begin with and helped justify my actions. I did not stay long before deciding to return home and try to get back into my room. I am here to tell you that getting back in was a lot more difficult that getting out, but after several unsuccessful attempts I managed to scramble up onto the edge of the porch. I got my balance and jumped for the window ledge. Hanging on for dear life I managed to claw and wiggle myself back up the brick wall and then drop down inside my room. I was covered with scrapes and scratches. Quickly I undressed and disappeared under the covers— completely undetected, which further proved that I should have been permitted to go to start with.

Several days passed and no further mention was made of the party. But then one day when I came home from school, my mother met me at the door. She was not smiling and asking me how my day had gone as she usually did. She definitely was not as happy as she could have been. "Did you go to Linda's party last Friday night?" she asked, trying to control her voice.

"You wouldn't let me go—don't you remember?" I answered as indignantly as possible.

"Well, I didn't think you did, but Constance said Maggie told her that the woman who works for Linda's parents said you were there." Constance worked for my mother and Maggie worked for the folks next door.

"Well, I wasn't. She must have been confused—probably thought somebody else was me because I understand there were lots of people there."

"Are you sure you weren't there?"

"Yes, I'm sure. I watched TV and then went to bed—remember? I... I need to go to the bathroom."

I dashed into my bedroom to get away from that look. Those eyes felt like steel beams running through me. Mother went back to the kitchen and I thought I had escaped once more, but then my grandmother's image of me started working. I really had not intended to lie about it and I wouldn't have had to if they had just been reasonable and let me go to the party like normal people. I could see my grandmother's face and smile and feel her arms around me, and the next thing I knew I was in the kitchen saying through my tears, "I did go to the party. I'm sorry. I don't know what got into me, but I just wanted to go so bad and I guess I just got carried away. I'm sorry I lied to you. I am sooo sorry. I'll never do anything like that again as long as I live."

Suddenly my mother's face and eyes filled with such hurt and disbelief. Questions followed—how did you do it, when did you do it, why did you do it? We were both so upset that I don't remember exactly what happened next except I spent a lot of time in my room after that. My daddy was furious and grounded me for what seemed like forever. Every time my mother looked at me she'd shake her head and say, "I just can't believe you would do such a thing. I never thought you would do anything like that? What would your grandmother say?" I knew exactly what she'd say—"not Presh!"

*Over forty years have passed since I went to that party and as far as I know Gran never found out, but my mother still brings this story up from time to time. She especially loved talking about it when I had disagreements with my children. And even now she shakes her head and says, "Why **did** you climb out that window? I still cannot believe you did it. What in the world were you thinking?"*

Well, I don't know what I was thinking. I guess I did it because I wanted to go to the party—after all I was trustworthy and fully capable of taking caring of myself. But at least I always knew what Gran would say— "not Presh."

-》》-《《-

Even though this story does not deal directly with loss, creating it gave me the opportunity to process some of the feelings I had for my grandmother. My visual images seemed almost like a visit with her and allowed me to feel her continuing presence in my life.

Confronting pain

My next significant loss was even more overwhelming. My first husband Win died suddenly of a heart attack when I was thirty-eight, leaving me with our three children—ages nine, thirteen, and sixteen. The shock of his death still blurs my memory of that period. I lived in a world of uncertainty as I struggled to cope with his death and all that had to be done. I was nineteen years old when we married and had gone from my father telling me what to do to my husband calling most of the shots. After his death, for the first time in my life I was completely responsible for myself and my three children. When the fog lifted, I had a lot to learn and do.

Everyone advised me to make life as normal as possible for my children's sake. Just before his death, I had graduated from college and started graduate studies in organizational psychology, so I stayed in school. Two weeks after his death I had to give a two-hour presentation on organizing your time, at a time when I could I barely function at all. I did not allow myself to adequately grieve for Win. I was busy trying to be super mom by compensating my children for the loss of their father. For the most part, I shoved my grief into the closet.

Many years later when I got involved with storytelling, I began to mention Win in a few stories without fully recognizing the feelings of loss, abandonment, and resentment his death had caused me. One such story revealed the problems I encountered with my children after starting to date, something I never dreamed of doing.

Dates and Names

Being single again at age thirty-eight after nineteen years of marriage was an eye opening experience. About a year after my husband's death, with the encouragement of well-meaning friends and family, I decided that I might be mentally and emotionally ready

*to start dating. I was wrong! Several friends knew men they wanted
to introduce me to, and I reluctantly accepted my first date.*

*While getting ready I was as nervous as a teen-ager waiting to see the
judge. All three children were hovering around and their advice was
priceless. My ten-year-old daughter said, "Now Mom, if he tries to
get fresh, tell him not on the first date."*

*Right before my date arrived, seventeen-year-old David said, "Mom,
if he has too much to drink, do not get in the car with him. Call me
and I'll come get you, no matter where you are." I wonder where he
had heard that before. When we returned later that evening and for
several times following, David was waiting up for me and met us at
the door. He stayed very close by until my date left. It was amusing
at first, but got to be a real drag. Finally I told him I appreciated his
concern, but he was not my father, and at my age, I didn't need
anyone to wait up for me.*

*Kathi, my fourteen-year old, didn't want me to date, period. She told
me she did not see why I had to go out with men—after all, I had
already lived my life. Her attitude stayed the same for a long time,
mellowing a little only after her Uncle Don came to my aid and had
a talk with her. He said, "You know, Kathi, if your mom doesn't
date and never finds someone she wants to marry, you'll probably be
stuck with her one day. It's the responsibility of the oldest daughter
to take care of the mother."*

*As I continued to date, the children always came up with nicknames
for the men I went out with. It was amazing how they were able to
zero in on names that were so fitting. The first was a radiologist they
named **The Curl** because he didn't have much hair. I have always
been aggravated by the way medical doctors introduce themselves as
"Dr. So and So." No other profession does that. One night in a
group, my date introduced himself as Dr. So and So and I followed
introducing myself as "Computer Programmer Mothershed," my
name at the time. When he looked puzzled, I said, "Oh, I thought
we were telling what we did."*

*Another of my dates was immediately named **Joe Studley** because
he arrived to pick me up wearing a low cut velour shirt and lots of
gold chains. He was actually a nice guy, but just a little too cool. The
evening got to be a bit long and it was one of those times I promised
myself if I ever got home, I would never date again. But the evening*

ended perfectly when we got home. Joe Studley came around the car to open the door for me and the handle fell off in his hand. It is awfully hard to look cool while you're holding your door handle.

*Then there was **Dipper Dan** - a nice, quiet, sedate, uninteresting, guy. BORING! His wife had run off to California, started hanging out with an itinerant musician, and left him with the kids. I don't blame her - I would have run off too.*

*Oh yes, **Charles Atlas** was a very strong guy who worked out a lot and looked like the after picture of any body building ad you have ever seen. His biceps were bigger around than my waist, and his shirtsleeves fit really tight—how else could they fit? David, who by this time had lost interest in my dates, walked through the room, did a double take and dropped the box he was carrying.*

Charles Atlas had been to chiropractic school for a while, and although he had not graduated, he said the Lord had taught him every thing he needed to know about back and neck problems. After dinner with friends of his, the wife asked him to adjust her neck, which he did. She reported that she always felt so much better when he did that. When he asked if I wanted him to check my neck, I replied, "No thank you, it's just fine and I never have back problems." He insisted and I finally said OK to just checking it. Before I knew what happened, a loud crack blasted from my neck, and I thought sure it must be broken. I reached up to feel the blood gushing forth. No blood, but that's the last time he touched my neck or me.

*I met **Bob the Babe** when I took sailing lessons. We had a great time and enjoyed sailing and many other things together. But my kids could not get over the fact that his age was seven years younger than mine. They harped on it so much that I became deathly afraid every time we ordered dinner that the waiter would say to him, "Well now, and what would your mother have to eat?" My son was the worst. If he drove by while I was jogging he'd shout, "you'd better run faster if you're going to keep up with the Babe."*

Finally, one day I had had it with him. I said, "David, I do not understand why you are having such a problem with this. You thought it was fine when I dated the Meal and he was fifteen years older. Why can't you handle somebody seven years younger? Besides, from a biological standpoint, it makes a lot more sense."

"Why?" he wanted to know.

"Because women live longer than men for one thing."

"What else?" he asked.

"I'll let you figure that out yourself."

There were others—**The Meal** was overweight, **Macro Man** talked constantly about all the food bargains he got at Macro - a quantity discount grocery, and **The Geek** was a systems engineer at the software company where I worked. After five long years of this torture, I had dinner one evening with an old friend who lived in Boston. He and I were discussing how the longer you stayed single, the more conditions you had for a potential relationship. He said, "In fact, you have so many filters, there aren't many of us that will fit through them all."

He was right. He did meet all my requirements! We started dating and a year and half later were married. I knew it had to be the right thing because the kids never came up with a nickname for him.

Resolving buried feelings

I thought I had handled my husband's death and gotten on with my life. Only after David's death did I realize how much I had ignored. Losing David forced me to explore my unresolved feelings related to Win's death. Much later I created a story called "The Wedding Ring," which I *initially* thought was about keeping your word and fulfilling expectations in life. In the story I told of keeping a commitment to a complete stranger even at the risk of exposing myself to a negative reaction from my husband. Everybody in the story did what he or she was supposed to do—except Win. Gradually I realized that the story contained a lot of anger directed at him because he had not kept his part of *our* agreement. Win died and left me alone to raise our three children. The insight I gained after David died helped me recognize my old anger and finally approach other untouched feelings. At last I understood that his death was not connected to his love for me.

Years later when my father died after a long battle with bladder cancer, many wounds needed healing. His years of alcoholism left emotional scars on a lot of people, myself included. When he became ill, I sensed sadness over the loss of our relationship when I was young. I was able to create a story, "It's Hard for an Eight-Year-Old to Understand," to help me unravel my feelings and forgive my dad. (The story appears in chapter ten.)

David's sudden death occurred the following year while I was still coming to terms with the loss of my father. My system was overloaded, and I doubted I would ever function again. Certainly I could never tell another story. I could not imagine having the desire to do anything that required thought or feeling.

I never stopped listening to stories even when I could not tell them. Slowly I began to see that telling stories was actually the best way to keep David alive—for others and for me. When I realized that stories were having a positive effect on my grief, I searched for stories to help me look at David's death in different ways. I shared memories of him with others and finally began to consider telling a story about my relationship with him. Embracing the importance of his life presented a challenge, but also a great opportunity.

All of the significant losses left me with the task of surviving not only the loss of a loved one, but also the change of my role in life as I had envisioned it. I spent time thinking about my first three significant losses, but never fully resolved them in my mind. For whatever reason I put them away in a special place inside and quit trying to figure them out. With David's death, the pain was too great to bury. Losing him set me on the quest to find meaning in my own life. Stories not only started me on the path, but also constantly showed me new directions along the way.

Embarking on a quest

Telling life stories a spiritual journey, although I did not understand that in the beginning. I was hooked on stories then, but told them primarily for entertainment. I still love to be entertained by a good story, especially one with humor, twists, and a surprise ending. But after a while, I knew storytelling offered a lot more than entertainment alone and noticed I was attracted to stories dealing with struggle and growth. Looking back, I know all the steps and stories were preparation for things to come.

"The Magic Mustard Seed" and "The Lion's Whiskers" provide good examples of stories about a quest for healing. Variant forms of both stories appear in folklore from several different cultures. The theme is finding resolution of a loss or problem, not in the sought object, but rather in the process of searching. The distraught individual must first seek a cure for the problem. The process of seeking, questioning, and taking action ultimately supplies the answers needed to begin to heal. In each story, the character seeks help from a wise man or woman and is told to procure an object to be used in a magic healing potion. Obtaining the object becomes the quest and requires planning, patience, perseverance, and boldness. In "The Lion's Whiskers," a whisker from the fiercest lion in the forest is actually procured but not used. In "The Magic Mustard Seed," the mustard seed from a home that knows no sorrow is never found, but the seeker learns that the source of healing is within. The wise one says, "Use what was learned in the quest and apply it to your life."

Both stories are variations of the classic hero's journey frequently found in mythology and contained vital clues for my healing process. Once I could no longer live in the depths of depression, I searched everywhere for guidance. Actively seeking understanding and healing led me to wonderful people, experiences, and stories. Each encounter added a unique piece to my puzzle of growth and understanding. Finding my purpose in life and figuring out how to accomplish it is the only way I know to honor those I love, both living and dead.

Once I started my journey toward recovery, I felt led to certain stories. Ideas I needed to examine further confronted me. Many stories contained healing messages and summoned me to learn and tell them because of their potential. In some cases, stories I had heard many times took on new meaning. *Were these stories really calling me, or was I reaching out desperately trying to grasp onto anything that made some sense?* I truly wanted to heal from the loss of my son and needed new insights in my search for answers. I did not even know what I was looking for, but I thought about and struggled with every aspect of those stories, trying to digest whatever they offered.

Others reported similar experiences. Carrie Wharton said many of the stories she has chosen for telling, as well as ones she has written, deal in some way with loss, death, or dying. She said, "These are not planned choices. I don't seek these themes out—somehow they find their way to me and I am drawn to tell them."

As I wondered if the stories that attracted me would have meaning for others, the strong visual image Clarissa Pinkola Estes described got my attention. Maybe my losses could become the roots that gave my life meaning and the stories could empower me in some way. Estes' image further confirmed that stories heal us by invading our beings and working within until we are changed. Stories become part of who we are. When I first created "Infinite Resource and Sagacity" and other stories about my son, I was still struggling with their truths. I wanted to believe their messages, but could not completely understand or accept them. Now, I wonder how I was able to compose the stories when I did. Encouraged by listeners, I continued the pursuit and my own stories worked on me. Every time I tell them, they become a more integral part of who I am. I finally realized my stories were healing me. *Where did these stories come from? How could they have come from me at a time when I had so many questions?* Now I know the stories came *through* me, from my son, to help in my healing.

Am I kidding myself thinking this way? Do I have delusions of grandeur? Why do I doubt the power of the universe and the power of stories to work in

> "For the most part, we tell stories when we are summoned by them, and not vice versa. Although some use stories as entertainment alone, tales are, in their oldest sense, a healing art. Some are called to this healing art, and the best, to my lights, are those who have lain with the story and found all its matching parts inside themselves and at depth.... In the best tellers I know, the stories grow out of their lives like roots grow a tree. The stories have grown them, grown them into who they are."
>
> Clarissa Pinkola Estes, Ph.D.
> *Women Who Run with the Wolves*

the world? I have seen that power working within me as I tell stories to others—as long as I am open to receive it. Likewise, I have felt healing power in the stories of others.

Crossing cultures

After my son's death I quit telling stories for a while. I could not even think of a story, much less tell one, as my brain closed down for self-preservation. Gradually as I reentered the land of the living, I saw stories as a way to seek comfort and to find meaning and understanding in my own life. I searched for stories that made me think, change, and grow in some way. A Scottish storyteller and friend, Ewan McVickers, told me about a time when he was listening to a story with an African storyteller. When the story was over, the African teller asked Ewan what the point of the story had been, thinking he missed it because of a cultural difference. Ewan said, "I don't think it had a point—it was just meant to be entertaining." His African friend replied, "Why would anyone waste time telling a story like that?"

Our society cannot fully grasp the importance of stories in a culture where they are the primary way to communicate beliefs and customs as well as convey traditional spiritual and moral values. For the African storyteller and his culture, stories were a way to impart understanding, teach values, reveal important things about life, and preserve the past. While stories were often entertaining, that was never their *primary* purpose. Africa is drastically changing today, but many native tales still offer strong, essential messages to help people think, grow, and heal. The same potential exists for our stories

Because stories put us in touch with our inner selves, they provide opportunities for growth. Even when a happy ending is not feasible, stories offer hope and understanding by exhibiting creative ways to deal with our problems. Seeing positive examples in stories opens us to new possibilities, as illustrated by the Japanese story "A Thousand Paper Cranes." In this true story, a young girl named Sadako suffered from leukemia after radiation exposure from the bomb dropped on Hiroshima. Sadako's best friend gave her a paper crane and told her that any sick person who folds a thousand paper cranes would get well. In Japanese folklore cranes live for a thousand years. Sadako's story of folding the cranes as her illness progresses is heart-rending and evokes all of the emotions surrounding death and loss. Certainly the story does not have a happy ending—Sadako does not live. Yet her determination and courage touched many lives and continues to affect others long after her death. A granite monument of Sadako with a golden crane perched on her outstretched hand stands in the Peace Park in Hiroshima. Her statue reminds and inspires, and her story shows us a creative way to approach dying and grieving. Through the story, Sadako still lives, for at least a thousand years. (A version of "A Thousand Paper Cranes" appears in *Stories for Telling* by William White.)

Stories cannot always end with everyone living happily ever after as in fairytales. Certainly many stories in real life do not. Once we understand and accept reality, we must look for ways to live and grow in spite of adversity. Uplifting stories like "A Thousand Paper Cranes" show us how to look beyond the grief and pain of loss to find new meaning in life. We take heart believing we can be better because of what has happened to us, if we acknowledge our loss and find ways to grow.

Even in the midst of great suffering and tragedy, incredible examples of transcendence exist. Viktor Frankl discussed the possibility in his book *Man's Search for Meaning.* Speaking about those who lived in the Nazi concentration camps, Frankl wrote, "If there is meaning in life at all, then there must be a meaning in suffering. Suffering is an ineradicable part of life, even as fate and death. Without suffering and death human life cannot be complete....

> "For Keats, the pains of human experience were not simply to be endured but to be learned from: they, as much as any sensory or aesthetic pleasure, nourished and transformed the soul."
>
> Rose Solari
> From the introduction to
> *Nourishing the Soul*
>
> ⇒⟫

Everywhere man is confronted with fate, with the chance of achieving something through his own suffering....It is just such an exceptionally difficult external situation [life in the camps] which gives man the opportunity to grow spiritually beyond himself."

Healing ourselves

Clearly, stories told from the heart have the most to offer and contain the greatest potential for healing. We listen to and tell some stories many times because we continue to learn from them. Maybe we are not ready for their full impact, so the message has difficulty getting through to us.

John Ward told me about the premature birth of his daughter. "Often times you never know until later when a story has proved healing for another. For a story to heal, I believe one must be open to the possibility. There are stories I read or tell again and again because I still need their therapeutic value. For example, my youngest daughter was a 'preemie.' The doctor said she would not survive. I refused to accept his words and through the intensive care glass partition, pleaded, 'Be a fighter, be a fighter.' She was, and she survived. She still loves to hear that story, as do I...as it continues to work its magic."

> "You tell a story until you no longer need to hear its message; then you put it away. Most of us simply tell our stories to make sense of our lives, and we listen to stories so others can make sense of theirs. We tell some stories again and again because we are in the process of living them out and learning their healing qualities."
> John Ward
> From his article
> "Storytelling and Healing"
>
> ⋘

When John told me his story, neither of us knew how important it would become to my family and me. Many months later, my daughter Wendy was expecting her first child and had a difficult pregnancy. She developed severe toxemia and had to deliver her baby six weeks early for health reasons. The baby boy weighed 5 pounds 3 ounces, which was amazing, but he had breathing problems and had to be taken immediately to the neonatal intensive care unit (NICU). The little guy was put on a respirator and had tubes running in and out of every possible spot.

That evening Wendy threw a fit to see him even though she was still having blood pressure problems. She and her husband went inside the NICU, scrubbed down, and put on hospital robes. My husband and I watched through the window as they looked down at their tiny baby without being able to hold him. Tears streamed down their faces. This was not the moment of their hopes and plans. In their eyes I saw pain, fear, disappointment, disbelief, and yet thankfulness that he was alive. I wanted to hold all of them and promise everything would be fine, but I knew it would bring little comfort.

All of a sudden, I thought about John's story and I started to say through my tears, "Be a fighter, be a fighter." When we returned to Wendy's room, I told her the story and we all started saying "be a fighter" to baby Davis every chance we got. He *was* a fighter and went home after only ten days in intensive care. I would like to believe our thoughts and positive energy helped his rapid progress, but I *know* telling the story that first night lessened our fears and helped us hang on to our hopes and dreams. *The healing power continues.*

Unexpected healing occurred following a performance of storyteller Doug Lipman. A listener reflected, "You never know what your story may be doing for some individual listening in the audience. During the performance we sang Doug Lipman's song about the rabbi and the three students, wherein the rabbi asks the students what they would do if they had one hour to live. Each student gives an appropriately pious answer, such as study the Torah or pray continuously. Then the students asked the rabbi the same question. He responds, 'I would go right on doing what I was doing, because all of life is sacred.' The audience enjoyed singing the song, but it wasn't until two weeks later that we got a letter from a woman thanking us for Doug's performance. She went on to tell how the story in that song had helped her thirteen-year-old daughter and her group of friends understand and cope with the death of one of their friends in a car accident."

Helping others

Almost all of the twenty-seven writers and storytellers I interviewed for this book confirmed my belief as they talked about the part stories played in their healing processes. Donald Davis said all of his own stories and those of his grandmother had been part of his healing process, but when asked how he used stories to help in the healing process for others, he replied, "I am not qualified to do this—I only tell stories." Yet many listeners and tellers find great healing insight in his personal stories. His statement indicates that the teller is only the vehicle and the story provides the catalyst. Carrie Wharton found answers for her grief and healing in Davis's story "Mrs. Rosemary's Kindergarten." A single line, "People die because they just get too old, too sick, or too hurt to get well," helped her and her children. Carrie said, "It doesn't get any simpler than that. I love that line."

"Stories can heal when we draw a parallel between our plight and the one detailed in a story. A personal story about Dr. Schuller's [Dr. Robert H. Schuller, minister and author of many inspirational books] daughter's loss of her leg inspired me to try to deal better with my loss of mobility after my stroke," Ginny Conrad explained.

Avis Fox said, "Ways to solve our problems come through in some stories, such as ways to find and remember happy stories and memories. For example, when Diane told 'Infinite Resource and Sagacity' and related finding the picture of her son and hearing him say, 'Hello, Mom, I'm still here,' I realized that every time I looked at a picture of my husband, I could revel in the idea that he would be saying, 'See Avis, I'm still here.' I knew those pictures could be real ones or in my mind."

Reaching out

A sixty-year-old friend recently told me he had never experienced a significant loss in his life. I wondered if he was just lucky or if he did not value the relationships in his life. We all eventually must face the loss of people, things, and situations. The value we place on what is lost determines its significance to us. In addition to coping with our own losses, as compassionate creatures we want to offer genuine help and comfort to others suffering from grief.

After the loss of my son, I asked storytellers to share with me stories with healing and growth themes. I was thrilled when tellers sent me stories they knew and thought would be useful to me. I received a gift from every one I heard, although probably not always what the teller might have intended.

One of the national storytellers who shared stories with me was Jay O'Callahan. I attended his workshop on the creative process years ago, and we renewed our friendship when he was a featured artist at the Florida Storytelling Association Camp. I told him about David's death, and we talked about healing stories. Following camp he wrote, "For me stories have been healing—healing of old wounds and blocks. Storytelling is like dancing with life—including all the old shadows. It's a chance to dance with all of life." He also sent two of his personal tapes and another tape containing an incident from the National Storytelling Festival in Jonesborough, Tennessee.

Jay told of finishing a performance and hurrying to his next venue when a woman named Susie Weber stopped him in the street and asked if she could tell him a story. Even though he had little time, something about her eyes and manner made him say, "OK, let's sit down." She reminded him of a time when he had helped her with a story he told in Michigan, and then began her story.

Jonathan

I work with children who are dying with cancer and several months ago was involved with an eleven-year-old boy named Jonathan who was dying with leukemia. Not long before his death, Jonathan told his family, "When I die, I'd like you to spread my ashes on Lake Michigan." So sure enough, after he died, his family went out on the lake in a boat one day and cast his ashes as he had requested. While they were still on the boat, a beautiful Monarch butterfly flew down to the boat and Jonathan's mother said, "Look, that's Jonathan!"

The next day they were out on the boat and a Monarch butterfly again flew down to the boat. Five-year-old Charlie, Jonathan's younger brother, said, "Look, there's Jonathan." The following day on the beach of Lake Michigan, Charlie was stirring the sand with a stick and he stirred up an old gray moth that had burrowed down in the sand. The old gray moth flew up and Charlie said, "Look, that's Jonathan—but today he's wearing a different shirt."

⇒〉〉⟨⟨⟨⟵

Jay was touched by Susie's story. At his next performance, he shared the healing way that a young boy named Charlie dealt with the loss of his brother—*knowing* that Jonathan was still with him even though he had changed his appearance. Stories like this one offer comfort and encourage the belief that those we have lost continue to be with us.

Discovering our story

Does the healing and growth that stories encourage come from listening to stories or from writing and telling them? When asked this question in my interviews, everyone answered both, although some had benefited more from one or the other. Myra Davis, who lost her teenage daughter in an automobile accident, said, "The only way I felt that I could continue was telling stories about Melanie, but we need to listen as well as tell or we will miss a true part of our soul."

Most of those I interviewed found the greatest benefit from first creating and then telling their stories. Some crafted their personal ones, dealing directly with their loss and grief, while others created stories with fictional characters and situations. In all cases, the stories struggled to find new possibilities to facilitate growth and learning.

A loss shatters us into many pieces and undermines our outlook on the world. We need a way to reclaim and sort out the fragments. Telling my story forced me to organize and resolve the confusing bits and pieces from my life enough to convey its meaning to someone else, a process that enhanced my own understanding tremendously. Obviously I could not have told a story convincingly if I did not believe it myself first.

Actually speaking words out loud reinforced them again and again. The first time I told the story about losing David was

> "Stories heal us because we become whole through them. In the process of writing, of discovering our story, we restore those parts of ourselves that have been scattered, hidden, suppressed, denied, distorted, forbidden, and we come to understand that stories heal. We are like a broken vessel, and story has the possibility of gathering us up again."
> **Deena Metzger**
> *Writing for Your Life*
>
> ⋘

incredibly difficult. Each time I tried it, I spoke with more conviction. I gained strength as I accepted my new reality, knowing I would never go back to being the person I once was. Stories taught me to change my perspective.

Personal stories, legends, mythology, Jack tales, and other folklore teach us we cannot get to the end of the road without the searching and struggling, even though most of us try to avoid it. Growth and healing occur in the strife and continue for the rest of our lives. Failure to recognize this basic truth results in stagnation; knowing and accepting it causes a giant step forward to a life of joy and fulfillment.

> "Story does not change what happened—nothing can change that. But stories can change our relationship to what has happened so that instead of being defeated by events, we grow from them."
> Donald Davis
> National storyteller and teacher
>
> ⇒》》

Finding answers

Stories enable us to learn even more, especially if we examine them closely. Storyteller and coach, Doug Lipman described in his book, *The Storytelling Coach,* the value of asking yourself questions about a story. "What is it about the story that you really love? What does it mean to you? What is its importance? What do you want to convey to your audience?" The questions help in figuring out what the story has to say. Searching within for the answers can be like going to a therapy session as you discover more about yourself.

Even though I would never impose *my* answers on listeners, understanding all those questions is an imperative part of story development and preparation for telling it to others. The story becomes clearer in my mind and reveals what I need to learn from the telling. Each time I analyze a story and find answers, I strengthen my beliefs. My responsibility is to decipher what the story means to me and tell it the best way I can. Then listeners are free to accept it, examine it thoroughly, and treasure it—or reject it if they choose.

Sharing in our stories what we have learned may offer the best opportunity to heal. As others share their feelings of grief and pain, we learn new ways to cope. Many people have changed the focus and direction in their lives due to losses they sustained. Most of us rock along in the rut of our lives until we are forced to examine questions we can no longer avoid. In his book *How Good do we Have to Be?* Rabbi Kushner quoted Albert Schweitzer, who said, "We must all become familiar with the thought of death if we want to grow into really good people....Thinking about death produces love for life."

My love of stories made them a natural place for me to look for answers. At a time when life held little meaning except as a source of great pain, stories offered comfort and started the search that eventually led to what I now see as my *storytelling voice,* or the reason I tell stories. The self-discovery process was such a gift—one that I want to enjoy and share with others—that brought growth I never dreamed possible before David's death. My revelations changed the way I look at the world and the people I meet. I have learned to value and be grateful for what I still have and to find joy in reaching out and sharing my experience with others. *Would I have reached this point if David were still alive? Why did I have to learn it this way?* I will never know all the answers in this lifetime. I only know what I must do because of what I learned after losing him. My feelings of commitment, expediency, and passion about the purpose of my life have bolstered my continuing desire to heal.

> "How is it that the heart, in the wake of a traumatic experience—one as tragic as the family shattered at the hands of death—causes and allows the human spirit to emerge with a greater sense of stamina, perseverance, determination, resilience and enthusiasm?... Whether we gained through facing everyday challenges, or from joy, pain and healing, many of the experiences in our lives trigger an opportunity for the heart to gain a deeper understanding, appreciation and acceptance of life—and of others."
> Bettie Youngs
> From the introduction to
> *Gifts of the Heart*
> ⋘

Many people struggle to survive overwhelming losses and are stronger because of it. All of the writers and tellers I interviewed are committed to acknowledging their losses in a straightforward way.

They open their lives and their struggles for their listeners and readers to see and find healing by doing so. They speak their truths and penetrate the hearts of listeners. The energy I feel as I write this book makes me shiver at times. When the same energy is present in a performance, whether I am telling or listening, I am once again overwhelmed by the healing power of stories.

Stories transform pain 9

Surviving the unexpected

Pain occurs when we have to grow through an unexpected change or experience. Since grief and suffering always result when we permanently lose something we value, we must find a way to transform the pain if we are to avoid a life dominated by loss. Stories abound with examples of transformation—frogs turn into princes, hags into princesses, water into wine, mice into horses, eggs into jewels, pumpkins into coaches, and straw into gold. If we can relate these images to situations in our own lives, we discover opportunities for healing. In addition, we can envision healing when an exit becomes an entrance, despair becomes hope, and hopelessness turns into believing.

At times, a casual comment, a discussion, a book, or a movie might temporarily affect our beliefs, values, or faith. When the message from a story resonates within us, stories can become the catalyst for a lasting transformation to take place. A lot of energy becomes available when pain is converted into something useful. When we run away from necessary change, pain consumes our energy and ability to function.

Transformation goes on around us all the time, and we usually think of it in a positive way, except for aging and death. Even when people are very sick and death is a welcome end to suffering, we do not understand the nature or the result of death itself. In its broadest sense, transformation implies an alteration either in the external form or in the inner nature of something. The life cycle of a butterfly symbolizes metamorphosis in a positive way as a caterpillar or larva becomes a dormant pupa or cocoon and then finally emerges as a beautiful adult. This positive transformation image offers a sense of possibility and becomes a comforting symbol of hope to many people.

Taking the risk to heal

Change involves risk when the end result is unknown. The outcome might be better *or* worse. Even making a positive change usually involves giving up something in order to gain something of greater value. A friend tells a story about a turtle that had always dreamed of flying like the birds. When he had the opportunity to become a bird, the turtle discovered he would have to give up his shell. The possibility frightened him because without a shell, he would no longer be a turtle. Further, if the transformation failed, he would be neither a bird nor a turtle; he would have risked everything and lost. The story ends by asking, "Which would you have chosen—to risk everything to be transformed and realize your life's dream *or* give up the dream and accept the status quo?" Not knowing the outcome of a choice is a stressful situation, and most of us are afraid to take the risk.

> "[The individual who accepts change becomes] someone who not only adapts to a stressful situation but finds something positive within it that enriches the individual's life.... [This approach to coping] has to do with the way we tell the story of our lives.... People who can transform the events of their lives into coherent stories that preserve integrity, compassion, and hope are transformational copers, and such coping is often associated with good health."
>
> Joan Borysenko
> "Minding the Body,
> Mending the Mind and Soul"
> *Nourishing the Soul*
>
> ⇒⟫

In her chapter "Minding the Body, Mending the Mind and Soul" in *Nourishing the Soul,* Joan Borysenko wrote, "We experience stress in our lives when an event requires us to adapt or change. The change could be anything from getting a new job to moving to having a loved one die." She explained that people cope with the resulting stress in one of two ways—either they resist the change, refusing to grow, or accept it and are transformed by it.

Following my son's death, I longed for the joy of having him in my life to overpower the pain of losing him. With the help of stories, I gradually began to look at the painful memories of my son and his death with new insights. Initially I just wanted answers that made sense. *How could a mindless insect kill my son? Why did he die at age twenty-nine?* Others might ask of their losses—*how could something harmful invade my body?* or *How could my spouse fail to honor a commitment to me?* or *How could something that changes my whole life happen without my permission?* Only when we transform our pain into stories do the answers begin to make sense.

Sudden loss forces us to choose whether we allow the grief from loss to consume us or do we risk letting the pain fashion us into something of greater value? Jeannine Auth remembered a sermon by Dr. William Sloane Coffin, Jr., who said after the loss of his son in an automobile accident, "The tragedy of human life is not that we suffer. What is tragic is suffering where nothing is learned, pain that doesn't somehow get converted into strength." Jeannine added, "I think story can teach us how to convert our pain." Further, stories can provide the channels to *transform* pain in a way that is meaningful, not only for us, but also for others.

Expressing the struggle creatively

As bereaved parents, Anne McCracken and Mary Semel found comfort by reading the works of writers who had experienced significant loss. Their book includes excerpts from selected writers who focused on mourning the loss of a child or sibling. Many of the writers created some of their best work following their losses, strengthened by new insights and depth of feelings resulting from their loss. McCracken and Semel introduced each chapter with their own thoughts and insights about the grieving process.

The expressions of grief and loss quoted throughout the book became the therapy that enabled both authors to survive. Several passages connected me with the writers and offered comfort as I read descriptions of my feelings expressed so beautifully and passionately.

McCracken and Semel said of Ralph Waldo Emerson that his "capacity for expression gave him the capacity to mourn" following the death of his five-year-old son who died from scarlet fever. Expressing feelings well leads to healing for the author, while hearing or reading the expressions allows recognition and connection for others.

In the early weeks following the loss of my son, I was numb and nothing mattered except that David was gone. People insisted on telling me personal stories of their own losses or the losses of others. I found I resented some of them, thinking *how dare anyone imply their grief was as bad as mine or that their loss was as significant.* My outlook was bleak. As strange as it seems now, I found recognition and comfort in reading the "Funeral Blues" segment of the poem, "Four Cabaret Songs for Miss Hedli Anderson," by W. H. Auden. The words of the last stanza described exactly the way I felt.

> *The stars are not wanted now; put out every one,*
> *Pack up the moon and dismantle the sun,*
> *Pour away the ocean and sweep up the woods;*
> *For nothing now can ever come to any good.*

Authors have written poems, plays, novels, short stories, and non-fiction to convey their struggles to discover meaning in their losses and lives following loss. Efforts necessary to complete creative work offer a way to transform pain and ultimately lead to healing. One of the great values of language and stories is the ability to record progress through suffering and loss. Language becomes a vital tool when used in the creation of a story that *must* be told.

Condensing thoughts and ideas, even in the early stages of grief when the expression of pain seems harsh and raw, leads toward more acceptance and understanding with the passing of time. In *Lament for a Son,* Nicholas Wolterstorff expressed his grief and gut-wrenching pain following the death of his twenty-five-year-old son from a climbing accident. He said in the preface that he wrote the book to honor his son and voice his grief as he made the emotional journey from the phone call announcing his son's death to his life a year later. In one passage he wrote, "Out of my self I traveled on a journey of love and attached this self of mine to Eric, my son. Now he's gone, lost, ripped loose from love; and the ache of loss sinks down, and down, deep down in to my soul, deep beyond all telling. How deep do souls go?"

In Wolterstorff's book, as with many others, I was amazed to find accurate descriptions of *my own grief* that I thought defied words. To read and digest his passionate feelings of loss helped me process my feelings by allowing me to more fully recognize them. In addition, as the book progressed, faith and hope gradually emerged out of his grief. Later Wolterstorff and his wife Claire wrote the text and commissioned a composer to create a requiem in honor of their son. As it moves from Part I, which "expresses the awfulness of death," to the end in Part VI, which "speaks of Christian hope," the requiem chronicles a beautiful transformation.

Telling the story

Being able to verbalize thoughts and feelings requires extensive searching within. Those in healing professions know the necessity of examining the wound inside rather than ignoring it and leaving it to fester. Therapist and storyteller Christine Reese believes stories have the power to be part of the healing process. She said, "The power comes from releasing the pain inside through the spoken work shared with an empathetic listener." The release and transformation of pain and grief has been called an exorcism of the soul.

Dr. John Taylor, my linguistics and research professor at ETSU, told the following story about his childhood relationship with his grandfather. Before telling it to our class, he made sure we knew he was not being disrespectful in *any* way, but simply using the words common in those days.

The Day I Lost Granddaddy

When I was a little boy, I loved baseball and my Granddaddy. In fact, my relationship with Granddaddy centered around our common interest in baseball. Granddaddy always wanted to know everything about my games—how many times I'd come up to bat, how many hits and runs I'd gotten, if I'd pitched, how many batters

I'd struck out, and how many outs I'd thrown. I could hardly wait to get to Granddaddy's house after a game, because I got to relive the whole game as I described every detail of my brilliance on the field that day. It made me feel so special because I had something to talk about that made Granddaddy excited.

In those days all of us boys would gather at the field, pick a couple of leaders, divide up, and play a game. We did not pay attention to size or color or anything—just whoever was there played—so those details were not important in my report to Granddaddy. But as we got older, things got more organized and we began to have fixed teams in the neighborhoods.

So it happened that one day our team played the team from the black neighborhood—and nobody ever beat them. But somehow on this day, we beat them and I pitched a no-hitter! I could hardly wait to tell Granddaddy. I ran all the way to his house, up the stairs, into his room and gasped out "Granddaddy, Granddaddy, you're not going to believe what happened today. We beat the colored team and I pitched a no-hitter!" He turned to me with a look in his eyes I had never seen before and he said, "Anybody who plays with niggers is not welcome in my house. Get out of here and don't you come back." I felt like I had been kicked in the teeth. Tears filled my eyes as I slowly walked down the stairs, out of the house, and headed home. I could barely see where I was going at times. I was so upset and confused and I never mentioned it to anybody. I didn't even know what to say.

I did go back to the house—it was actually Grandmother's family home. In fact, I went there many times to family gatherings and so forth, but my relationship with Granddaddy was forever changed. We never talked about baseball again. In fact, we never talked about anything much ever again. Nobody even seemed to notice the difference—nobody except me.

The hurt and loss was so deep and so great that I never told anyone about it until recently—almost fifty years later. After I was a grandfather myself, I could not imagine how that could have happened. But for all these years it has nagged at me—even made me feel ashamed of Granddaddy at times. As I grew older and wiser to the ways of the world, I gained understanding of the incident. But it was only when I told the story to someone that I began to have some insight and to realize how powerful Granddaddy's cultural

beliefs and his upbringing had been, even though he was a good,
Christian man. It took telling the story to transform my pain so that
I could once again love Granddaddy.

The capacity to forgive his grandfather came with telling the story.
In addition, now he can look back and see the situation as it really
was. Dr. Taylor explained, "Grandmother was personable, witty,
intelligent, and wealthy, and Granddaddy had none of those attributes
and nobody much valued his opinion." As an adult Dr. Taylor
realized that "those lowest on the totem pole often exhibit the greatest
amount of prejudice to make themselves feel more important."

Understanding the past

Dr. Taylor's story has helped me deal with the confusion and
disillusionment I felt from my own past of growing up in the south.
Many of the racial issues I questioned as a child were answered in
ways I did not understand and could not accept as I got older. I felt
betrayed and misled by my parents, grandparents, and others, and
only in later years gained some insight about why they told me the
things they did. I know they were loving, caring people, but their
answers of "that's just they way things are" and "she likes to eat by
herself" fell short when I asked "Why do we have separate drinking
fountains?" and "Why can't Opal eat lunch with us?" Children
seemed to accept answers more readily back then than they do
today—certainly more than my children ever did.

When I was a child, the beliefs of adults generally mirrored the
beliefs of their parents and the times. As children they had not been
allowed to ask questions at all. Through guilt and intimidation, as well
as out of love and respect, children just accepted their parents' beliefs.
After World War II, established belief systems began to break down,
as people were exposed to new and different situations. Many people
from my generation questioned a lot of things, no longer accepting the
old answers in the face of conflicting evidence.

I struggled with my past misunderstanding for many years and my
loss of innocence was painful, though not uncommon. Other students

in my linguistics class had experienced similar situations. They all agreed that Dr. Taylor's story provided perception and sensitivity that gave them a new way to look at past events they had not fully understood. In some cases, they had never explored their hurt and confusion because the incidents were too painful to discuss or examine. Listening to Dr. Taylor's touching story offered a way to look at the past and transform the pain, just as he had done. Sharing stories like this one has the potential to create acceptance and understanding among people of all races, cultures, and backgrounds.

Everyone has confusing and hurtful experiences growing up. When the memories are buried within and never talked about, such experiences become harmful. Eighty-six percent of those incarcerated in California experienced a significant loss in their family. Most children in institutions are dealing with loss issues that they were never able to process. Matthew Heavilin, who lost three younger brothers before he was twenty-four, says that children are often the forgotten grievers and yet have many baffling problems following loss. Matthew and his mother Marilyn coauthored a book entitled *Grief is a Family Affair.*

Being able to talk about feelings related to grief is important. Dr. William Worden conducted an extensive study with Harvard University to look at the factors that contribute to a successful resolution of children's grief. Dr. Worden and his team tracked children, age five to sixteen, who had lost a close family member, most often a parent. The results of the study appear in Dr. Worden's book *Children and Grief.* Worden found that children who were able to share memories and stories of the deceased were more likely to resolve their grief issues than those who were not. This occurred more often when the mother was the surviving parent, probably because women are usually more comfortable discussing feelings. This positive finding clearly indicates the importance of children being encouraged to talk about their loss and explains why problems frequently arise when this opportunity is not available.

Several years ago, a young woman told me that as a child she had been raped by a neighbor and had never told anyone. She knew if she had mentioned the rape when it happened, her brothers would have killed the man and gone to prison for murder. She could not bear that thought, so she kept everything inside for years. She had never told anyone in her family, instead suffering major problems in her life and marriage, which ended in a divorce. In addition, she warned her young daughter everyday about how vicious men could be and constantly cautioned her to be on guard when any male was around.

We talked about the likelihood of her daughter growing up with a warped view of men and the world, and with an unhealthy sense of fear. I asked if she thought *any* men were decent, and she reluctantly acknowledged the possibility. She began telling me about the incident in great detail, her anger and fear still very evident as she relived the horror of the experience. I asked her to tell the story again even though it was painful to remember. After a while, she said, "What a relief to finally get this out. Thank you for asking about it and listening. Somehow it doesn't seem so horrible now." The last time I heard from her, she was planning to be married again "to a wonderful man." Perhaps being able to tell the story of her loss enabled her to transform some of her deep fear and hatred to love.

> "Writing has helped me enter fully into my sorrow. In doing so, I began to discover that there are gifts hidden in the grief experience. Although there has been great sorrow from Derek's death, there has been great joy in sharing and helping others with their own sorrow.... Writing is a creative expression that has helped me keep my commitment to grow through the experiences I face and to live in the present rather than the past."
> Phyllis Davies
> *Grief: Climb Toward Understanding*
>
>

Releasing grief

In his book *Embracing Their Memory,* John Harvey discussed the necessary conditions for full healing from loss, including opportunities for story development and storytelling. Harvey said these opportunities "...involve the release of emotions that build up after a loss. This release is necessary for the survivor to recover. In their stories of loss, grief, and healing, many people have provided powerful examples of transforming even the most crushing forms of loss into rays of hope and meaning for themselves and others."

After the loss of her son in a commercial airline collision, Phyllis Davies wrote *Grief: Climb Toward Understanding,* which was her "survival notebook." Using a technique called "clustering" that she found in a book entitled *Writing the Natural Way* by Gabriele Rico, Davies wrote lyric prose pieces to help in her own healing process and later collected them in her book to encourage others "in their struggle across their own mountains of loss." Another son was stillborn and she feels close to both sons as she writes, transforming her own pain into creative words for healing herself and others. This transformation is the same one available whenever a story is created and told.

In her book of poetry entitled *The Garden Where All Loves End,* Melissa Morphew wrote a poem based on a true family story about a relative from several generations back. I have included it to show how grief and loss can be processed through the use of words and images and converted into something beautiful and wonderful.

To Feel The Eggshell

The first time my heart was broken
Mama handed me a dustpan and a broom.
Then she told me this story:

My great-aunt Ophelia had two children.
One day the little ones followed a cloud
of lavender butterflies into the woods,
enticed by the wind-chime flutter of wings.

By suppertime they hadn't come home.
Ophelia called and called. But no answer,
only the silence of early lightning bugs, glowing
green-gold in the branches of the pear trees.

Late that evening, she and Uncle Benny
finally found their babies, arms and legs akimbo
like sleeping rag dolls, face down
in a patch of deadly nightshade—

their mouths full of blackish berries,
their fingers grubby with purple juice.

And burdened by the weight of her name,
what could Ophelia do but go crazy?
Benny caught her wandering their garden
in her pink flannel gown, clutching a turnip,
mumbling Italian sonnets to the arch-angel Gabriel.

He hated to do it, but Uncle Benny
sent her to the state sanitarium.
He cried when the doctors took her away,
sprinkled his overalls with her lemon verbena,
wore her aprons while he plowed.

The doctors put Ophelia to work washing dishes,
great stacks of heavy green-rimmed plates.
She scrubbed for four weeks straight,
night and day, chanting strange prayers:

"Dear God, thank you
for the blue delphinium,
the long-handled rake.
It's good to feel the eggshell
crack against the bowl.
Bless the mole and weevil.
Let us have fennel-seed cake for dinner.
The world is weary with the smell of mothballs."

The doctors took her for a hopeless case.
Told Benny breaking the spell of a mother's grief
was more difficult than catching moonlight in a jelly jar.

But one morning, the kitchen sweet
with the scent of mock orange,
Ophelia stared hard out the open window
and told the nurse standing guard:
"I'm tired of washing dishes.
If you let me go home,
I promise I won't be crazy."

Ophelia had another baby,
a little girl born with puckered fingers.
She named her Belladonna.
Rocked her to sleep every night humming
"Au Claire de la Lune."

⇒≫≪⇐

This poem showed me how Melissa coped with loss at the deepest level and worked to change her feelings through writing poetry. We witness Ophelia gradually transform her grief by learning to be thankful for the small things in life as she washed dishes and made the decision to heal. The poignant image "breaking the spell of a mother's grief was more difficult than catching moonlight in a jelly jar" rang true with my feelings of grief and reinforced how inadequate ordinary words often are in describing loss. Strong images framed with words can connect to the mind and heart with the power to transform our pain and offer comfort.

Finding possibilities

Working through the exercises in Gabriele Rico's book, *Pain and Possibility,* leads to the awareness that "the impulse to transform pain must come from within, no matter how much we initially resist it, and that our own words on a page are the gentlest, most powerful means to impel us toward new ways of seeing, being, heal-ing....Only your own personal language has the power to mirror you, has the power to nurture, heal, and help....What helps is to direct your pain into constructive acts, thus transforming it. Writing is one of these acts. Writing gives shape and form to your feelings. Writing opens the wilderness of feelings for explorations, and the

> "As the orange already exists as potential in the orange blossom, so possibility already lies within our pain. When we relearn to face pain, we discover choices we didn't know we had. If we deny it, emotional confusion can quickly become utter anarchy; if we learn to be receptive, it becomes absolute potential."
> Gabriele Rico
> *Pain and Possibility*
>
> ⇒≫

emerging patterns in your writing lead to gradual insights, occasional life-changed epiphanies, but mostly a wary grace....Spilling your pain onto the page is healing; holding it in is as unfruitful as holding your breath. Letting go leads to life."

As a storyteller, I believe recognizing and creating your own story is important. Even greater power comes from telling the story to others, allowing it to become ingrained in your consciousness and memory. Personal narrative offers the opportunity to transform painful memories from the past to new stories of meaning and significance. Wrestling with the details of our loss primes the pump so that transformation occurs as the story pours out.

Changing our story

Others believe that writing a story can actually change the way you look at the characters and events. Tristine Rainer believes we are able to change the past by how we remember it, and how we remember the outcome of events is up to us. In her book *Your Life as Story*, Rainer advocates the use of autobiographical narrative in order to tell our story based on what we have learned. This ability to view again or *review* our story gives us the opportunity to get it right or at least find the lost meaning. Whether a story is written or told, the enhanced version *becomes* our reality and gives us a new way to view our world.

Carrie Wharton said, "I believe that those who have experienced loss in their lives and who have stared it in the face and not run from it, are forever changed. Their perspective is different. I would give anything to have my mother and my husband here with me now, but I am thankful for the deep, rich, soulful experience of loss. Pain brings with it tremendous growth and fresh perspective on living. I believe it has made me unafraid to feel deeply—to dive into and wallow in feeling, even pain, and come up smiling. Because of this I tend to look for and seek out the things in life that make me feel deeply. Stories do that for me and I quickly recognize their power. I want to be a part of that power—giving to others the gift of feeling and growing." Carrie obviously has been touched so greatly by her experience of loss that she has no choice but to share what she has learned with others through the stories she tells.

Sharing our knowledge

Many writers and storytellers are driven to share what they have learned through the creation of their stories, particularly if the results have been life changing. Processing events through the structure of stories helps authors deal with their own disappointments and losses by providing an outlet for emotions. The impact of sharing the story with others encourages additional expression and can validate undisclosed feelings of the listeners. Both the teller and listener facilitate a change in each other.

> "Stories are the greatest healing and teaching art that we have. Through stories, we transmit values, ethics, traditions, memories, and identity. One way to retrieve our souls is to ask ourselves what our favorite stories are, to repeat the ones that we find most healing and comforting, and to remember which ones we especially want to pass on to others."
> Angeles Arrien
> "Walking the Mystical Path with Practical Feet"
> *Nourishing the Soul*
>
> ⇛

In our society very few ways of expressing feelings are deemed acceptable, which may partially explain the increase of inappropriate behavior, especially among young people. Certainly some violent outbursts occur because outlets for releasing normal feelings simply are not available. Unexpressed feelings build an urgency that eventually explodes much like a volcano erupts from underground pressure. Telling and listening to stories provide an escape hatch to address problems *before* they become so volatile. If diffused and properly channeled, destructive energy and behavior can be transformed into something healing and productive. And that is just the beginning, for stories have the power to change lives.

When I look back at everything I have learned about pain, suffering, grief, and loss since my son's death, I am overwhelmed. It saddens me to think that David had to *die* for me to learn it all, and I cannot help but wonder if there could have been another way—an easier way. I feel obligated to him and to myself to learn everything possible from my experience, and then use my knowledge helping others deal with loss. If I fail to live up to my commitment, then his death and all the pain and suffering I have experienced will be for nothing. He taught me so much about living, and his short life was far too meaningful to waste.

The only way I can honor David's life is to share what I have learned in my struggle to make sense out of why *he* died and why *I* am still here. Figuring out how to transform my pain was necessary for my sanity. Sharing my stories affords me the opportunity of finding ways to heal and grow and helping others do the same. Telling stories is the only way I know to spin gold out of straw.

Stories establish control and closure 10

Understanding control

As we go through life, we foolishly believe we control so many things. But if we live long enough, we will experience loss, by death or otherwise, which makes us realize what little power we actually have over our lives. The sudden feeling of having no control compounds the overwhelming feeling of the loss itself. With the passage of time, we eventually come to know that the only thing we can significantly influence is our *own* attitude and behavior—how we react to things that occur and how we choose to live our lives as a result of those happenings.

Following a loss, people frequently report feeling that *all* the events in their life are completely out of control. Some occurrence altered their lives dramatically, and they were powerless to affect the outcome. So the ability to control anything seems impossible and leads to feelings of despair.

Many people, especially men, often run away from pain because they have not been taught how to live with it—i.e. to grieve the loss so healing can begin. They are often perceived as feeling no pain though they probably feel it very deeply but don't know how to express it in a way that is satisfactory or acceptable to themselves and the world, so they avoid it. Maybe they feel personal failure because they couldn't avoid or prevent the loss, and don't like the feeling of loss of control.

In the beginning this realization is a bit depressing, for it is easier to rationalize or blame events and our behavior on someone or something else. When David died and I discovered I was not in charge of the events of my life, I felt like a victim or pawn being whisked about randomly. I questioned the value and validity of all the choices I made. *What difference did anything make?* Gradually I realized that even though what happened to me was beyond my control, I *was* responsible for my outlook on life and the decisions I made about my future. I could stay sad, bitter, inactive, and depressed, which would accomplish nothing except to let David's death have victory over me too, *or* I could choose for my life to be meaningful in a way that honored David—filled with joy, adventure, excitement, love, and growth. Further, I could decide to keep everything I learned and encountered to myself, *or* I could reach out to others to help them create the best possible versions of their own life stories. Every morning of my life *I get to choose* a path that affirms life or death. While the statement may seem too dramatic, anyone who has experienced significant loss and the resulting pain and confusion, knows its truth.

> "Loss deals with disruptions of relations with people and things: losing one sense of place and finding another. Loss leaves so much unfinished business, things not said. Control is valued, both socially and morally. Loss shows no control and hints of moral failure and being irresponsible."
>
> Arthur Frank
> *At the Will of the Body*
>
> ⇒⇒

I had considered these ideas at several times during my life, but after David's death everything became more urgent. Once I decided to do more than merely survive, I began to explore opportunities for learning and growth. Since my story had not ended, I had to find out what was going to happen in the next chapter. I needed to expand my horizons and my mind because old patterns were no longer sufficient. I wanted to be involved with storytelling, but I was not sure how.

In *Cold Sassy Tree* by Olive Ann Burns, the young boy and main character, Will Tweedy, reflected that life is like reading a good book—you never know how the next chapter is going to turn out. His statement encouraged me. No matter what happened in the middle chapters of my life, the outcome of future chapters was ultimately up to me. While I could not determine all of the events entering my life,

I could choose my response to those events. As I learned about others who had experienced loss and chosen to endorse life through their actions, I felt hope that I might be able to influence the direction of my own life once again.

Taking control of your story

At some point, most storytellers see *everything* as story. A friend recently said, "Everything in my life has become a story. I look at everybody and hear what they are saying as part of a bigger story." *Perhaps my life was a story, too.* This realization offered a way to regain some sense of order in my life.

In his book *The Healing Art of Storytelling,* Richard Stone said that the act of telling a personal story changes the way we feel about the event. The book is filled with examples of how to make sense of stories about loss and suffering. Stone wrote, "By telling the story, I am no longer the victim of circumstances beyond my control. I have wrested back control by the simple act of description, turning what seems to be a failure in almost every way into a heroic saga of survival."

"The process of writing allows the writer to get more control of thought and feeling and renders them relatively less confusing as they are bound and grounded in the written word," according to Therese Rando in her book *Parental Loss of a Child.* The same is true for stories to be told. Certainly issues and feelings must be examined internally before they can be effectively communicated to listeners. Nothing makes sense in the beginning, but during necessary emotional homework of the

> "Writing stories has helped me to cope with all kinds of situations all of my life. In stories I could make happen what I wanted to happen."
> Sue Alexander
> Author

> "Stories are a way of giving structure to your thoughts about your loss and in a way, to your life. It's how you see your life."
> David Holt
> Musician and storyteller

creating and crafting process, rambling thoughts melt down to their essence.

> "Sharing my personal stories with audiences has been very helpful, too. After you have held your experience up for many people to examine, you have the power to control it. It no longer controls you."
>
> Elizabeth Ellis
> Storyteller and teacher
>
>

After Ginny Conrad had a stroke, she walked with a limp and lost the use of her right hand. Ginny has used stories to heal from a number of losses in her life and acknowledges the role they had in helping her adjusting to the loss of mobility from her stroke. She said, "There's nothing wrong with my mouth or my heart and mind, which are filled with stories waiting to be told. Have I been healed by stories? My goodness, yes...even though I can't, my stories dance and run and jump and bubble and bounce."

Her comments reminded me of a story attributed to Martin Buber that several tellers I interviewed mentioned. In the story Buber's grandfather had been paralyzed for years when someone asked him to tell a story about his great teacher, the holy Baal Shem Tov. The grandfather explained how his teacher hopped and danced while he prayed. As Buber's grandfather became involved in telling the story, he arose and began to jump and dance to demonstrate how his famous master had done, and his lameness was healed. Telling the story about his teacher had healed him. (A version of Buber's story entitled "Story to Heal" appears in *The Sower's Seeds* by Brian Cavanaugh.)

> "The word is a defining aspect of our humanity. Not to use it is to throw away a gift. We are not complete if we do not use words to express who we are."
>
> Ann Aldrich
> *Notes from Myself*
>
>

I write and tell stories about my son and his death to help me understand myself better and find meaning in the loss. I have included other life experiences in my stories for years, and the examination process brings greater understanding every time. Somehow creating a story shows me that I can exert influence over an event, whenever or whatever it might be. There are no short cuts—I still have to give attention to all aspects of the situation and the resulting emotions. Maybe my previous storytelling experiences prepared me to create and tell stories about my son, but I know the ability to create meaningful stories is accessible to anyone who explores it. I watch people from all walks of life experiencing this power when I lead workshops on using stories to heal.

In *Notes from Myself,* Ann Aldrich wrote that writing in a journal lets us see the full dimension of our lives. The same holds true for developing our stories.

Finding ways of expression

Most people are likely to convey their feelings through a familiar art form or mode of expression. We all use whatever tools we know how to use to express ourselves and deal with our emotions. Part of the creative process itself helps to foster healing because we have produced and controlled our output.

My daughter crafts beautiful handmade jewelry and says her creations come out of the wounds from the losses in her life. The same is true for many artists. For example, a musician would be inclined to compose music to help express feelings and deal with loss. Cindy Bullens recorded a CD of her music entitled "Somewhere Between Heaven and Earth." The life and death of her eleven-year-old daughter Jessie, who died of cancer, inspired the creation. Cindy believes the results may be the best music she will ever make. She remarked, "Today I choose to live, inspired by the joy of living that my little red-headed spit-fire imbued in every moment she was here on earth.... May we all find peace in the simple beauty of art, music, and nature."

While many other creative processes exist as sources of healing, creating stories is accessible to everyone. We *all* use language and are inherently storytelling creatures. Sharing stories that reflect what we have experienced and learned in life further contributes to our healing process and reestablishes a sense of control in our lives.

Delivering our message

Noted writer Elie Wiesel has a strong conviction about being sent here to deliver a message. Wiesel experienced terrible loss early in his life and survived living in the concentration camps during the Holocaust. His writings contain strong images filled with powerful feelings—horror and pain mixed with joy and passion. He uses stories to describe events, people, and feelings that could be communicated in no other way. As a messenger to all people of the world, he shares his insights on the questions that confront anyone who thinks deeply about the meaning of life, certainly those who have experienced significant loss. He imposes meaning on his experiences through his stories and books, bringing closure to the pain he has suffered. He believes that not speaking out is inexcusable for those who have struggled and learned from their suffering.

In his book, *Elie Wiesel: Messenger to All Humanity*, author Robert McAfee Brown wrote of Wiesel, "In listening to him we may be shattered. The risk is always present. But there is another possibility— the discovery that, *in spite of everything*, it is still possible to sing and shout defiance, to fling down a challenge to despair, and even, in powerful and incomprehensible ways, to initiate and respond to occasions for rejoicing." Brown recognized that story is the connecting link between our world and Wiesel's. He sensed that Wiesel was a teller of tales when he heard him begin a story by saying, "You want a description of the indescribable? There is no way to describe the indescribable. But let me tell you a story."

Because we are all potential messengers, we have things to share *if* we listen and comprehend our message. Many distractions close our minds, making it difficult to stay on track. The possibility of missing the message altogether seems impossible, and yet can happen. Not all of us can speak as eloquently and with such passion as does Wiesel, but what a waste to fail to deliver our message in the best way we can. Stories offer a way to proclaim the truths of our lives as we reconcile our past and move into the future.

Healing a painful past

In her book *Composing a Life,* Mary Catherine Bateson described the memoir she wrote about her parents by saying, "It completed my grieving for them and allowed me to work through much that was incomplete and unspoken between us." Her memoir became a book entitled *With a Daughter's Eye: A Memoir of Margaret Mead and Gregory Bateson.* Writing the story helped her find closure in her relationships with both of her parents. Processing memories as she wrote the book offered opportunities for reconciliation, which led to feelings of control she had never experienced prior to their deaths. Writing helped her revisit and heal those relationships.

So much is incomplete and unspoken when we lose a loved one. Many *if only* statements following loss indicate things we wish we had said or done. Frequently heard is "I didn't even get to say goodbye or I love you." Since all opportunity for new interaction is gone, guilt feelings often develop. A bereaved parent expressed remorse, "If only I had known my son was going to be killed, I would have bought him that bicycle he wanted so badly." Though we can never go back in time, writing and telling our stories *does* give us another chance.

Following the death of his father, storyteller Michael Parent said, "Giving the eulogy, which was filled with little stories about him, was very healing for my mom, my brother, and me. My dad and I clashed in many ways. We made peace about ten years before he died and our relationship improved steadily and significantly until his death. When he died, I found that my being able to tell the stories about how he'd really ticked me off (and vice versa) allowed me to get to the stories about the things he did that had made me proud of him. It was in that spirit that I convinced the priest who said the funeral Mass to let me give the eulogy for my dad. In it, I

> "I process memories, feelings and people through stories. In story I can thank and honor those whom I never got around to thanking...the passage of time takes away all we invest in. Stories of these people and places redeem the value of the investment."
> Donald Davis
> National storyteller
>

pointed out that my dad had often been difficult, but that if you truly paid attention, you could see past his crusty outer layer to a compassionate, intelligent man of integrity."

> "It is not enough for the bereaved parents to mourn the death of the deceased child. The parents must also mourn secondary losses that occur as a result of death. Too often these secondary losses are not identified and grieved for, especially when they are symbolic, such as the loss of parenting the child or loss of the part of the self. Additionally, the parents must grieve for the dreams, hopes, fantasies, and expectations that they had for and with the child."
>
> Therese Rando
> *Parental Loss of a Child*
>
> -≫

The healing that took place in the relationship was empowered by the stories Parent shared. His stories validated his father as an individual, led to acceptance of the entire person his father was, offered reconciliation, and helped to bring closure to their relationship. Healing the relationship enabled Parent to accept the significance of the loss that followed when his father died. The entire process helped heal Parent and others who knew and loved his father.

In *Parental Loss of a Child,* Therese Rando discussed secondary losses. She explained the importance of identifying all of the unfinished business tied to the issues surrounding the original loss. Stories provide a direct way to process all of these painful issues. Recognizing and talking about these additional losses are the first steps. Then a story can help to focus on resolution and healing. Stories always offer a way to show or say whatever is needed—including "I love you."

Sharing insights

Some of my son's closest friends have been unable to come to terms with his death even after seven years. David was an integral member of a very close group of friends who had known each other since high school. Everyone acknowledged that David provided the catalyst for the group relationship and the craziness they experienced together. The wife of one friend told me that her husband still could barely mention David's name. Another of his closest friends refused to be a pallbearer at David's funeral because he was too overwhelmed with his own sense of loss and grief. The group has scattered now, and those that still get together rarely talk about David, according to one of them. I felt such sadness and concern for those young men and knew David would have done something about it.

While writing this book I wondered if sending some of my stories to David's friends might help them, since getting them all together is no longer possible. My story coach, John McLaughlin, encouraged me by saying, "If you can show those guys how to grieve through these stories, you will be giving them a gift they can use for the rest of their lives." After a lot of thought, I agreed and mailed copies to them. After all, this book is about healing through stories, and I do believe in it with all my heart.

I sent "Oktoberfest," "Infinite Resource and Sagacity," and "Boilie" (all are included in this book) because each of them represents a different aspect of my grief process. "Oktoberfest" expresses the raw grief and dramatic irony I felt at the time of his death. "Infinite Resource and Sagacity" shows how memories and stories helped my healing process. "Boilie" represents a creative way to continue to have an active relationship with David. I enclosed a letter with the stories, asking them to share their favorite David memory or story with me.

Several of David's friends expressed gratitude for helping them to recognize their loss and allowing them to talk about it. Some sent memories and stories to me. One young man responded that my stories were "so David" and "brought back countless memories of how David could interact with people on a completely different level." He continued, "It is funny how stories can get you back in touch with something you've lost." The healing venture showed all of us ways to acknowledge what he meant to us by keeping him in our lives.

How many times do I have to be shown the value and importance of sharing stories? If I believe in it so strongly, why do I hesitate to follow through with my feelings and intuition at times? I have all the evidence I need, from my own experiences and from many others who generously shared their thoughts and convictions with me. Perhaps my reluctance comes from not wanting to impose my beliefs on others, and yet failure to share what I have learned withholds the wisdom I have gained. I have *never* had someone say, "I wish you had not told me that story." I am convinced that David is my guide and muse, helping me to use stories in situations that need healing. I simply must learn to relax and rely on his lead. After all, now *he* is the man of infinite resource and sagacity.

Gradually I began to see the importance of sharing my stories and what I have learned through them, although I still need to be reminded from time to time. Goodness knows I have experienced a number of significant losses and struggled to find meaning and purpose in my life. Surely my insights from this spiritual journey *could* be useful to others. Sharing the knowledge would honor the loved ones I have lost, help me live my life with passion and purpose, and make my suffering worth the struggle. Stories were the obvious way to find opportunities for reconciliation and change, and to reestablish feelings of control over my life. Imagine the irony of finding a better version of myself through David's death.

Dying with no regrets

My mind often returns to David's funeral and the story my cousin Wayne told as part of the eulogy. The last time Wayne saw David was at the end of the Bike Ride Across Georgia (BRAG) several months earlier. He and David had both ridden in the weeklong mountain bike ride, but had not seen each other until the last day due to the large number of bikers. At some point during the ride, David was drafting too closely behind one of his friends and had taken a spill—known as road surfing. When Wayne saw David skinned up from head to toe, he asked, "Well David, how did you like the ride?" With a huge grin on his face, David replied, "It was wonderful!" Wayne continued, "David lived his life with a spirit of adventure and always found the fun in whatever he was doing. He had figured out how to live and always lived his life to the fullest. And that is why his death at a young age is such a tragedy to all of us. But even more tragic is a life lived long but not lived at all."

That story always brings a smile to my heart and tears to my eyes, as does every memory of him that someone shares with me. Hearing shared memories is so important to those who have lost a loved one as the only new memories can come from other people. The stories may cause tears to flow, but they also bring comfort and joy, supplying more insight into the life of the deceased.

I have known several people, including some hospice patients, who approached the end of their lives with regrets for things they had not done. One woman with terminal cancer said, "We always planned to travel when we retired, and I waited to do so much. Now, I can't go anywhere because of my illness." Another said, "I always wanted to go back and finish college, but didn't take the time and now it's run out."

I contrasted death in advanced years with David's death at age twenty-nine, trying to decide which was more tragic. The answer, of course, is that death is always tragic when it closes an unfulfilled life. Some people fail to live fully even though their years are many, while others race through lives cut short. This realization altered my thinking. I found comfort envisioning David now—soaring through time and space, still growing and relishing it all. In time I felt I had to live my life the way David had chosen to live his. The story told about David at his funeral helped me make that choice.

"It took years for me to finally write the story of the father I never knew as he died when I was quite young. He played banjo in a vaudeville orchestra. Listening to banjo music was a strong connector. It was also necessary for me to invent plausible stories about him to bridge the gap. Finally, to come to grips with the loss, I wrote a story about him based on press clippings (my only legacy). I published the story for my children. In the process of writing and visualization, I was able to reach beyond time and find resolution. Our own personal stories can frequently be the most positive message for ourselves and others."
John Ward
Writer and consultant

Recovering lost relationships

Telling a story can enable people to explore feelings of loss that had always seemed beyond their reach. By contributing a link to a painful relationship, these healing stories can give shape to something that has been missing or forgotten. Renewing lost bonds through stories can bring the understanding needed to establish control over childhood perceptions and ultimately lead to new acceptance and closure.

"My story was one of loss at a young age of a relationship and a lifestyle. It occurred not by death, but from my father's addiction to alcohol. The loss became a secret inside of me that I felt shame and embarrassment over. Once I began to tell the story these debilitating emotions began to heal."

Christine Reese
Therapist and storyteller

⇒》》

The coping skills I developed as a child to deal with disappointment and loss were primarily escape and denial, which resulted in confusion and lack of understanding. When my father lost his job and we had to live with my grandparents in another town, my life turned upside down. Excuses were made, and we talked about it very little. Years later I was able to understand and accept this loss through a story I created at a healing story workshop. At last I was able to ask questions and discover the answers from an adult perspective. I certainly never could have found answers until I knew what the questions were.

I tell the story to explain how dealing with an unpleasant situation in a story can eventually bring acceptance and healing—even years later. In workshops with hospice volunteers, the story illustrates how healing and closure can be facilitated with terminally ill patients. The value of life review and storytelling is widely accepted, as found in numerous studies. The rewards are great as patients see their lives having value, even in situations they previously might have viewed as failures. Switching the focus to the *process* instead of the end result can be therapeutic. Telling their stories helps people realize they did the best they could at the time. (Many examples of reminiscence exercises such as "Where were you born?" and "What was your first job?" can be found in the appendix of Richard Stone's book *The Healing Art of Storytelling*.)

Closing unresolved issues

When my father was dying of cancer, I wrestled with unresolved issues related to his years of alcoholism and lost time and opportunities. During that turbulent period, my mother, brother, and I experienced many losses—Daddy lost jobs, and we all lost our financial and social status, our home, and feelings of self-esteem. I had dealt with many of these issues through the years, especially during his illness as he talked a lot about his life stories. His father had been killed in a train accident when my dad was only four years old, and his life growing up was filled with problems as his mother struggled alone to raise him and his brother.

In the fall of 1992 I was trying to cope with the problems of his illness compounded by my daughter's approaching wedding. In the midst of everything, I signed up for a workshop entitled "Storytelling—the Healing Art." Clyde Annandale and Renee Brachfeld were the leaders of the workshop to be held at the monastery in Conyers, Georgia. Everybody thought I was crazy to attempt it, but I strongly felt the need to attend.

On the way to the monastery, I stopped to see my dad and realized that he was very close to death. He could barely talk, but in a weak voice said "I love you too" when I told him I loved him as I was leaving. I drove to the workshop wondering if I should be going, but still feeling that I needed to be there even though I did not know why. The setting was beautiful and serene in those old Benedictine buildings built of stone. The workshop leaders shared wonderful healing stories with the group on the first night. The following day we participated in a series of exercises that caused us to discover areas in our lives that needed healing. We were encouraged to look for a story that needed to come out.

As I completed each assignment, a story about the relationship with my dad began to emerge. I was able to identify some of my negative feelings about him. I had gained more understanding of his alcoholism as I grew older and no longer lived at home, but had never put to rest the many disappointments I felt as a child. Even though as an adult I was not consciously aware of my childhood feelings, they still played a significant role in my relationship with him.

For the first time, I openly talked about my childhood embarrassment and confusion and brought my feelings to life in a story. Each of us shared our story with a partner and facilitated the other's creation process. Late in the day we started telling our stories to the entire group. I was not sure I could tell the story while my father was still alive. It seemed a betrayal of him somehow and, of course, was extremely emotional for me. Fortunately time ran out that evening before everyone took a turn, and the rest of us were to finish the next morning.

My sleep that night was fitful, and early the next morning Renee came to my room to tell me my father had died during the night. The monk that had taken the call had the details and wanted to see me. I dressed quickly, found him, and listened as this gentle, holy man told me what he knew. My biggest concern was for my mother, but the message said family members were already with her. I do not even remember what the monk said to me, just that my experience with him was peaceful and comforting. I returned to my room, packed to leave, and went to say goodbye. Clyde asked if I would tell my story before leaving, and with his encouragement I agreed to try. We both felt I might find healing in telling it. When the group gathered after breakfast, Clyde announced that my father had died and I would be leaving soon, but wanted to tell my story.

It's Hard for an Eight-Year-Old to Understand

When I was eight years old, I figured out that things went a lot better around our house when my daddy got home from work in time for supper. When he wasn't late, we had a great evening. Mother was a good cook and we'd all eat together, then sit around the table and talk about things we'd done that day.

But when Daddy was late getting home, things got tense. We could not even get through supper without arguments and fights. My younger brother and I would always knock over our milk or spill something on the table. Mealtime disasters just seemed to come out of nowhere.

One evening Daddy was late getting home, but because it was summer with plenty of daylight, I was still playing outside. I had learned that the best plan on those late evenings was to stay out of sight as much as possible. We had just gotten back from a super vacation to Florida—we always had so much family fun at the beach. I had brought back some Spanish moss, which Daddy had hung up high in a tree in our backyard. Although the moss never survived the winter, we tried it every year. That night I decided that the moss needed water, so I hooked up the hose to shoot the water high up into the tree.

Just as I got started, Daddy called me inside to get ready for bed and I yelled that I'd be there in just a minute. But I kept watering that moss—I really wanted it to survive. Daddy came to the back door again and said, "Diane, I told you to come in the house right now."

Again I yelled, "I'm coming—just a minute," and still continued spraying my moss. About that time he started out of the house toward me, and I don't know what got into me. He was still dressed in his business suit and necktie, and when I saw him coming toward me—well, the next thing I knew I had turned the hose on him, full blast. And the water was coming out hard—it had to have a lot of force to get all the way to the top of that tree.

As you can imagine, my daddy was not pleased with that reception and he started running toward me. I dropped the hose and ran around the back yard, then up the steps and into the house. I was in the hall when he reached me. I was scared to death and he was in some sort of altered state by then. He grabbed me and began hitting me and hitting me. I fell to the floor screaming as he continued to hit and kick me. It seemed like a long time passed. My mother was threatening to call the police, and she and my brother were crying and screaming at the top of their lungs. Finally he stopped or paused, and I got away from him and flew into my room. I got into bed and cried myself to sleep.

We never mentioned the incident again. That's the way it was in my family. But that night lying in my bed, I wondered how it was that someone who loved me so much—and I knew that he loved me—could hurt me so badly. You see I didn't know anything about alcohol and how drastically it can change someone. I was only eight at the time, but it's still hard to understand.

⇒⟫⟪⇐

My story is very personal and I had never written it down before putting it in this book. I included it here because it has helped others get in touch with past hurts and losses when I have told it in healing story workshops. Even though I am not sure the story is finished, it shows how telling a story can piece together feelings and events that foster a sense of closure following a painful situation.

The story touched everyone in the room and offered me a chance to revisit a painful part of my life, which eventually redeemed my relationship with my dad. Exposure to the power of story felt like a gentle, healing wave washing over me. Several workshop participants told me months later that they would never forget the impact my story had on them. One woman said her childhood had not been exactly like mine, but she had received mixed messages of another type from her parents. Hearing my story had helped her recognize the truth of her situation and acknowledge the effects on her development. Others said the story had enabled them to see things from the past they needed to address. Somehow naming the beast had set it free.

And so it was with me. I was able to find forgiveness and closure in a relationship that had been troubling all my life. The story had been the key. Telling the story let me control the past rather than the other way around.

Stories restore the future 11

Envisioning a future

Following a significant loss, the future we envisioned is no longer a possibility. In the early days after a loss, we cannot even imagine a future of any kind, except one filled with grief and pain. Only when stories come back into our lives can we begin to make sense of things enough to realize that as long as we are still breathing, we have more life to live. Gradually memories and stories can restore, or *re-story,* the future.

Driving home from a Compassionate Friends meeting one night, I realized that many of the people at the meeting had not been blessed with the gift of story. Some seemed to see the tragic loss of their child as the conclusion of their own life, ending with a terrible nightmare. I felt the same way, especially immediately after David's death. As I searched for ways to heal and reasons to go on living, I gradually saw the events surrounding David's death as only *part* of his story. His life was bigger than his death, and even his death was not the end—the last page had not been written.

> "After a significant loss, all you have are the stories. The only way I found myself getting through the loss of my Melanie is through her stories. Some were funny and some heart breaking because they were her dreams and now the dreams were gone. Without stories there is no past or future."
>
> Myra Davis
> Florida storyteller

Although drastically changed, my life and my relationship with him continued even though the future was unclear.

Recognizing that I could influence the rest of David's story helped me regain feelings of self-confidence and enthusiasm that I completely lost when he died. Like all stories, his story and mine had a beginning, a middle, and an end. *If the stories were not finished, how would they turn out?* I could affect the outcome in a way that honored David and kept his memory alive, or I could let his death destroy both of us. The choice was mine to make. David wanted so much from life, and now his final chapter depended on me. *But where did I start? Could stories play a part? Which ones?*

Asking questions

Our reasons for telling stories influence the stories we choose. The traditional reasons for telling stories differ for men and women, although both told their stories primarily in small family settings. Historically, men's stories have been to entertain, answer why questions, and record events. Women, on the other hand, have told stories to establish feelings of community, teach life's lessons, and serve as memorials to people and things gone by. My own grandfather introduced me to Brer Rabbit and Uncle Wiggly and described how the boll weevil ruined the cotton crop. My grandmother told me life stories about her mother, grandmother and other family members.

Many present day storytellers focus on their performance techniques since they often tell stories to large audiences who want to be entertained. Knowing the audience helps determine what stories will be appropriate in different situations. Certainly, stories told in a festival environment are different from those told at a battered women's shelter. As tellers, we gradually become more aware of preferred venues and favorite stories and may choose to focus our time and energy in those areas. Discovering why you tell stories, or anything you do, can lead to valuable insights.

Defining new goals

Seeking the answer to why I wanted to tell stories helped me focus on my new life goals and ways to accomplish them. I discovered that I wanted to use stories to help others see creative solutions to problems in life by affirming their abilities and strengths. Perhaps I could offer hope because of my own experiences with loss and the different ways to approach healing—some that were helpful and some that were not.

As discussed in chapter one, failure to deal with loss does not work long term. Only when we are willing to *feel* everything and face the depth of our loss can we expect to come out whole on the other side. We cannot chart a new course until the old one has been sufficiently mourned. Then we begin to find hope for the future and gain a sense of what might be possible. Once we have found our way, stories can encourage us on our new path.

We have to develop new outlooks in order to face our new future. The loved ones we have lost never age. They are forever enclosed in a time window that precludes any future memories or new stories, while we continue to grow older and move further from our past. The gap widens over time as new events occur and our lives change even more.

> "Because we have let ourselves experience grief, because we suffered the depths of aloneness, because we took time to reflect on our experiences, we have arrived at a new place.... We can now imagine our lives extending out into the future, something that did not seem possible, or even likely, earlier in our grieving."
> Elizabeth Harper Neeld
> *Seven Choices*
>
>

Feelings of separation and loss increase. The only link back to the past and our lost relationship is a story.

Mary Carter Smith is a performing folklorist who lost her only child when he was twenty-nine years old. She has been telling stories for over twenty-five years and calls herself an urban American griot. According to editor Jimmy Neil Smith in his introduction of her in *Homespun,* "In the months and years following Ricky's death, Mary had to struggle against the very despair from which she had labored to rescue others. Mary believed always in our common humanity—and the power of her stories. During those troubled times, she continued her travels, performing the stories and songs she used to console, comfort, and strengthen—not only those to whom she spoke but also herself, in her own dark moments." Smith quoted Mary as saying, "For through Ricky's death, I have come to believe even more in my work, my duty, and I have committed myself anew to truth, freedom, justice, and peace for all peoples, black or white, young or old, free or in bondage. My stories are my message."

Creating new memories

Eventually I found a way to have a new experience that included David. About a year after his death, I longed for new experiences to replace past interests that could no longer be the same. I found several things that offered possibilities—a physically taxing Outward Bound trip, a trip to Tanzania as part of a professor's research with tribal stories, and an Oceanic Society Expedition swimming with dolphins to study behavior and communication. When my two daughters expressed an interest and agreed to take a week off from work, I signed us up for Bahamas Project Dolphin, and we began making plans. We were still suffering greatly from David's death and hoped the trip might provide a way to spend some healing time together. The information from Oceanic Society Expeditions said we would be swimming in strong ocean currents and recommended building swimming stamina and practicing with snorkeling gear. The experience led to a story.

Boilie

Our entire family has always been drawn to the water and boats and dolphins. We went to Marineland years ago, when David was four years old and Kathi was only one. David immediately fell in love with Nellie—the main performing dolphin in the late sixties. (Nellie was born in 1953 and is the oldest living dolphin born in captivity. She still loves to perform and interact with people at Marineland today!) We bought David a leather dolphin, which he named Nellie and slept with for years.

We spent a lot of time on the water in our boat when the children were young. David later became a certified diver, Kathi won a lot of blue ribbons competing on a swim team, and Wendy swam laps everyday during the summer. We always said the children were part fish. So a trip to swim with spotted dolphins was a good fit.

Kathi, Wendy, and I flew to Lucaya, Bahamas and boarded the Calypso Poet, a fifty-foot trimaran sailing vessel that was our home for seven days. The three of us were assigned the two aft cabins, which were joined by a tiny head. Ten people lived aboard, including the captain, the cook, the head researcher, and her assistant. We spent part of the first day practicing our snorkeling techniques along a reef, and then headed out across the Bahama Banks to the research site. Kathleen Dudzinski was researching dolphin communication for her Ph.D. Using lectures and videos she taught us about marine mammals, concentrating on the spotted dolphins we would be observing and interacting with in the wild. She had selected the location for her research because the waters of the Bahamas are warm and crystal clear and the Banks was a huge sandbar with relatively shallow depths. Numerous spotted and bottle nosed dolphins inhabited the area. In addition, a nearby shipwreck attracted divers and the curious dolphins.

Captain Geoff took us to the secret coordinates of the research location using the boat's Global Positioning System. We were assigned to watch teams and schedules to look for dolphin in the area during daylight hours. As soon as we anchored the boat, Kathi and Wendy went for a swim and found the water warm, but the current strong. They had just struggled back aboard when one of the watch team members yelled, "Dolphins at two o'clock!"

Kathleen threw on her gear, grabbed her camera, and dove into the water in a flash. She quickly assessed the situation—seven or eight dolphins and no predators—and signaled us to join her. My daughters were exhausted from their swim, and I stared at the large ocean swells with a little concern. Meanwhile Kathleen was swimming with them, and they welcomed her like an old friend. They obviously recognized her as they swam along side brushing against her arms and legs. When two young women jumped in, one immediately popped up shouting with delight, "One touched me!"

I could not stand it any longer. I grabbed my equipment and flipped into the water, adjusting my mask and snorkel. Two dolphins immediately greeted me by staring directly into my eyes. We had been instructed not to invade their space in any way—to let them initiate all contact. As I stared into those eyes, the strangest feeling came over me—as if I recognized them. I don't know which of us was more curious and I felt a strong urge to reach out, but I resisted. After a moment they started swimming, touching me gently with each pass. I totally forgot about the seas—hardly remembered to breathe—and tried to recall what we had been instructed to do. Look for identifying markings, observe behaviors, and listen for sounds accompanying those behaviors. I did the best I could, but was far too excited to be very accurate. Kathleen filmed and recorded as the dolphins interacted with her, each other, and us. They twisted and flipped and spiraled to the bottom like underwater acrobats.

For five or six minutes a young dolphin stayed right with me—#34, a class three male juvenile with scattered spots. Spotted dolphins get more spots as they age (don't we all?) and the young ones have very few. The more familiar bottle-nosed dolphins are larger and darker than the spotted variety. After about ten minutes, the visit was over and the dolphins disappeared as quickly as they had arrived. What a rush that had been watching them all frolic around us, jumping and diving and playing and swimming at unbelievable speeds. Only then did I realize how exhausted I was and could barely climb back on board.

My daughters were amazed at the scene they had witnessed from the boat and could hardly wait for the next group to arrive. We did not wait long before the next call came, "dolphin at six o'clock—three, no five, no eight or nine," and the process repeated.

Kathleen's enthusiasm for her work rubbed off on us and made us want to learn everything about our new friends. She shared her research findings—definite sound patterns related to specific behaviors, "signature" whistles unique to each dolphin, courting and mating behaviors, jealousies, parenting, and on and on. We began to recognize some of the dolphins by name—Doubledot, Topnotch, Hook, Macho—and other unnamed ones by number, including #34. Researchers and volunteers had named many of the dolphins in the Bahamas Project, but some still had only numbers. We learned about the work of Oceanic Society Expeditions and their numerous marine related projects.

We soon talked like experts ourselves in our reports to Kathleen following the encounters, "Double Gash interacted with Halfmoon making a clicking and pulsing beep—behavior somewhat aggressive. Ridge and her calf both very friendly, with constant clicking by Ridge."

One day no dolphins came, so we loaded into the dinghies and searched for them. The dolphins love to play in the bow wave of the small rubber boats, and after several passes around Calypso Poet we attracted them. We flipped backward out of the boats like Navy frogmen to get into the water. Kathi and Wendy swam a long time one morning with a mother dolphin and her calf and could not believe how willingly the mother shared her baby with them.

We found a lot of quiet time—to rest and talk and think. The actual time in the water was short, but by the end of the day we were exhausted and filled with wonder at all we had seen and learned. We talked a lot about David and told the others about him and why we were there. We knew how much David would have loved all we were doing and at times actually felt him with us. In fact, the research assistant reminded us of David because of his fascination with life and passion for his work. Alejandro told us stories about his research and his life growing up in Mexico and one night even sang a Mexican lullaby for us.

We wanted to cling to the beauty and peace and healing we were experiencing. The day before heading home, Kathi and Wendy suggested that we pool the money we would have spent on presents for David and each other that Christmas and donate it to the Project Dolphin Fund to adopt and name a dolphin. They already knew the name—Boilie—the name they always called their brother. Nobody knows exactly why they called him that—something to do with his calling one of them "girlie" one time—but he had been Boilie for years. We talked to Kathleen and chose number thirty-four, the class three male, since I had connected with him on that first day in the water and we played with him so often.

*According to the researcher's latest reports, Boilie still swims in the warm, crystal clear waters of the Bahamas. We have never been back to swim with him, but we do not have to see him to **know** he is still there.*

The trip is still shaping into a story even as I write this book. The whole experience was enlightening and healing for my daughters and me. We all treasure the memories and the framed pictures of Boilie hanging on our walls. The trip and the story showed us a way to include David in our lives even after his death and gave us back a future with him.

I feel David's presence so much in my life and in what I do that he continues to be a vital part of my future, although certainly not in the way I expected. I feel his presence in my current home even though he never visited me here. Almost every day I think about ways to include him in a story or an incident. Keeping him in my life is easy when I share a story with listeners and see them express recognition. My biggest thrill comes when people say they can see David through my eyes.

I still have self-doubts and my nagging inner critic gets me down at times saying *who do you think you are and what do you know that is so red hot and would interest anybody else?* But most days, when everything is working and my attitude is positive, I know I am on the right track.

Helping each other

We must believe our stories are worthwhile. Each person's insights are unique and might supply exactly what someone else needs to hear. Susan Klein always has her students affirm themselves and their work by saying, "I am valuable and what I have to say is important." At times I repeat this affirmation over and over to convince myself of its truth. Fortunately I have had many people encouraging me along the way, and I am grateful for them and their support. I now believe part of my mission as a storyteller is to encourage others to share their stories so we can all heal each other. The following story showed me how helping each other *works!*

Heaven and Hell

There was once a woman who was so good and kind and loving that even the angels in heaven took notice. Because of her generosity to everyone else, the angels decided that they wanted to give her a wonderful gift. They discussed all sorts of possibilities—gold, jewels, a new wardrobe, stocks and bonds, a winning lottery ticket—but nothing quite seemed to fit. Finally one of the angels suggested that they allow her to choose her own gift and they all agreed. The angel who made the suggestion was picked to fly down and tell the woman the news.

So down, down he flew and found the woman preparing the food in a homeless shelter. The angel approached the woman but was told he would have to wait. When the meal was served, the woman asked the angel what she could do for him. He replied, "Nothing, my good woman. I have come to do something for you. Because you do so much for others, all of the angels have decided to grant you anything you wish."

The woman thought and thought and finally said, "I would like to see for myself what heaven and hell are like. That is what I would like to know more than anything."

The angel thought that was the strangest thing he had ever heard, but he had said anything she wished, so how could he refuse? He waited until she finished with all of her duties at the shelter. Then he took her by the hand and off they flew—down, down, down until they reached the gates of hell.

The woman looked inside and could not believe her eyes. She had always been told hell was a terrible place, but she gazed into a beautiful banquet hall. The tables and chairs were ornately carved, and incredible china, silver, and crystal covered the exquisite table-cloths. Platters of food lined the tables—meats, fruits, and breads— food of every description. Never had the woman smelled such aromas or seen such a feast, but as she stepped closer she heard moaning and cries of agony and pain. The people looked emaciated, as if they were starving to death. Tears streamed down their faces. Then she saw that the people were shackled to their chairs and their arms were covered with sleeves of metal so they could not bend their elbows. While they could reach out and touch the food, they could not bring it to their mouths.

The woman could not bear to hear that awful wailing sound. The angel took her by the hand and they turned to leave. They started the ascent—up, up, up until they arrived at the gates of heaven and stopped once more. Again she could not believe her eyes for she saw the same scene as in hell—everything was exactly the same....the banquet hall, the tables, the silver and crystal and china, the platters laden with food—even the chairs with shackles and the people with sleeves of metal. She quickly entered, but heard no cries of pain and sorrow. The people here looked happy and well nourished. They were smiling and laughing and some were even singing. How could this be possible?

*And then the woman saw that even though the people in heaven
could not bring all that wonderful food to their own mouths, they had
discovered the source of true happiness. They were reaching out,
filling their hands with food, and feeding their neighbors.*

Versions of this story appear in the folklore of many different
cultures, establishing its universal theme. The Chinese story describes
people using chopsticks that are too long to feed themselves. In the
Irish version, people are trying to eat stew from a pot with spoons that
are too long to reach their own faces. All of the variations affirm the
only real difference between heaven and hell is that in heaven people
are feeding and helping each other. What a wonderful metaphor to
show the necessity of others assisting to encourage healing and
wholeness. Doing our part in the process is empowering. When we
feed each other, we foster healing for everyone, including ourselves.

Making new commitments

Listening to the stories and comments of those experiencing loss
always assists their grieving process. As I recalled how I had been
helped along my healing journey by other bereaved parents, I knew I
wanted to stay involved with Compassionate Friends to offer hope
and understanding to others. Helping as freely as others had given to me offered me the chance to give back to the world some of what I received and learned. The privilege of being able to share my struggle and growth inspires me to learn even more. If this helps others, then I am doubly blessed as my healing continues.

As part of this commitment I tell a healing story each month to the local Compassionate Friends

> "I took Melanie's story to schools and classrooms to show children how beautiful she was and how she helped our community, and then how in one short span of time, a total of seven seconds, her life was over. I needed to let children know how important seat belts were. If telling and sharing her story helped saved one life, then it was worth it."
> Myra Davis
> Storyteller

group I facilitate. I look for opportunities to tell stories and teach healing story workshops for other groups as well. Sometimes we discuss the stories, but most often leave them to work in each listener.

Many people speak of a strong desire to *give back* after a time of receiving so much from others. Some bereaved parents establish community projects to increase public awareness of the cause of their child's death. If this effort can prevent additional deaths, the parents feel their losses have served a purpose.

In *Nourishing the Soul*, Zalman Schachter-Shalomi talked of the importance of having role models for women participating in home birth. He said, "[It was] crucial to have someone there who had already been through the process, who could tell them what they might expect and what they should do about it. If someone can tell us what we are likely to encounter and how we might handle it, then what seems like a terrifying process becomes accessible and replicable; we can do it again, and we can show somebody else how to do it as well." His comments apply to any experience. Telling a story often provides a role model and offers encouragement.

> "...we can use our major losses to grow stronger and give back to others through learning from our own pain....it is decidedly more empowering to confront loss than it is to run from loss."
>
> John Harvey
> From the Preface to
> *Embracing Their Memory*
>
> ⋘

In his book *Timeless Healing*, Herbert Benson wrote about a survey conducted by Allan Luks, executive director of Big Brothers/Big Sisters of New York City. Benson said, "In a survey of thousands of volunteers across the nation, Luks discovered that people who help other people consistently report better health than peers in their age group. Luks calls this phenomenon 'the helper's high' [associated with] increased energy, a sense of euphoria and long-term effects of greater calm and relaxation. The overall rewards noted in Luks's survey were reaped from helping strangers, not just family and friends." The positive side effects Luks describes result when someone reaches out to help another who has experienced loss. This *helper's high* contributes to the healing experience inherent in telling stories.

Offering our gifts

After my healing from loss began, I had a strong desire to share with dying people the things I knew about staying alive through stories. I also wanted to hear their wisdom about approaching death, the ultimate loss. I resumed my work as a volunteer with hospice patients, from whom I already had learned so much about living. Coming to terms with David's death had given me an even greater appreciation of life. Using stories to explain my outlook further refined my own understanding and made me realize how precious and meaningful our time on earth can be.

David Oldfield wrote in *Nourishing the Soul,* "The wisdom of heroic myths and rites of passage is clear: the treasures won on the soul's journey are not possessions to keep, but gifts to offer." This wisdom must include understanding how the lessons learned can best be shared with others. Giving away the treasures we have won restores a future filled with meaning and promise. Oldfield continued, "Compassion—the willingness to be present and to suffer with others—is an astonishingly potent healing force, and compassion springs from shared stories."

Many opportunities and methods of helping others heal and grow exist, but my experience with loss leads me to others who need stories to find their way—just as I did. Working with hospice volunteers and patients, The Compassionate Friends, battered women's shelters, and others provides me opportunities to share meaningful stories. Listeners provide encouragement when they respond to stories with their insights. Interacting with people at that intimate level forms strong bonds. These relationships fill life with meaning. Having fresh dreams and goals creates a new vision of the

> "Others who haven't experienced the death of a loved one don't know how important it [telling the story] is and often don't want to hear all the details. But the person who experienced it needs to tell all of that. It's therapeutic for the person in grief to tell his or her story, and because of my experience I'm a very good listener."
>
> David Holt
> Musician and storyteller
>
> ⇛

future to replace the one that was lost. My vision includes giving to others the stories that find their way into my life.

Richard Katz learns healing stories and techniques from the indigenous groups with which he works. In his chapter in *Sacred Stories* entitled "The Wisdom of Ancient Healers," Katz said the knowledge should be used "only to serve the people, not for personal gain." He has been told many times, "This healing is a gift...it comes to us from the Creator of all things." Katz added, "And then it follows that whatever healing knowledge we have been given is to be offered to others as a gift."

Christine Reese's belief in the healing power of stories was strengthened so much by her own experience that she is creating a workshop related to sacred stories. She envisions "a workshop guiding participants through a format designed to facilitate a person to tell his or her story or journey to make sense of it—to find forgiveness, healing, and encouragement for the future." When you have gained so much from stories yourself, you naturally want to help others find the same benefits.

> "The simple act of reaching out to help anyone is always therapeutic, and sharing my personal stories about loved ones is not only a way to reach out to someone who is suffering, but it enables me to keep my loved ones alive in my heart and my life."
>
> Jeannine Auth
> Writer and storyteller
>
>

Ada Forney was already involved with storytelling when she lost her granddaughter. She said, "[The experience of using stories] confirmed my belief in the power of stories to change us, to touch us, and to heal our pain. It made me more determined to find a way to spread the word and to help heal others with the power of a story."

Changing the perspective

Stories helped me realize that David's life had been a gift to me, which turned out to be a big step in my healing after his death. A hospice chaplain gave me a tape entitled "The Creative Handling of Grief" by Episcopal minister John Claypool, who had lost his ten-year-old daughter. I listened to that tape at least fifty times, usually while driving my car. Each time, I heard something new and different from Claypool's thoughts and stories. The tape was the same—I was the one who was changing.

At first I disagreed with and resisted everything Claypool said, but gradually embraced most of his beliefs. To illustrate the difference between gifts and entitlements, Claypool told a simple story about the gift of a green Bendix washer to his family when he was a child. Friends of his parents stored furniture in the basement of the Claypool home during the war. His family used the stored washing machine and became accustomed to having it in their home. Young John, whose job was to wash the clothes, resented the intrusion in his life when the people returned and reclaimed their washer along with the other furniture. John's mother reminded him, "The washer never was ours to begin with. It was just our good fortune that we got to use it at all. It was not our possession, but a gift. As such, the response to its loss should be different. Since it did not belong to us, we need to use the occasion of its being taken away to give thanks that we had it in our lives for a while."

Claypool said when he remembered the story one night after his daughter died of leukemia, the way he looked at her life and death changed. He began to be thankful for the gift of her life and all she had meant to him.

The first time I heard the story I bristled at the suggestion that David's life had been a gift or was in any way comparable to a green washing machine. Listening to the story at least made me think about it. Gradually the story worked on me, and I was drawn to listen to it again. The more I thought about its concept, the more I saw the connection. The story eventually helped me put things into perspective and see David's life and death differently. I do not mean that I was reconciled to his death or that I ever will be. I will certainly never understand it, but I started looking for ways to show my gratitude for the wonderful gift of David *instead* of concentrating on how much I had lost.

Recovering joy

Only when I recognized how much of a gift David really was, could I be grateful for his presence in my life. At last the joy of having him became greater than the pain of losing him—a feeling I thought was impossible. I finally decided to celebrate the twenty-nine years I had with him. The decision helped my life move in a new direction.

The timing of my encounter with Claypool's tape definitely played a part in how I received the message. My strong desire to find healing had opened my mind and heart. I certainly became more receptive as days passed, but what about the story itself? Its power spoke to me in all stages of my grief—giving me a fresh message each time I heard it. The insights triggered responses in my brain, which led to acceptance of new ideas.

In the beginning I believed David belonged to me and had been ripped away unfairly. After all, I was his mother and had carried him inside my body for nine months. My feeling of protest did not permit any healing to take place. The idea contained within Claypool's story eventually opened my mind and heart to possibilities I might never have considered on my own. Expressing in words what actually happened is difficult, but I know the power of that simple story contributed to the transformation.

Later, a phenomenal thing happened. I gradually began to see what I was supposed to do with my new insights and the rest of my time on earth—tell stories to help others deal with life and loss and find meaning and purpose in their lives. What a concept! I found a reason to get up in the morning and be excited about life. I went from feeling I had no future to seeing one filled with adventure and meaning.

Without stories in my life, the outlook for the future would be bleak indeed. Thank goodness for all those memories and stories, not only the ones of David, but all the healing stories that surrounded me in the past *and* the ones I will hear and tell tomorrow. Because of them, my future is once again filled with anticipation and joy.

Stories offer hope 12

Raising expectations

Stories impart hope, which opens the door for healing to enter. Because stories *do* accomplish all the miracles discussed in this book, hope automatically follows. When we struggle to stabilize our beliefs enough to convey them to others, a ray of sunshine almost always shines through. The sharing of this hope—not false hope, but genuine hope founded in what has been learned—is a *vital* part of the healing process.

Jenna Eisenberg tells stories of hope every day to patients in her chiropractic practice. "To patients who have a certain problem, I tell about someone else who had that problem resolved. To patients who are in the midst of losing a parent to death, I listen and if appropriate share some of the stories of my mother's or father's death and what I learned about them or me

> "I believe stories have the power to heal both the teller and the listener because ultimately stories are about hope. That is why we tell them, and that is why we listen. For the teller, it is a way to try and give order to a situation where there seems to be none, to reach out and gather all the mystical little fragments together that we know must have meaning, and then try to fit them into something that we can understand; something that makes sense. This is when healing begins—when we can acknowledge the depth of our loss, identify our hope, and begin to tell the story."
>
> Jeannine Auth
> Writer and storyteller

or us that was helpful in grieving and healing." Jenna's patients often tell her later how one of her stories made a difference for them. Learning how others were helped raises the expectations of patients, thereby increasing their chances of improvement.

Encouraging survival

As we share stories of endurance and resilience with others, we reinforce the possibility that they too can survive. A simple story can help someone else decide to be a survivor, while reminding ourselves of the wisdom and power the story holds for us.

Immediately following a significant loss, even believing that survival is possible does not engender much hope. Merely existing in a life of suffering and pain is not an appealing prospect, especially if no change is expected in the future. At this point, the healing power of stories lies in their capacity to offer hope—not only to survive, but to go beyond and lead a *normal* life again, even though normal has changed.

The stories I heard at Compassionate Friends meetings offered me such hope. I was unable to participate or speak in any way at first, but I listened. Every person in the room had experienced the loss of a child, and yet still talked, worked, and functioned in a normal way. As I heard the stories of their losses, I wondered if I would ever be able to smile, laugh, and share with others. The hope of returning to life again came through their stories and nurtured those of us who needed something to hang onto.

After attending many meetings, I am still moved by the intense grief of those whose losses are recent. Their acute pain quickly brings back feelings I had in the early days after David's death. The bereaved often say that when

> "The stories people tell have a way of taking care of them. If stories come to you, care for them. And learn to give them away where they are needed. Sometimes a person needs a story more than food to stay alive. That is why we put these stories in each other's memory. This is how people care for themselves."
> Barry Lopez
> Badger's comments in
> *Crow and Weasel*

their grief was the worst, stories of hope were the only thing that kept them going.

Emotions of hope and happiness were not part of my daily routine after David's death. But as I found the needed feelings in stories, I gradually moved them back into my life—when I was ready to accept them. It was impossible to feel joy when I was consumed with grief. I laughed if someone said something funny, but feeling joy and passion was out of the question. Stories I heard and some I already knew slowly offered hope by providing a model or example that I could strive toward.

Trying to make sense of my experience taught me who I am and what is important in my life. The sorting out process showed me inner truths and strengths that I did not know I possessed. Stories filled my tank after a long dry spell and made me realize that I could find *healing* even for problems that could not be *cured*. The realization convinced me that life and joy could be found and led me to a new understanding of the old saying, "Where there's life, there's hope." I now believe we all need to hear stories of hope—again and again.

Inspiring others

In *The Artist's Way,* Julia Cameron wrote, "Your own healing is the greatest message of hope." Her statement explains why the story of someone who has survived a loss and is seeking answers offers such inspiration to others. I have witnessed this inspiring power in action when I tell the story of losing my son and struggling to heal. Listeners frequently tell me that my story offers them the encouragement that survival and recovery are possible. I do not doubt their sentiments, for I know the stories of others help me along my path.

Even after believing that recovery might be possible, two questions still faced me—*Where do I go from here?* and *How will I live my life in light of what has happened?* As I searched for the answers to these questions, I heard a story that demonstrated a different way to look at adversity. Tommy Oakes, a wonderful storyteller and caring teacher, shared this story about a man named Orville Kelly.

MTC

Orville Kelly went to his doctor one day because he had been feeling mighty poorly. After a lot of poking and prodding and testing, the doctor told Orville that he had terminal cancer and had only a few months to live. Stunned by the news, Orville went home and told his wife. They cried and screamed and prayed and did everything else people do when receiving such devastating news. After agonizing over the loss of so many hopes and dreams, Orville and his wife sat down to figure out exactly how they wanted to handle the news and what they wanted to do with the time he had left.

*They hit upon an idea and decided to **celebrate** the fact that he had cancer. The way they chose to celebrate was by throwing a huge party and inviting all of their family and friends. They sent out the invitations and everyone came. After the food had been served and everyone was full and happy, Orville stood up and thanked them for coming to the party. Then he announced that the reason for the party was to celebrate his diagnosis of terminal cancer. You could have heard a pin drop. He said they had decided to celebrate whatever came their way. As part of the plans, they were going to start a new club and invited everyone present to become a charter member. The group would be called "MTC"—Make Today Count.*

And that is just what they did. At last report MTC had grown to sixty chapters around the country, and Orville Kelly lived a long time—by celebrating each day and making today count.

This story encouraged me even though the answers to many of my questions remained unclear. Sometimes I could not *make today count.* On those days I felt miserable and depressed all day. Gradually I realized the choice *was* always mine. I thought about "MTC" a lot and have told it many times now after sensing that somebody needed encouragement. The story reinforces my belief that we face the choice when we wake up each morning to determine how we live that day. Telling "MTC" allows me to share my discovery with others. Telling it over and over helped me finally to get the message too.

Once a friend, whose daughter had died from cancer, had just been diagnosed with uterine cancer herself and happened to be in my audience. I had not planned to tell "MTC" that day but when I saw her, I had to share the story. She thanked me later and told me how much that simple story had helped her attitude. She said she thought of it whenever she started feeling sorry for herself. She realized the option for her to make every day count was always present and that she alone could choose how to make that happen. Knowing she could make the choice gave her some control over a situation that was seemingly beyond her control.

Any time we can celebrate something about the loss we have experienced, we are on the right track. "I personally find a healing balm associated with being able to tell stories about my loved ones and to celebrate their uniqueness, and their continuing role in my life" wrote Jeannine Auth.

> "Loss is an opportunity for self-reflection of a kind not otherwise available. Because we can choose how we experience loss, we can be more than victims. Choice can turn the worst circumstance into an experience of value. Our human capacity to choose how we use each day, however limited our choices, is a gift."
> Arthur Frank
> *At the Will of the Body*

Living our hero's journey

Many stories about loss end with a sense of hope no matter how bleak and desperate the situation appeared along the way. Getting to hope from despair is the core of the human struggle. The hero's journey of mythology and everyday life is everyone's ultimate story of survival.

Although I had been involved with storytelling for a long time and had certainly heard of the hero's journey, I had never thought about its significance for me personally. Even though many storytellers such as Joseph Campbell and Sam Keen have written extensively about the journey, I thought it was reserved for characters in myths and legends or perhaps an extraordinary person of today. As I read *The Gift of Stories* by Robert Atkinson, I began to see the journey as something more than an interesting story structure. I experienced a real awakening as I recognized the hero's journey within my own life.

A life-changing event, such as a significant loss, most often initiates the hero's journey. Variations in the course of action are numerous, but several basic elements are always present:

⫸ The hero or heroine faces a problem brought on by uncontrollable circumstances or self-induced behavior.

⫸ As a result of the problem, the hero must leave home, emotionally or physically, and struggle to find new answers and solutions.

⫸ The hero faces numerous choices during the struggle, including accepting or rejecting the challenge; leaving behind the old way of life; falling into many pitfalls along the way; encountering wise helpers, mentors, or fools to help in the search; and experiencing the breakthrough.

⫸ The hero gains the knowledge necessary to solve the problem, reach the physical goal, or gain understanding.

⫸ The hero returns to a life to use the newly found knowledge to help others.

Lasting solutions do not come easily or quickly or without struggle. Odysseus was gone from home for *twenty years*—ten years fighting the war and another ten years trying to get back home from Troy. It is an epic tale of a hero's return to find that life as he knew it had changed—big time!

Recognizing the hero

Maybe the word *hero* had been the stumbling block to my understanding. The hero or heroine is not only a person of great strength and courage who is descended from the gods and admired for great exploits and achievements—he or she can also be simply the central character in a story. I certainly do not qualify for the first definition, but I definitely am the central character in a story—my story. Seeing my life as a mythic story opened my eyes. I immediately saw the events in my life in a new light. Next I needed to figure out what I had learned in my struggle and how to use my new knowledge to make a difference in my life and the lives of others.

As I learned more about the classic mythological voyages and quests, I felt overwhelmed with the power of my growing understanding of the big picture. I previously had read tales of heroes, such as *Vasilisa the Beautiful, Ulysses, Sir Gawain and the Green Knight,* and other Arthurian legends, never realizing they were guides for every person's quest for meaning. Interpreting the events in those stories as analogies and metaphors relating to incidents in my life gave me hope that I might be victorious in my quest. I discovered necessary steps for fulfillment and realized that the struggles—fighting the dragons or giants or grief or depression—were imperative for reaching the goal.

We all must set out on the hero's journey many times in our lives— starting school, going away to college or our first job, breaking away from parents to be married, having children, finding a career, dealing with losses and new beginnings, accepting our aging process, and ultimately dealing with our own death. Each stage is a journey in and of itself. Our entire life is a hero's journey of epic proportion, but only if we accept the challenges to learn and grow along the way.

Many different disciplines, such as education, developmental psychology, and traditional twelve-step programs, follow their own version of the mythological process. The journey begins with the birth, the surrender, the crisis, or the quest for knowledge. The middle stage is the transition, awakening, or learning period. At the end comes the resolution, return, new beginning, recovery, or application of the

6"A hero ventures forth from the world of common day into a region of supernatural wonder: fabulous forces are encountered and a decisive victory is won: the hero comes back from this mysterious adventure with the power to bestow boons on his fellow man. The standard path of the mythological adventure of the hero is a magnification of the formula represented in the rites of passage: separation— initiation—return."

Joseph Campbell
The Hero With A Thousand Faces

knowledge learned. The final stage embodies the spiritual quest that gives our lives meaning as we share our bounty with others.

Refusal to start the journey occurs frequently in myth and popular tales, as well as in actual life situations. According to Joseph Campbell, the person who refuses the call "loses the power of significant, affirmative action and becomes a victim to be saved." Reasons abound for refusing to begin the journey, such as contentment with the status quo, fear of the unknown (the devil you know is better than the one you don't know), distraction by other things, or seemingly easier paths. None of these reasons were viable options for me as I struggled to regain my life—I had to find meaning in order to do more than exist.

Expanding awareness

Although following my son's death I felt more like a victim than a hero, my personal journey was definitely underway. Loss and the resulting separation was the obstacle challenging me to begin. When my life drastically changed, I had to expand my awareness and outlook to find new ways to live. The initial steps on my journey offered great challenges. I had little energy or enthusiasm for anything because of depression and suffering. As much as I hated the internal and external struggles, I am convinced now that little growth takes place without them. Opportunities for learning and growth exist all the time, but a crisis adds a sense of urgency. I plunged into explorations that I would not have taken the time to examine unless forced to do so. My obsession with finding resolution grew and eventually led me to new joy and purpose I could never have imagined. The process continues, and my vision is clearer than ever.

Comprehending that steps in the classic journeys of mythology and legends were repeated in personal stories empowered me. Accepting my role and obligation to continue learning helped me regain a feeling of control over my final destination, provided I stayed true to the search. I no longer felt like a tiny mouse trying to run through a maze that had no path leading out—only dead-ends and false paths with the ever-present fear of the impending cat's paw. My growing understanding prepared me to answer the challenge that losing David had presented. Having a goal or mission offered hope even when I was unsure of the precise steps to take. *Perhaps instead of erecting a stumbling block, his death could open new doors.* I was *determined* to learn from my struggle so I might end up with something worth sharing. This vision and hope initiated a new enthusiasm and excitement for living.

Laughing pain away

One of the most significant turning points in my grief process came as I gained a deeper understanding of the Storyteller's Creed, found in the introduction to several of Robert Fulghum's books. As mentioned in my story "Infinite Resource and Sagacity," David gave me a framed copy of the creed the last Christmas he was alive. I treasured it and read it over and over again after his death. Not completely grasping the significance when my grief was new, I knew those words somehow connected to David and to my healing. One line that continued to jump out at me is "[I believe] that Laughter is the only cure for Grief."

It is widely accepted that laughter has a powerful healing effect on all our systems, based on studies, our personal experiences, and the writings of others, such as Norman Cousins in *Anatomy of an Illness.* Laughter provides a break, even if only temporary, from whatever is bothering us. Laughing through our tears helps us realize that happiness and joy are still possible.

Stories provide an excellent way to share humor with others. The resulting laughter always gives an emotional lift, improving both physical and mental states. Following her battle with breast cancer and the surgical loss of part of her body, Tennessee storyteller Peggy Kenny recalled the importance of "a visitor who told me the story of her experience with breast cancer. Her present good health gave me hope that I could be okay." Later Peggy worked with other cancer patients, using stories of how she and others had coped successfully. When patients were ready, she also described humorous incidents related to having surgery and using the prosthesis. Being able to laugh at stories of things like a "blow-up bra" lifted patients' spirits and gave them hope.

In his book *Gesundheit,* Patch Adams said he learned early in his medical career that "medications rarely alleviate human suffering." After his mother's leg was amputated, he used his gift of humor to help her adjust to loss. As his mother awoke following her surgery, the first thing she saw was Patch with his red clown nose looming over her. He said, "Well I guess you know what it's like to have one foot in the grave!" He explained, "She laughed and continued for years to tell the story to others with glee. It could not bring her limb back, but it did spark her hope for continued enjoyment of life." In addition to the obvious medical benefits, Dr. Adams is convinced that humor is vital in healing the problems of individuals, communities, and societies.

Providing comic relief

My cousin, Jan Reeves, and her two young daughters, Mollie and Annie, provided a wonderful example of how healing laughter can be when they visited me at David's home a few days after his death. Knowing I was a storyteller, the girls asked me if I would tell them a story. At that point I could barely remember my name, much less a story. In fact, I could not think of a single story that I knew, so I told them I would do it another time. Then they asked if they could tell me a story. Jan suggested they go outside to play, but I encouraged them to go ahead with the story. They decided to tell "Jack the Giant Killer," a story I had heard many times.

Even though I remember very little from those first days after David died, I still vividly remember the girls' story. Their telling of it was hilarious. Six-year-old Mollie started the story but soon forgot what happened next and asked eight-year-old Annie, "Then what happened?" Annie took over the telling, but after only a few words, Mollie yelled, "Oh yeah, I've got it, now I've got it," and she resumed telling the story. Soon she forgot again, and again Annie came to her rescue. This scene repeated quite a few times before the tale finally concluded. By that time, tears of laughter were running down our cheeks. What a breath of fresh air the story and those two precious children brought to me. Even in the midst of my most intense grief, I was able to relax and laugh because of their story. That first genuine laughter after David's death gave me hope to think that laughter might be part of my life once more.

In *Finding Joy,* Charlotte Kasl related a story that continued to bring her comfort. In a phone conversation following the death of Kasl's mother, her beloved aunt Margaret Wickes MacDonald said, "Now don't forget to laugh." Reflecting on her aunt's advice, Kasl wrote, "That was such a help, because I was caught thinking I had to be grim all the time because my mother had died." Later she and her sister were able to find healing as they laughed and cried together remembering things that happened with their mother.

In *Healing and the Mind,* Bill Moyers recorded an interview with Dr. Michael Lerner, president and founder of Commonweal, a health and environmental research center in California. Lerner said, "Expressing the feeling or emotion that's going on now clears the way for what may be next. Laughter and joy come mixed in with the very intense emotions of pain and sorrow and anger."

One of Aesop's fables entitled "Joy and Sorrow" shows how interconnected laughter and pain can be. In the story, twin sisters named Joy and Sorrow constantly argued over which of them was preferred by man. Since they could not reach an agreement, they decided to let King Minos settle the argument. Even Minos could not convince them to live together peacefully and finally decreed that they should be chained together forever, so that each would always be close to the other. The last verse of the fable reads

> *Thence comes it that we never see*
> *A perfect bliss or misery;*
> *Each happiness has some alloy;*
> *And grief succeeded is by joy.*
> *The happiest mortal needs must own*
> *He has a time of sorrow known:*
> *Nor can the poorest wretch deny*
> *But in his life he felt a joy.*

Remembering funny stories

Florida storyteller Nancy Case said her interest in stories and storytelling goes back to her childhood and her father, her primary model of a storyteller. When her father died after a prolonged illness, her family was emotionally and physically exhausted. They did not think they would be able to make it through the funeral service and even dreaded attending. But something happened at the service when the preacher told a funny story based on an experience he had shared with her father. Case remembered, "It was so hilarious that we all found ourselves laughing, something we had not been able to do for days. And when the service was over, we started sharing funny stories of our memories about Dad and we laughed all the way to the cemetery. We couldn't believe how much better we all felt."

A story Case 's family heard prompted their own memories and stories. Their outpouring of laughter seemed like a miracle as it relieved a lot of built-up tension and caused a transformation in her family. Case remembered, "The stories told at the funeral had a great healing effect on the whole family. It helped us to focus on the joy of having him with us all those years instead of the terrible, long, drawn-out dying process and our overwhelming loss."

> "Telling stories about Daddy is always therapeutic for me and helped me work through the grief process. As I tell stories about my dad, it's like he's with me again. I feel a closeness to him when I tell his stories and know he's laughing along with us somewhere. It has helped me to get past the cloud of grief that hangs over you when someone close has died."
>
> Nancy Case
> Storyteller and librarian
>
> ⇒⇒

Case found hearing the personal stories of others also had a healing effect on her. She added, "Stories about the deceased that are joyful and humorous have been the most helpful. When you think of life as a story, you begin to see that there is sadness, drama, and much humor. After the most terrible event, it is healing to be able to see the humor that is almost always there. Stories that focus on the positive aspects of life allow you to, in a way, re-write history in a more positive light in your own mind. Almost anything can be looked at more than one way. Telling happy stories about the deceased makes you feel warm and happy too."

Lifting the weight of grief

Many people use humor to deal with the emotions they feel following a loss. After losing her husband, writer Louise Colln "wrote and had published several articles on learning to live without Bud—buying a car, traveling alone, etc. All, perhaps strangely, were from light to humorous. One was about a cantankerous lawnmower that I sold three times." Similarly Margaret Lawrence consciously seeks humorous stories to tell now so she can offer laughter and encouragement to others, remembering what helped her following the death of her son.

> "I have found the most help when I have taken the facts of my losses and woven those into stories. Funny stories helped me most—stories that find that speck of humor that lives in every situation."
>
> Christyna Jensen
> Tennessee storyteller
>
> ⋘

Jenna Eisenberg said, "When I need encouragement, I listen to tapes of stories that inspire me or make me laugh or let me escape from my own circumstances for a while." Sometimes we do need to escape, and stories can provide the diversion that allows our systems to relax for a while. After a mental break, we are better equipped to face difficult situations. In addition the story might provide some insight that will help us cope.

After the loss of her daughter, Myra Davis found she needed to tell her stories even more than before, "because it took me away from reality and let me escape into a world of my very own. I wanted to hear the laughter of children, for that made me happiest. I needed to know that I was doing what my children always wanted me to do." So she quit teaching school after fifteen years to become a professional storyteller, which got her through the darkest times of her life.

> "Telling stories was part of my healing process because it gave me something to do in order to keep from thinking about my loss. Of course, I was escaping, but sometimes you just have to do that for a while...at first."
>
> Ginny Conrad
> Teacher and storyteller
>
> ⋘

Believing in the power of stories

In his chapter "Stories That Need Telling Today" found in *Sacred Stories,* Matthew Fox wrote about the many dangerous and debilitating stories existing in our culture today. Fox said these harmful stories need to be replaced with "fuller stories that satisfy the heart, the mind, the imagination, and the quest in every one of us for justice and peace, for the return of blessing to our daily lives." He continued, "Healthy people base their lives on healing, authentic stories. Empowerment comes through the process of telling those stories.... The spirit is fed and moved when people tell their true tales, with all their inherent grief but also with possibility and hope....There is passion behind our yearning to tell stories. When we become aware of what is in us, it is altogether natural to announce it, pronounce it, produce it, and give birth to it."

> The human will to find healing "...is epitomized in people's stories of loss and recovery. The act of telling these stories is a timeless antidote to the feeling that there is no hope in dealing with loss. Just as loss is continuous and inevitable in human experience, so is the capacity of humans to tell of their loss and thereby find light and the hope and will to live."
> John Harvey
> *Embracing Their Memory*
>
>

The storytellers I interviewed for this book attempt to convey a sense of possibility and hope through their stories because of the function stories provide in their own lives. Michael Parent had been a professional storyteller for a long time before his losses occurred, but said, "I gained a new appreciation of the wide-ranging power of stories as a result of these losses and their aftermath."

The realization of the powerful role stories play in healing from loss grows within me each day as I expand my outreach to others. The possibilities seem endless as I hear the many ways storytellers, healing professionals, and individuals help listeners to grow through stories. Sharing stories from the heart *always* activates hope and fosters great potential for healing.

A friend cross-stitched a plaque for me that said, "When you get to the end of your rope, tie a knot in it and hang on." Stories were the knot at the end of my rope—stories about David, stories from my life, stories from folklore and literature, and other people's stories. I *did* hang on to them searching desperately for the keys to open doors that had slammed shut.

Stories turned out to be the keys. Gradually I realized the incredible power they had to open hearts and teach us to grieve, render meaning from chaos, penetrate barriers with images, preserve and perpetuate memories, validate listeners as individuals, connect us to the universe, expand imagination and creativity, enable growth and learning, transform pain, establish control and closure, restore the future, and offer hope. The stories were there all the time. I just needed to find them.

Appendix 1

How and Why Stories Heal:
A Look at the Healing Power of Stories

Prospectus for
Dr. John Taylor
EDFN 5950
Summer 1997

Diane Rooks
East Tennessee State University
253-66-3865
June 18, 1998

Table of Contents

Chapter   Page

I.   Introduction 227
     Purpose..228
     Significance..228
     Sample...229
     Assumptions 229
     Delimitations 229
     Operational Definitions 230

II. Review of Literature.....................................231

III. Procedures 235

     References...236
     Appendix A 238

CHAPTER 1

Introduction

"The relationship between stories and healing is receiving serious attention today." (National Storytelling Association, 1994) Many storytellers speak of the "power of story" in a way that implies that stories have the power to promote healing and wholeness and growth. Does this healing occur in the teller or the listener? What part do stories play in the successful resolution of grief after experiencing a loss? How and why does healing take place?

Following the death of my son, I found and continue to find both listening to and telling stories to be important parts of my healing process (Rooks, 1998). Others have told me that after a significant loss, they experienced healing through stories. Many people have expressed an interest in this subject following workshops or programs containing healing stories. Some therapists use stories with clients and give examples of people who have been helped after telling their stories. Articles and books have been written stating that stories help with the healing that occurs following a loss, but little has been written about how that healing occurs. Stories offer us win-win situations—the magical power to heal both the listener and the teller (Cotter, 1998). Cotter further states, "Stories heal, yet we have no way of knowing whom they heal or how they do so."

Having experienced this healing power of stories first hand, I am anxious to explore the subject further by talking in depth with others who have also found stories to be healing. Finding out what those individuals think took place and understanding how this healing occurred can have beneficial results not only to those who have experienced loss, but also to those involved with healing professions, such as storytellers, mental health counselors, therapists, clergy, teachers, and physicians.

Purpose

It is the purpose of this research to explore through naturalistic inquiry how and why stories heal. Qualitative studies are ideally suited to uncovering a jointly created reality through narrative interviews (Riessman, 1990). I chose this method to begin to understand a process about which very little is written. In addition I plan to compile a list of stories that have been healing to other storytellers for themselves and their listeners. This will encourage tellers to use "the power of story" by including healing stories in their programs and will promote the use of stories in the healing professions.

Further research could be done by asking the same questions to storytellers and non-storytellers to see if a significant difference existed between the two groups. However, because I want to gather this information for myself and to share with other tellers, I have restricted my research only to storytellers who have experienced a significant loss.

Significance

Because all people experience loss of many different kinds, it is important to find ways to help in the grief resolution process. Because the death of a significant loved one is considered to be the greatest loss a person experiences, understanding ways to heal from this loss is a valuable lesson not only to those who have experienced loss, but also to anyone wishing to help others deal with loss. Experts agree that the loss of a child is the loss people fear the most and the one from which healing is most difficult. Therefore many of the storytellers chosen to be interviewed will be ones who have lost children. Those experiencing other significant losses will be interviewed also to show that stories help in the healing process following any type of loss.

It is my belief that research on the subject will encourage others to tell stories to bring about healing. In addition, having a list of healing stories will be useful to anyone wishing to help others heal through story. Sanders (1997) speaking of the power of stories to help us deal with suffering, loss, and death says "like so many characters, we are lost in a dark wood, a labyrinth, a swamp, and we need a trail of stories to show us the way back to our true home."

Sample

The 12 initial subjects are storytellers who have experienced the loss of a significant loved one, in most cases the loss of a child. In addition, the questionnaire sent to the subjects will ask them to list other storytellers who qualify as subjects, specifically those who have experienced significant loss. If this does not result in the desired 25 subjects, I intend to query the Storytell list/serv on the Internet for volunteer subjects who qualify and are interested in participating.

Assumptions

1. It is assumed that all of the subjects selected are storytellers and have experienced a significant loss.
2. It is assumed that the subjects have used stories for their own healing as well as for helping others.
3. It is assumed that the subjects will be completely candid in their answers and not give answers they think the researcher wishes to hear. (This could be a limitation of the research.)

Delimitations

1. The research will continue until at least 25 have been interviewed.
2. Only subjects who are storytellers and have experienced a significant loss will be interviewed.
3. The initial 12 subjects are tellers I know personally or have heard tell stories; the rest of the subjects will be recommendations from others or volunteers from the Internet.

Operational Definitions

The following definitions will be used by the researcher to conduct this study:

1. Healing stories - stories offering hope and containing positive messages about dealing with loss.

2. Significant loss - the death of a loved one resulting in the disruption of normal behavior.

3. Grief - natural reaction to loss.

4. Positive resolution to grief - learning to manage and negotiate in life following a significant loss.

CHAPTER 2

Review of Literature

Sanders (1997) points out that Aristotle, with his theory of catharsis, is only one in a long line of commentators who have recognized the healing power of stories. Sanders refers to "the root meaning of healing, which is to make whole." Stone (1996) says that research shows that stories filled with positive, healing images can create a physiological state that biochemists associate with health, relaxation, and emotional well-being. Traditional cultures have used stories and storytelling as part of the healing process for centuries. Fairy tales, poems, and parables all make use of a literary device known as metaphor to convey an idea in an indirect yet paradoxically meaningful way (Fazio, 1992). The use of metaphor often helps listeners to see their own situation in a way that direct confrontation cannot. The literature of folklore, myth, and fairy tales contains stories that help people explore their own lives and find insight into their own loss (Wright, 1996). Sedney, Baker, and Gross (1994) point out that stories and rituals have long been recognized by family therapists as playing an important role in healing. This has consisted of therapists telling stories to their clients as well as the clients telling their own stories.

Putting our life's events into the form of a story can help us bear a burden or see with a clearer perspective. The stories of our lives carry a great power because we tap into ageless, universal themes that become deeply familiar to us when we tell our stories (Atkinson, 1995). Constructing stories can be understood as one phase in the process of organizing and making sense of our experiences. This narrative mode is well suited for reinterpreting and accommodating inconsistent information, as well as for helping people think about situations that involve conflicts or contradictions. Taylor (1983) proposed that this form of reinterpretation is often a powerful and beneficial feature of cognitive coping; specifically, people interpret their cancer or trauma as serving to bring about positive, desirable outcomes in the long run. When asked by a hospital administrator about ways to improve the hospital's healing operations, Moore (1992) recommended "a time and place where patients could tell stories about their illness and hospitalization with a real storyteller or someone who would know the importance of letting the soul speak and find its images."

One of the first tasks for survivors of loss is to understand what happened (Baker, Sedney, & Gross, 1992). Telling the story about the loss can help begin to achieve this understanding as the survivor struggles with explanations that are acceptable. It can be seen as a way to make sense of something that makes no sense. When confronted with a confusing and contradictory array of information, people will try to make up plausible stories to tie it all together.

Riessman (1990) noted that it is possible to accomplish a positive self through narrative retelling of key events from the past, healing discontinuities by the way the narrative account is structured. Individuals can do this on their own or be guided by a trained therapist. Stories can serve both as ways of interpreting experience and as means of communicating to others. Baumeister & Newman (1994) state that stories can be understood as exercises in self-interpretation, by which people make sense of their experiences. In addition, stories are accepted as effective means for teaching others as shown by spiritual leaders who use parables and stories to make their messages more comprehensible to listeners.

In *A Child Dies,* Arnold (1983) says that following the death of a child, parents search for meaning and ways to fill some of their emptiness. In this process, parents often find comfort in memories. Arnold further says that memories can be shared with others through stories and recollections of special days and events, and that these memories keep the dead alive and preserve and protect the lost loved one. The death of a child often causes the bereaved parents to undertake work that would benefit others, thereby increasing the greater good. This need to show purposiveness is one of the motives for the construction of stories and may be a vital first step toward understanding an event (Baumeister & Newman, 1994). Creating and sharing these stories can be seen as helping to heal others.

Telling the story of what happened begins to relieve some of the strong emotions that always accompany the experience of loss. These strong emotions include helplessness, loss of control, dissociated feelings, and a sense of disbelief. Since stories often capture emotions, telling stories can provide emotional relief, help make an experience meaningful, and bring people together (Sedney et al., 1994). Estes (1992) says that stories are medicine and "they have such power: they do not require that we do, be, act anything—we need only listen." She further says that although some use stories as entertainment alone, tales are, in their oldest sense, a healing art. Some are called to this art and "in the best tellers I know, the stories grow out of their lives like roots grow a tree."

Taylor, Aspinwall, Giuliano, Dakof, and Reardon (1993) state that positive stories about similar others going through stressful events are perceived as more helpful and reassuring than negative stories. In three separate studies they found that positive stories have beneficial effects on mood by making people happy and reassured; positive stories are seen as providing a good role model; and they provide hope and encouragement. In addition, the most effective stories may come from similar others, especially those who have undergone the same experience. This seems to be confirmed by organizations such as Compassionate Friends and Alcoholics Anonymous where members are encouraged to tell their story to promote healing of themselves and others. These self-help organizations understand the transforming power of telling stories and being heard.

The concept of the wounded healer appears in numerous publications (Moyers, 1993; Remen, 1996; Moore, 1992). This may explain why wounded people are often healed by other wounded people. In describing the value of the twelve-step program of Alcoholics Anonymous, Alston (1994) asserts that the paradigm of wounded healers telling their stories to each other is an important contribution of our society to the larger world community. When members reach out to one another, they simply tell stories of their "experience, strength, and hope." Remen (1996) says "only other wounded people can understand what is needed, for the healing of suffering is compassion, not expertise. It is the wisdom gained from our wounds and from our experiences of suffering that makes us able to heal." She found the stories of others who were suffering to be inspiring, moving, and important and realized that the truth in those stories began to heal her. Further, she found that listening to another's story was perhaps the most powerful tool of healing since it allowed the teller an opportunity for wholeness by hearing truth in themselves and feeling valued by others. Thus listening is healing for both the listener and the teller.

While some of the literature referenced concerns storytellers in social settings, much of it involves therapeutic storytelling in a client-therapist relationship. Although the settings are different, communication is the important aspect of human behavior being exhibited in both situations. Because both types of storytelling are done with a specific purpose in mind, healing seems to take place. Perhaps that is the key—telling the story with an attempt at under-standing what happened which leads to gaining some meaning and perspective. Atkinson (1995) says we tell our stories because they: 1. expand and enhance our experiences; 2. give words to our thoughts; 3. connect us to the human community; 4. validate life experiences; 5. cleanse by causing acceptance and healing; 6. entertain by evoking feelings; and 7. allow sharing with others. All of these contribute to the power of stories to aid in the quest for wholeness. Personal growth and therapeutic acceptance of the past show the value of reminis-cence and storytelling (Newbern, 1992).

CHAPTER 3

Procedures

Each of the 12 initial subjects will be contacted to explain the purpose of the research and to determine their willingness to participate. The questionnaire (see Appendix A) will be mailed to those who express an interest. When the questionnaire is returned, a follow-up interview will be conducted based on subject response and the need for any clarification. Additional subjects (from recommendations or the Internet query) will be contacted and sent the questionnaire with a follow-up interview. This procedure will be followed until at least 25 subjects have responded to the questionnaire and interview.

After receiving responses from the subjects, the process of compiling the data will begin. A research paper will be written using subject responses and other information acquired from additional reading. In addition, a list of healing stories and books that have been recommended by the subjects and the researcher will be compiled as part of the research paper.

A copy of the final paper will be sent to all subjects who participate and are interested in reading the results of the study. It is hoped that the study will prove interesting and important enough to use the information, quotes, examples, and stories as the basis for a book on how and why stories heal.

REFERENCES

Alston, T. (1994). Storytelling: A tool of healing for Vietnam veterans and their families. *The legacy of Vietnam veterans and their families: 1994 National symposium papers.* Pittsburgh: United States Government Information.

Arnold, J.H. (1983). *A child dies: A portrait of family grief.* Rockville, MD: Aspen Systems Corporation.

Atkinson, R. (1995). *The gift of stories.* Westport, CT: Bergin and Garvey.

Baker, J.E., Sedney, M.A., & Gross, E. (1992). Psychological tasks for bereaved children. *American Journal of Orthopsychiatry, 62,* 105-116.

Baumeister, R.F., & Newman, L.S. (1994). How stories make sense of personal experiences: Motives that shape autobiographical narratives. *Personality and Social Psychology Bulletin, 20,* 676-690.

Cotter, M. (1998). Can stories heal? *Storytelling World, 14,* 4.

Estes, C.P. (1992). *Women who run with the wolves.* New York: Random House.

Fazio, L.S. (1992). Tell me a story: The therapeutic metaphor in the practice of pediatric occupational therapy. *American Journal of Occupational Therapy, 46*(2), 112-119.

Moore, T. (1992). *Care of the soul.* New York: Harper Collins.

Moyers, B. (1993). Wounded healers. *Parabola, 18,* 3.

National Storytelling Association (1994). *Tales as tools.* Jonesborough, TN: The National Storytelling Press.

Newbern,V.B. (1992). Sharing the memories: The value of reminiscence as a research tool. *Journal of Gerontological Nursing,* 18(5), 13-18.

Remen, R.N. (1996). *Kitchen table wisdom—Stories that heal.* New York: Riverhead Books.

Riessman, C.K. (1990). Strategic used of narrative in the presentation of self and illness: A research note. *Social Sciences and Medicine,* 30(11), 1155-1200.

Rooks, D.L. (1998). Infinite resource and sagacity. *Storytelling World,* 14, 13-14.

Sanders, S.R. (1997). The power of stories. *The Georgia Review,* Spring, 113-126.

Sedney, M.A., Baker, J.E., & Gross, E. (1994). "The Story" of a death: Therapeutic considerations with bereaved families. *Journal of Marital and Family Therapy,* 20, 287-296.

Stone, R. (1996). *The healing art of storytelling.* New York: Hyperion.

Taylor, S.E. (1983). Adjustment to threatening events: A theory of cognitive adaptation. *American Psychologist,* 38, 1161-1173.

Taylor, S.E., Aspinwall, L.G., Giuliano, T.A., Dakof, G.A., &Reardon, K.K. (1993). Storytelling and coping with stressful events. *Journal of Applied Social Psychology,* 23, 703-733.

Wright, B. (1996). *Sudden Death* (2nd ed). New York: Churchill Livingstone.

APPENDIX A

Questionnaire for the Storyteller

Include any details and descriptions that you are comfortable sharing.

1. Do stories have the power to heal individuals following a significant loss? Explain.

2. Have stories been part of your healing? Telling stories or listening to them?

3. What type of stories have you found healing? Personal stories, myth, folklore?

4. How do you think stories heal? How have they healed you? Be specific if possible. For example, were any of the significant points in your healing process related to stories?

5. Do you find stories that deal directly with loss helpful? Stories that deal with loss through metaphor?

6. List stories which have been a part of your healing. Stories that you believe would be healing for others.

7. Do you know other storytellers who have used stories/storytelling to deal with loss? Please list them if you think they would be interested in participating in this study.

8. Have you used stories to help in the healing process for others? How? Do you find this therapeutic for yourself?

9. Briefly describe the loss you experienced. Did your interest in stories/storytelling occur before or after your loss?

10. Would you be willing to be quoted in my research paper? If so, would you prefer to be quoted by name or indirectly?

Appendix 2

List of Healing Stories
including author and source when known

Story	Author	Book or Source
A Bargain is a Bargain	Irish folktale	*Fair is Fair*
Apple Tree	Penninah Schram	
C-R-A-Z-Y	Donald Davis	
Christmas Box (The)	Richard Paul Evans	*The Christmas Box*
Clown of God (The)		
Cow-Tail Switch (The)	Harold Courlander (African folktale)	*The Cow-Tail Switch*
Cracked Vase (The)	Rachel Naomi Remen	*Kitchen Table Wisdom*
Dancing Lass of Anglesy (The)	Scottish folklore	
Dancing Healers (The)	Carl Hammerschlag	
Dark Candle (The)	Ada Forney	
Death in a Nut	Duncan Williamson	*A Thorn in the King's Foot*
Disasters and Blessings	Chinese tale	
Doll Story (The)	Reader's Digest	
Edna Robinson	Jay O'Callahan	*Homespun – Smith*
Elijah	Penninah Schram	

Story	Author	Book or Source
Emperor Moth (The)	Gail Rosen	
Fall of Freddie the Leaf (The)	Leo Buscaglia	*The Fall of Freddie the Leaf*
Firebird (The)		
Gift of the Magi (The)	O'Henry	
Giving Tree (The)	Shel Silverstein	*The Giving Tree*
Godric	Frederick Buechner	*Godric*
Good Grief	Granger E. Westberg	*Good Grief*
Grand Canyon (The)	Donald Davis	*The Grand Canyon*
Grandfather Clock (The)	Heather Forest	
Grandfather Death	Folklore	*Grimm's Complete Fairy Tale*
Happy Man's Shirt (The)	Duncan Williamson	*A Thorn in the King's Foot*
Happy Prince, (The)	Oscar Wilde	
Heaven and Hell	Unknown	*Stories for Telling – White*
How Do You Spell God?	Gellman & Thomas	*How Do You Spell God?*
Iron John	Folklore	*Grimm's Complete Fairy Tales*
Jenna and the Troublemaker	Hiawyn Oram	*Jenna and the Troublemaker*
Land of No Death	Stanley Robertson	*Land of No Death*
Lessons of Love	Melody Beattie	*Lessons of Love*
Lettie and the Rose	Penny Ruip	
Lion's Whiskers (The)	Somali tale	*Peace Tales – MacDonald*
Listening for the Crack of Dawn	Donald Davis	*Listening for the Crack of Dawn*
Little Women	Louisa Mae Alcott	*Little Women*
Littlest Angel (The)	Charles Tazewell	*The Littlest Angel*
Love You Forever		
Magic Mustard Seed aka Cure for Sorrow	Folklore	*Stories for Telling – White*

Story	Author	Book or Source
Marriage of Sir Gawain (The)	England	
McGoogan Moves the Mighty Rock	(children's book)	
Mrs. Rosemary's Kindergarten	Donald Davis	
My Mother Sings	Bill Suiter	
My Mother's Hands	Stephanie McKinnon	
Nadia the Willful	Sue Alexander	*Nadia the Willful*
Nana Upstairs & Nana Downstairs	Tomie dePaola	*Nana Upstairs & Nana Downstairs*
Nixie on the Mill-Pond	Folklore	*Grimm's Complete Fairy Tales*
Old Joe & The Carpenter	Pleasant deSpain	Appalachian folktale
Old Man and the Great White Heron (The)		
One My Darling	Diane Wolkstein	*The Magic Orange Tree*
Owl	Diane Wolkstein	*The Magic Orange Tree*
Pollyanna		
Red Lion	Persia	
Refuge	Terry Tempest Williams	*Refuge*
Sailing the Flying Ship	Mary Hamilton	*Sailing the Flying Ship* (audiotape)
Seal Skin	Folklore	*Iceland*
Shepherd(The)	Eric Kimmel	*Days of Awe*
Sorrow Tree(The)	Folklore	*The Sower's Seeds-Cavanaugh*
Story to Heal	Martin Buber	*The Sower's Seeds – Cavanaugh*
The Missing Piece	Shel Silverstein	*The Missing Piece*
There's No Such Thing as a Dragon	Jack Kent	*There's No Such Thing as a Dragon*
This Too Shall Pass	Folklore	*Wisdom Tales - Forest*

Story	Author	Book or Source
Through a Ruby Window	Susan Klein	*Through a Ruby Window*
To Sir, With Love		
Vasilisa the Beautiful	Folklore	*Russia*
Wee Lass in the Yellow Frock	Stanley Robertson	*Nyakim's Windows*
Weeping Lass at the Dancing Place (The)	Scottish folklore	
When Bad Things Happen to Good People	Rabbi Harold Kushner	*When Bad Things Happen to Good People*
Where to Hide God?	Folklore	*The Sower's Seeds - Cavanaugh*

Appendix 3

The Scottish View of Death and Dying
Its Reflection in Their Stories and Songs

Diane Rooks

East Tennessee State University
Appalachian-Scottish & Irish Studies
Summer 1997

Contents

Preface and Acknowledgments 246
The Scottish View of Death and Dying 247
    Its Reflection in Their Stories and Songs
References Cited 260
Additional References 261
Appendix 262

Preface and Acknowledgments

This paper is not intended to be an exhaustive study of the subject, but rather a compilation of the ideas, impressions and experiences I gained during my three weeks in Scotland (July 12 - August 3, 1997) with the cultural exchange group from East Tennessee State University. During this time I was able to interview some local people to gain insight into the Scottish view of death and dying. In addition, I explored this idea at many of the places the group visited and had the opportunity to do research on the topic at the library at the School of Scottish Studies and at the main library of the University of Edinburgh. Information is included from several books purchased in Scotland that I felt would aid my understanding of the topic. I know I only scratched the surface of this fascinating topic, but the results made the journey worthwhile. This topic interested me as I attempted to find new insights following the death of my son. He died September 29, 1993 from an allergic reaction to an insect bite. As I struggled to make sense of something that made no sense, I needed a bridge between my world and David's, and I found it in the people and stories of Scotland.

I would like to thank all of the people at the School of Scottish studies and the University of Edinburgh library who answered my questions and helped me find information that I needed. I especially appreciate the thoughts and time that Stanley Robertson, Christine MacIntyre, Roy Pedersen, Barbara McDermitt, Donnie Shedlarz, and Colin Geddes shared with me. Their insights enriched this paper, my time in Scotland, and my life. In addition, I would like to thank Stevan Jackson for his guidance and for the opportunity to have this experience, which was both enlightening and healing.

Diane Rooks
January 27, 1998

The Scottish View of Death and Dying
Its Reflection in their Stories and Songs

Diane Rooks

The Scottish proverb "Oor first breath is the beginning o daith" seems to characterize the traditional view of death throughout Scotland. Death is a natural part of life and should not be feared. This healthy and positive conclusion is reflected in the stories and music of Scotland and still believed by many of its people.

Margaret Bennett in *Scottish Customs from the Cradle to the Grave* says there are many proverbs of Scotland concerning death that echo this universal idea. When death occurs suddenly or unexpectedly, we may hear folks remark "Daith comes in and speirs no questions" or "it's no particular who it takes awa." (from Willie McPhee in March 1992)

In the book *Scottish Endings - Writings on Death,* Dean Ramsay is quoted from his *Reminiscences of Scottish Life and Character* (1858) as saying that the older generation "spoke of things hereafter as positive certainties, and viewed things invisible through the same medium as they viewed things present." Death is seen as a transition, and not as annihilation. Many references to it are life affirming and not threatening or filled with dread.

This leads to the question posed in the above mentioned book— "Do the Scots have a special relationship with death?" From the numerous songs and stories dealing with the subject and the ease and even joy with which Scots speak of death, the answer to the question seems to be a resounding YES.

In the introduction to *Scottish Endings - Writings on Death,* James Robertson says of the book, "There is certainly as much humour in it as morbidity. We should take our cue from it, and not be so mealy-mouthed about the single, inevitable, incontrovertible fact of all our existences. Discussions of death should not be excluded from daily life; those most at ease and ready to talk about it are often those who live most fully and enthusiastically." He mentions a tale from Archibald Geike about an old couple who were upset at not receiving an invitation to the funeral of one of their friends. "Never you mind,

Tammas," said the wife, "we'll be haein a corp o' our ain before lang, and we'll no ask them."

The acceptance of death as part of life and the willingness to talk of death and of those who have died can be seen in many aspects of the Scottish culture. It becomes evident that death is not seen as the end, but rather a deeper dimension or extension of life. In *Scottish Lore and Folklore*, Ronald MacDonald Douglas says, "From birth to death seems a natural enough sequence of events—at least to the Scot; for, to us, death has never held the fears that it holds for some of the world's peoples. Death has never meant the end. We have always thought of death as another beginning, as a re-birth, and as a rebirth to something better. And this faith we held long before the Christian doctrine of the Immortality of the Soul was brought to us to lighten our Pagan hearts! Indeed, there is much to prove that our distant ancestors held very decided views on spiritual re-birth, and the notion of another and brighter world beyond. From our Celtic forebears there has come the beautiful legend of *Tir-nan-Og*, the Land of Eternal Youth; and other legends, too, of invisible other worlds." There are references to a Celtic other world where the "natural and the spiritual dance together in a green harmony."

Stories about experiences with those who have died or spirits from the 'other' world are common, and spoken of with belief and conviction. In his book, Douglas relates a personal encounter in great detail after first stating his own skepticism with such events. His experience involved hearing a piper on numerous occasions which others verified hearing also. He investigated it thoroughly and found no explanation except that of a ghost piper, who on one occasion led a "ghost-army" that "passed clean through the house, and went off southwesterly...and faded into the night." He says that thousands of stories similar to this one exist in Scotland and "even the most hard-headed Scot has to admit at times that there may be something in at least some of the ghost stories with which our Scottish history and our folklore is packed."

Communing with the dead seems to be common and many examples are found in folklore, current stories and many of the ballads. David Buchan in *Folk Tradition and Folk Medicine in Scotland* relates several stories where a husband or wife continued to communicate with a spouse who had died. In one case, the wife always took snuff to put on her husband's grave when she went to consult with him on financial matters "so that he might regale himself with it till her next visit."

Numerous examples can be found which reflect the idea that the spirit continues living even after earthly death occurs. The familiar song *The Bonnie Banks o' Loch Lomond* reflects the old Celtic belief that if death occurs in a foreign land, the spirit will return to Scotland by an underground way—the Low Road. In Greyfriar's Church in Edinburgh, a small card for purchase contained this message from Bishop Brent:

What is dying? A ship sails and I stand watching till she fades on the horizon someone at my side says, "She is gone." Gone where? Gone from my sight, that is all; she is just as large as when I saw her...The diminished size and total loss of sight is in me, not in her, and just at the moment when someone at my side says "she is gone," there are others who are watching her coming, and other voices take up a glad shout, "there she comes!"...and that is dying.

In the museum at New Lanark, a quotation from Christian Livingstone, a widow, said, "Remember us...we live on in the things we touched and handled in our lives...." Also at the New Lanark museum from Letitia Flood, a spinner at the mill started by Robert Owen, "We are the past...but part of the future too."

This belief in the continuation of the spirit explains the openness and willingness to talk about dying and loved ones who have died. In 1997 at the Aberdeen train station, the following tender message from Debbie Gemmill was displayed on a window:

Oh little one if I had known it was to be our last day together I would have done it all differently. I would have taken you to the beach to hear the waves and to the mountains to feel the snow. I would have shown you rainbows and Christmas trees and ferris wheels. Or maybe I would have done exactly what I did. Sing you to sleep, tuck you in with Teddy, and whisper goodnight.

On a very different note, a toast from Mrs. Martha Reid of Perthshire found in *Tocher* No. 9 (1973) reads:

Here's to the World that runs upon wheels
Daeth is a thing that every man feels
If life wis a thing that money could buy
The rich would live and the poor would die.

Many people in Scotland today, especially in the highlands and islands, still hold the traditional beliefs about death and dying. The following excerpts from an interview with Christine MacIntyre from South Uist on July 26, 1997 confirms this. "Birth, living and death are all parts of life. People here (on South Uist) are not afraid of death. When someone dies, it is because they are chosen. Even the children here understand death. They see it around them as part of everyday life. They are not kept from it and are always taken to funerals and to the home when the body is still there and encouraged to touch it and say goodbye. The body is always kept at home for people to visit before it is taken to the undertaker. Even if death occurs in a hospital, the body is taken home first."

Responding to how people who have lost a loved one deal with that loss, she said, "With great fortitude and strength because they know that the person who has died—all their troubles are over. The people who are left take on the troubles so the person's spirit can go free. When someone is dying, friends and neighbors offer to sit with the person so they aren't ever alone and this also relieves the family. My grandmother died several months ago and I sat with her and nursed her while she was dying. The day before she died, she was unconscious and I was sitting next to her holding her hand. She opened her eyes and looked at me and said my name. I'm certain that she recognized me. Then she looked at the foot of the bed with a smile and a look of recognition in her eyes. I'm certain that she recognized her husband, her mother, a couple of sisters—others that have gone on before her. Then she closed her eyes and died a few hours later."

Asked if she still felt close to her grandmother's spirit she said, "Oh yes, she's in everything I do."

When I told her about my son's death and my struggle to find understanding and healing, Christine replied, "You should come here. I believe you would find peace here—from the place itself and the people who live here. You're welcome to come stay with me and my family. Three months ago a young lad died and the whole island turned out for the funeral and are still taking food and visiting with the family. People are so supportive here, especially when there's a death of a child or a young person. We are more natural with death here than other places. In South Uist the women go to the cemetery for the burial, but in North Uist and other parts of the islands and highlands, they don't. Only the men go to bury the dead body while the women go home to prepare the food."

The views expressed comfortably by Christine focused once again on death as a natural thing with the conviction that it is a transition to a better dimension which is still accessible to those who are left behind.

At the Gaelic College of Subhal mor Ostaig, a beautiful poem (see appendix) is on the wall of the big barn, now the community hall. Roy Pedersen of Highland & Islands Enterprise explained that the poem had been written by a man who lived nearby named Donaidh Caimbeul. Donaidh tended sheep and lived with his mother. He supported the Gaelic school in its early development and did a lot of the physical labor and support to get it started. When he was in his forties, he fell in love with an American woman and they planned to be married. Late one evening he had an automobile accident and was killed. With no apparent reason for the fatal crash, no one understood what had happened. But everyone believes and feels that his spirit is present and still very much a part of the college. Another poem (see appendix) on the wall there reflects the poet Angus Peter Campbell's feeling of being connected to those who were forced from their lands during the Highland Clearances. He says they are still alive in their songs and prayers, and in his memory, conscience, blood, bones, head and poetry.

During an interview with Roy Pederson on the ferry from Isle of Skye to Maillig on July 27, 1997, Roy was very interested in Christine's thoughts about death and dying and said he agreed with her. I told him I found her beliefs and openness to talk about them very comforting, because few people talked about death in the United States or hardly acknowledged that a death has taken place. He responded, "I think death is sanitized and hidden from folks in the States and to some extent from the people in the larger cities of Scotland. I think the views expressed by Christine are more prevalent on the islands and in rural areas of Scotland."

When asked if he had any thoughts about what happens to people after they die, he said, "I have thought about that lately because of something a good friend told me. This was my very best friend in school—we were so close and did everything together, but had somehow lost touch and hadn't seen each other in 25 years. The friend decided to look me up and after searching, he found me. We got together and it was just like old times—like no time had passed at all. During the evening he told me his father had passed away. I knew his father well and had been with him on many occasions years ago. He said the strangest thing happened one day when he was especially missing his father—they used to hike in the woods together a lot, so he went up to a stream where they had been many times—I had even been with them once or twice and knew the place. They would go there because his father liked to get water from the stream for mixing with his Scotch whiskey. My friend took a large container with him to get water that day. He said while he was up there he actually felt his father's hand on his elbow which is where his father frequently touched him while they talked. He felt close to his father in that spot, and the feeling on his elbow was real and convinced him that his father's spirit was actually there. Hearing my trusted friend talk about that with such certainty made me think a lot about life after death."

An exploration of the Scottish view of death and dying naturally leads to the traveller tradition since it is closely related to and reflects the Scottish tradition itself. Because the travellers isolated themselves from other people and because their oral culture was vital to their beliefs, much can be learned from them. In recent years, researchers from the School of Scottish Studies discovered what a treasure the traveller community had preserved in their stories and songs. Many feel that the recording and preservation of traveller traditions and stories was done "just in time" as their way of life began to disinte-grate and older storytellers died. In an article on the Internet entitled "The Language of Traveller Storytellers," Hamish Henderson said, "They still keep alive an ancient and vital oral literature that makes theirs one of the most dynamic folk cultures of Europe." In the same article, the function of traveller storytelling was described, "As well as entertaining, it strengthened family bonds; reinforced values, attitude, customs and beliefs in the community; helped cope with strong feelings like fear and anger; and provided a template for psychological development."

In an interview with traveller Stanley Robertson at a ceilidh at the School of Scottish Studies, July 19, 1997, I expressed my interest in the Scottish view of death and how it reflected in their stories and music. Stanley replied, " People who've passed are not gone—they are just beyond the veil. Sometimes I feel so close to them I feel as if I could reach through the veil and touch them. Just before my Auntie Jeannie died, a voice clearly said to me "this is the last time you're going to see your Auntie Jeannie." I went to her house and sat with her until my father came in, then I kissed her good-bye and started walking home. When I arrived, the phone was ringing and I knew she was dead. I returned to her and went with her body to the funeral home. On the way there, she sang to me and taught me a song I had never heard. And I know this song and sing it today. So I know people who have passed from this life are not gone—they are trans-formed to another dimension. And death is really just another part of life. I have been a Mormon for 35 years and one of the reasons is because they have a different way to look at death. My wife and I are married for eternity—for all time." (Author's note: Stanley's Auntie Jeannie was Jeannie Robertson, who is acknowledged by many as one of the greatest traveller storytellers and singers of ballads. Much of her tremendous repertoire was recorded and preserved by the School of Scottish Studies prior to her death. Stanley says he learned a lot of his stories and songs from her.)

I commented that Americans don't like to talk about death and Scots seem much more willing to talk about it. And Stanley replied, "The American Indian view of death is much like the Scottish—they talk openly about it, but most Americans don't. I think if you've ever lost a loved one, you know they are not really gone. I've actually gone beyond the veil myself—several times—and had the opportunity to look around and see things. It wasn't my time to go, and so I had to come back. But I've seen it and you'd be surprised how close your loved ones still are—they are all around you—they touch you and help you more than you can know."

I told Stanley that my son died four years ago and I felt close to him at times, but found it frustrating not to be able to communicate with him and had difficulty accepting his death. He took my hands and said, "Your laddie's work was finished in this world—he's gone on to do his work in the next. I wish I could tell you all I know—all of the examples that I could give you."

Responding to the question "Are you talking about your gift of Second Sight?" Stanley replied, "Yes, I have the gift and my mother had the gift. She told me one day as we were riding past a building that she would die in that spot on Christmas Day. Over twenty years later, she did become sick and went into the hospital there and died on Christmas Day." (Author's note: 'Second sight' is the ability to have prophetic visions and according to Shari Cohn who has researched it extensively in Scotland, "Detailed written accounts of second sight from the 17th century onwards are consistent with modern-day accounts collected by folklorists and ethnologists and reflect the cycle of birth, life and death.")

As he was signing my copy of his book Land of No Death, Stanley said, "This is the most important Jack tale of all—you know Jack had conquered all things and all realms except death which he does in this book. All Jack tales are about his growth and change and this is the last Jack tale. You should get my other book Nyakim's Windows and read all of the stories in it, especially the last one, "The Wee Lassie in the Yellow Frock." They will help you understand how close we are and how much we interact with those beyond the veil."

Barbara McDermitt in her dissertation said, "Traveller children were taught to accept death as something natural, not something to fear" and "The very fact that Stanley (Robertson) has so many stories featuring Death points up how fine a line travellers place between the world of the living and the dead, and how realistically they accept death as a natural extension to the life cycle." Responding to the question "How do travellers feel linked to their ancestors?" in an interview on July 28, 1997, Ms. McDermitt said, "They keep them alive by telling their stories and singing their songs. They believe they can visit their spirits or be visited by them."

Further in the dissertation, Ms. McDermitt recounts a number of traveller legends and family stories as examples of their beliefs about and acceptance of death. She maintains that all of the songs and ballads Stanley sings and all of the stories that he tells are expressions of his traditions and beliefs. She concludes "as is evident in the case of Stanley Robertson, traveller beliefs and superstitions are integral to traveller experience, narratives, memorates, legends and tales. Stories seem to have borrowed from beliefs and beliefs from stories."

Another well-known traveller and storyteller, Betsy Whyte, reflects the traveller beliefs about death as she describes her reaction to her father's death in her book, *The Yellow on the Broom*. Even in her distraught condition she began to realize that "grief is no more than a form of selfishness." As she focused on the traveller custom of living close to nature, the memories of her father's stories and laughter comforted her and she gained strength and calmness from the beauty of the plants and life around her and was "ready to take up life again."

David Sibley in his book *Outsiders in Urban Societies* says of the travellers, "We might add that there is no separation ... in their cosmology between life and death. My own observation is that the dead are referred to in the present tense for years after death ... and the birthday of the person is remembered as if he were alive."

One of the many examples of traveller stories reflecting their view of death can be found in "Death in a Nut" which is recorded in *A Thorn in the King's Foot* by another well-known traveller storyteller, Duncan Williamson. In his book *Alias MacAlias,* Hamish Henderson says "My own personal favourite among all the stories is "Death in a Nut." Here the story has deeper moral and philosophical implications than is general in folk-tales; the story spells out poignantly the universal tragic truth, human and animal, that there is veritably no life without death." The story shows how life itself stops when Death is captured by Jack and put into a nut in order to prevent Death from taking Jack's mother. When Jack realizes what he has done, he must release Death so that life can continue for everyone.

May the Devil Walk Behind Ye! is another of Duncan Williamson's books which contains stories collected and recorded by his wife, Linda Williamson. In the preface, Linda says these twelve folk tales "are interesting because they incorporate the Scottish travelling people's beliefs about evil, temptation and suffering. Religious expression shines through these stories; they are expressive of a traditional attitude towards death. For Duncan, as for all travellers, life is a simple force, a force deeply felt."

In Stanley Robertson's book, *Nyakim's Windows,* the stories are based on dreams that Stanley had and all are concerned with occurrences in the "other" world. Several of the stories are related to the traveller view of death. The story called "The Warning" seems to be based on Stanley's own experience with his Auntie Jeannie as many of the details are similar. In the story he says, "...and this great love they hid for each ither wis stronger than the cords of death." After the auntie's death in the story, as the young man, Ashley, looked down on her body, he said, "...he felt as if she wis still speaking tae him frae beyond the veil. It wis as if her spirit wisnae awa frae her yet and that they were still communicating by telepathy." He concludes the story by saying, "Many ither times he felt her influence and he aye said that his Auntie Laurie often used tae help him. Sometimes Ashley thought that the veil between this world and the next gets very thin, and that ye could feel a presence, almost at yer side."

The story entitled "The Visitor" also found in *Nyakim's Windows,* deals with Second Sight or the "gift o the foresight" as Stanley calls it. The main character, Dundonald is "a very special laddie and chosen by the ancients tae receive mair wisdom than usual." Another story of Dundonald entitled "Astral Travel" reveals more about his gift. "Noo some folks say that a fine cord, like an umbilical cord, attaches yer spirit tae yer body; and though the cord is very elastic and can reach tae realms far beyond oor wildest dreams, there is a limitation upon the cord and the Silver Curtains is as far as it can stretch. Beyond that, the cord breaks (an aa o the great secrets o life are contained beyond!)

So if ye reach as far as the Silver Curtains then ye are very near aa these secrets." This gift and the visions are to be used by Dundonald to help other people.

In the introduction to "The Wee Lassie in the Yellow Frock," Stanley says, "Ye see, time is the chatry (stuff, goods) that life is made oot o and there is nae beginning or end tae it—for it's aa een roon...(all one around, a circle)" In the story, a young traveller lad plans to take his own life but is prevented when he stops to help a young girl wearing a yellow dress. He had never seen her before and never sees her again until he returns from war to his wife and child and discovers that the young girl in the yellow dress was his daughter who was not born until seven years later. Stanley closes by saying, "Ye see, the past, present and future are aa really tied intae een anither as one and sometimes wi dae get glimpses o whit tae us seems like different times." This story and many others reveal Stanley's deeply spiritual nature.

Insight into how music reflects the Scottish view of death can be seen at Balnain House—Home of Highland Music—in Inverness. "Ho Roinn Eile" a song in one of the exhibits was "for widows who have not graves to tend, the sea is the element they must address. There is no more poignant expression of that sense of loss than this lament—with wonderful imagery the music rises and falls like the sea itself." The words of the song are

O, Alan of the brown hair, mouth of tender tones...
How it grieves me that your bed is seaweed;
that those who wake you are the seals,
your tall candles the shining stars
and your violin music the sea."

A ballad of "The Great Silkie" and other silkie stories reveal a belief that those who die at sea are not really gone, but rather have gone to live with the silkies (seals which have the supernatural ability to become human.)

Many of the Scottish ballads seem to suggest that the Scottish people respond to death and loss "with a stoical resignation rather than with resentment, and their stoicism is sustained by a deep but unsentimental sense of fidelity," according to Edwin Cowan in the chapter of "The Border Ballads" in his book *The People's Past*. He includes the ballad entitled "The Lament of the Border Widow" which he says "reflects on appropriate grief in a society where excessive lamentation was regarded with disfavour, and where action and mourning are consciously displayed without mawkishness or self-indulgence." This suggests that excessive lamentation would not have been consistent with the prevailing view of death.

In the introduction to *Scottish Ballads* edited by Emily Lyle, Ms. Lyle says "one feature that has been remarked upon in Scottish ballads is that they have an especially strong element of the supernatural, sometimes experienced directly at meeting with supernatural beings, and sometimes through dreams and prognostications." One of the ballads in this collection is "Sweet William's Ghost" where Margret's true love Willy has died and his spirit returns to her to ask for her "faith and troth." Verse 9 says,

My bones are buried in yon kirk-yard,
Afar beyond the sea,
And it is but my spirit, Margret,
That's now speaking to thee.

And once the ghost "left her all alone," Margret "closd her een...and dy'd."

"The Wife of Usher's Well" found in the same book tells of a woman whose three sons went away and were killed. They later returned home and she had a feast for them, but they had to leave when the cock crowded after saying "Fare ye weel, my mother dear!" And so the spirits of her son came to comfort her after death.

A final example of a ballad reflecting the Scots belief in spirits living on after death is Will Ogilvie's "The Raiders" found in the afterword of *The Illustrated Border Ballads* by John Marsden. The ballad speaks about tramping horses with reckless men—"the ghosts of men that died"— that ride up the glen to bring the writer a horse that he might ride with them. He heard their voices in the wind and was convinced that "A troop of men rode up the glen and brought a horse for me!" The images created with the words in this and others ballads are vivid indeed. Marsden comments that the photography in his book suggests "how the very landscape of river ford, peel tower and remote hillside seem to be haunted by ghosts who might ride out of history at any moment, the thin sunlight glancing off their spearpoints and the thunder of hoofs echoing back from the surrounding fells."

In summary, the stories and music of Scotland are filled with images of death and the spirit world which exists after death. These images reflect the traditional beliefs that Scots had in years past and continue to cherish today. This acceptance of death and dying as a part of life and the firm conviction that death is a transition to another state of being which continues to make contact with the living can be seen in all parts of Scottish life. The following was written in 1894 by Robert Louis Stevenson in the *Weir of Hermiston* and can be found in *The Scottish Quotation Book* edited by Joyce and Maurice Lindsay:

> *For that is the mark of the Scot of all classes: that he stands*
> *in an attitude towards the past unthinkable to Englishmen,*
> *and remembers and cherishes the memory of his forebears,*
> *good or bad; and there burns alive in him a sense of identity*
> *with the dead even to the twentieth generation.*

This sense of identity manifests itself throughout the stories and songs of Scotland, perhaps because feelings and emotions of people speak most clearly through the power of story—both spoken and sung.

References Cited

Balnain House exhibit, Inverness,1997.

Bennett, Margaret, *Scottish Customs from the Cradle to the Grave,* Edinburgh:Polygon, 1992.

Bishop Brent, Quotation, Bristol:Tim Tiley Ltd.

Buchan, David, *Folk Tradition and Folk Medicine in Scotland,* Edinburgh:Canongate Press Ltd., 1994.

Cohn, Shari, 'Second Sight' lecture notes, Edinburgh:School of Scottish Studies, July 1997.

Cowan, Edward, *The People's Past,* Edinburgh:Polygon, 1991.

Douglas, Ronald MacDonald, *Scottish Lore and Folklore,* New York:Crown Publishers, Inc., 1987.

Henderson, Hamish, *Alias MacAlias,* Edinburgh:Polygon, 1992.

Lindsay, Joyce and Maurice,ed., *The Scottish Quotation Book,* USA:Marboro Books Coro., 1991.

Lyle, Emily ed., *Scottish Ballads,* Edinburgh:Canongate Press Ltd., 1997.

MacDermitt, Barbara, A Comparison of a Scottish and American Storyteller and their Marchen Repertoires (dissertation), Edinburgh:University of Edinburgh, 1985.

MacDermitt, Barbara, personal interview, Edinburgh, July 1997.

Marsden, John, *The Illustrated Border Ballads,* London:Macmillan London Limited, 1990.

Martin, Andrew,ed., *Scottish Endings - Writings on Death,* Edinburgh:National Museums of Scotland,1996.

MacIntyre, Christine, personal interview, South Uist, July 1997.

Pedersen, Roy, personal interview, Skye, July 1997.

Robertson, Stanley, *Land of No Death,* Nairn (Scotland):Balnain Books, 1993.

_____, *Nyakim's Windows,* Nairn:Balnain Books, 1989.

_____, personal interview, Edinburgh, July 1997.

Sibley, David, *Outsiders in Urban Societies,* Oxford:Basil Blackwell Publishers, Ltd., 1981.

Tocher No. 9, School of Scottish Studies, Edinburgh,1973.

Whyte, Betsy, *The Yellow on the Broom,* Edinburgh:W&R Chambers,Ltd., 1979.

Williamson, Duncan and Linda, *May the Devil Walk Behind Ye!,* Edinburgh:Cannongate Publishing Limited, 1989.

_____, *A Thorn in the King's Foot,* Harmonsworth(England):Penguin Books Ltd, 1987.

WorldWideWeb, The Language of Traveller Storytellers, www.arts.gla.ac.uk/www/english/comet/starn/crit/langtrav.htm

Additional References

Beith, Mary, *Healing Threads*, Edinburgh:Polygon, 1995.

Bruford, A.J. and MacDonald, D.A.ed., *Scottish Traditional Tales*, Edinburgh:Polygon,1994.

Jarvie, Gordon ed., *Scottish Folk and Fairy Tales*, London:Penquin Books Ltd., 1992.

Tocher No. 40, School of Scottish Studies, Edinburgh,1986.

Williamson, Duncan, *The Broonie, Silkies and Fairies*, Edinburgh:Canongate Press, 1985.

_____, *Don't Look Back Jack!*, Edinburgh:Canongate Publishing Ltd., 1990.

_____, *Fireside Tales of the Traveller Children*, Edinburgh:Canongate Publishing Ltd., 1983.

Appendix

Spark

The white heat of the sun
Is softened by the woods
A breath of wind plays on the leaves
Amid the quiet of pool and lochan.

The songs of the fiddle are on every side
Mixing people and cultures
Coming together in the music—
The music and heritage of our ancestors
Appearing in our thoughts and hopes

The hope of no soldier in Ireland
No chants at Ibrox*
And no poverty on the streets of our cities.

Hope in the steps of Cape Breton
The fiddle of Ireland, Scotland and Cajun
The Tree of Strings* and Brazilian clave*
And poetry moving the heart.

And when you leave
Spread the spark of this brightness
And hold fast the joy of the music
As a jewel in your breast forever

Donaidh Caimbeul

On the wall of the big barn at Sabhal Mor Ostaig Gaelic College on Isle of Skye

*Ibrox - football (soccer) stadium in Glasgow
*Tree of Strings - harp
*Brazilian clave - musical instrument

The Song of the Sabhal

In a sense, Sabhal Mor Ostain   (The Big Barn of Ostaig)
stands as a memorial to the Highland Clearances, built
for the big farm here whilst the people themselves were
being turfed overseas: it may be that times have changed.

The many students
who never saw either a book or college
but saw plenty peat-ploughs, woodplanes and poverty
who were flung over to Canada:
"village Hampdens" they were called in the cold language
that gave them nothing but exile, homesickness and death.
Their graduation is in the rocks of the Highlands
their education in the hay, in the corn, in the very air
the poor people who never saw a college
alive with their songs and prayers
in my memory, in my conscience, in my blood
in my bones, in my head, in my poetry—
the barn for the animals, and Canada for the people
put that into your computer and make a hi-ho-ro-heir* of it.

Angus Peter Campbell

On the wall of the big barn at Sabhal Mor Ostaig Gaelic College on
Isle of Skye

*a song and dance

Bibliography

Adams, M.D., Patch. *Gesundheit!*. Rochester, VT: Healing Arts Press, 1998.

Aesop. *Treasury of Aesop's Fables*. New York: Crown, 1973.

Albom, Mitch. *Tuesdays with Morrie*. New York: Doubleday, 1997.

Aldrich, Anne Hazard. *Notes from Myself*. New York: Carroll & Graf, 1998.

Alston, Tina. "Exploring Feelings through Storyimaging." *Storytelling* (May 1995).

Atkinson, Robert. *The Gift of Stories*. Westport, CT: Bergin and Garvey, 1995.

Auden, W. H. *Tell Me the Truth About Love*. New York: Vintage Books, 1994.

Bateson, Mary Catherine. *Composing a Life*. New York: Atlantic Monthly, 1989.

Benson, M.D., Herbert. *Timeless Healing: The Power and Biology of Belief*. New York: Scribner, 1996.

Blum, Ralph & Loughan, Susan. *The Healing Runes*. New York: St. Martin's, 1995.

Brody, Ed; Goldspinner, Jay; Green, Katie; Leventhal, Rona & Porcino, John, eds. *Spinning Tales Weaving Hope*. Philadelphia: New Society, 1992.

Brown, Robert McAfee. *Elie Wiesel:Messenger to All Humanity*. Notre Dame Indiana: University of Notre Dame, 1983.

Browne, Renni & King, Dave. *Self-Editing for Fiction Writers*. New York: HarperPerennial, 1994.

Bullens, Cindy. "Somewhere Between Heaven and Earth" (musical CD). New York: Artemis Records, 1999.

Burns, Olive Ann. *Cold Sassy Tree*. New York: Ticknor & Fields, 1984.

Cameron, Julia. *The Artist's Way*. New York: G. P. Putnam's Sons, 1992.

Campbell, Joseph. *The Hero with a Thousand Faces.* New York: MFJ Books, 1949.

—————. *The Power of Myth.* New York: Doubleday, 1988.

Canfield, Jack; Hansen, Mark; Aubery, Patty; & Mitchell, Nancy. *Chicken Soup for the Surviving Soul.* Deerfield Beach, FL: Health Communications, 1996.

Cassady, Marsh. *Storytelling Step by Step.* San Jose, CA: Resource Publications, 1990.

Cavanaugh, T.O.R., Brian. *The Sower's Seeds.* New York: Paulist, 1990.

Claypool, John. *Tracks of a Fellow Struggler.* Dallas: Word, 1974.

Coles, Robert. *The Call of Stories.* Boston: Houghton Mifflin, 1989.

Courlander, Harold & Herzog, George. *The Cow-Tail Switch.* New York: Henry Holt and Company, 1986.

Cousins, Norman. *Anatomy of an Illness.* New York: W.W. Norton & Co., 1979.

Csikszentmihalyi, Mihaly. *Flow: The Psychology of Optimal Experience.* New York: HarperPerennial, 1991.

Davies, Phyllis. *Grief: Climb Toward Understanding.* San Luis Obispo, CA: Sunnybank, 1987.

Davis, Donald. *Telling Your Own Stories.* Little Rock: August House, 1993.

Dinesen, Isak. *Out of Africa.* New York: Crown, 1987.

Ehrenpreis, Anne Henry. *The Literary Ballad.* Columbia, SC: University of South Carolina, 1970.

Eisenberg, Carla. *A Moment Changes Everything.* Wheaton, IL: Moon Mountain, 1998.

Estes, Ph.D., Clarissa Pinkola. *The Gift of Story.* New York: Ballantine Books, 1993.

—————. *Women Who Run with the Wolves.* New York: Ballantine Books, 1992.

Finger, Charles. *Tales from Silver Lands.* Garden City, NJ: Doubleday, 1924.

Frank, Arthur. *At the Will of the Body.* Boston: Houghton Mifflin, 1991.

Frankl, Viktor. *Man's Search for Meaning.* New York: Washington Square, 1985.

Fulghum, Robert. *All I Ever Needed to Know I Learned in Kindergarten.* New York: Villard Books, 1989.

Gerard, Philip. *Creative Nonfiction.* Cincinnati, OH: Story Press, 1998.

Gibran, Kahlil. *The Prophet.* New York: Alfred A. Knopf, 1923.

Goldberg, Natalie. *Writing Down the Bones.* Boston: Shambhala, 1986.

Harvey, John. *Embracing Their Memory: Loss and the Social Psychology of Storytelling.* Needham Heights, MA: Allyn and Bacon, 1996.

Heavilin, Marilyn & Heavilin, Matthew. *Grief is a Family Affair.* Menifee, CA: The Proverbial Solution, 2000.

Hillman, James. "A Note on Story." *Parabola,* IV:4 (November 1979).

Hobbie, Douglas. *Being Brett.* New York: Henry Holt and Company, 1996.

Hotchkiss, Vern. *Of Death and Recovery.* Eau Claire, WI: Heins, 1993.

Kasl, Ph.D., Charlotte Davis. *Finding Joy: 101 Ways to Free Your Spirit and Dance with Life.* New York: HarperCollins, 1994.

Kent, Jack. *There's No Such Thing as a Dragon.* New York: Golden, 1975.

Kubler-Ross, MD, Elisabeth. *On Children and Death.* New York: Macmillan, 1983.

――――. *The Wheel of Life.* New York: Simon and Schuster, 1997.

Kushner, Harold S. *How Good do we Have to Be?* Boston: Little, Brown and Company, 1996.

――――. *When All You've Ever Wanted Isn't Enough.* New York: Summit Books, 1986.

Lewis, C.S. *A Grief Observed.* New York: Bantam, 1976.

――――. *The Problem of Pain.* New York: Macmillan, 1962.

Lopez, Barry. *Crow and Weasel.* New York: HarperPerennial, 1993.

MacDonald, Margaret Read. *Peace Tales.* Hamden, CT: Linnet Books, 1992.

Maguire, Jack. *The Power of Personal Storytelling.* New York: Jeremy P. Tarcher/Putnam, 1998.

Martin, Joel & Romanowski, Patricia. *We Are Not Forgotten.* New York: G.P. Putnam's Sons, 1991.

――――. *We Don't Die.* New York: G.P. Putnam's Sons, 1988.

McCracken, Anne & Semel, Mary. *A Broken Heart Still Beats.* Center City, MN: Hazelden, 1998.

Meade, Erica. *Tell It by Heart.* Chicago: Open Court, 1995.

Metzger, Deena. *Writing for Your Life.* San Francisco: HarperSanFrancisco, 1992.

Moody,M.D., Raymond. *Life After Life*. New York: Bantam, 1976.

Morphew, Melissa. *The Garden Where All Love Ends*. La Jolla, CA: La Jolla Poets, 1997.

Moyers, Bill. *Healing and the Mind*. New York: Doubleday, 1993.

Mullins, Mattie Carroll. *Judy*. Baltimore, MD: Recovery Communications, 1998.

Neeld, Elizabeth. *Seven Choices*. New York: Clarkson N. Potter, 1990.

Neufeldt, Victoria, ed. *Webster's New World College Dictionary*. 2d ed. New York: Macmillan, 1996.

Oceanna. "The Healing Power of Story Listening." *Storytelling World* (Summer/Fall 1998).

O'Donohue, John. *Anam Cara*. New York: HarperCollins, 1997.

Ornish,M.D., Dean. *Love and Survival*. New York: HarperCollins, 1998.

Pearmain, Elisa. *Doorways to the Soul*. Cleveland, OH: The Pilgrim Press, 1998.

Puryear, Anne. *Stephen Lives!*. New York: Pocket Books, 1992.

Rainer, Tristine. *Your Life as Story*. New York: Jeremy P. Tarcher/Putnam, 1998.

Rando, Therese. *Parental Loss of a Child*. Champaign, IL: Research Press, 1986.

Remen,M.D., Rachael Naomi. *Kitchen Table Wisdom*. New York: Putnam, 1996.

Rico, Ph.D., Gabriele. *Pain and Possibility*. New York: G.P. Putnam's Sons, 1991.

————. *Writing the Natural Way*. Los Angeles: J. P. Tarcher, 1983.

Robertson, Stanley. *Land of No Death*. Nairn, Scotland: Balnain Books, 1993.

————. *Nyakim's Windows*. Nairn, Scotland: Balnain Books, 1989.

Rosenthal, Norman. *Seasons of the Mind*. New York: Bantam, 1989.

Rosof, Barbara. *The Worst Loss: How Families Heal from the Loss of a Child*. New York: Henry Holt & Co., 1994.

Schiff, Harriet. *The Bereaved Parent*. New York: Penguin, 1977.

Siegel,M.D., Bernie. *Love, Medicine, and Miracles*. New York: Harper & Row, 1986.

Shakespeare, William. *The Complete Works of William Shakespeare.* New York: Walter J. Black, 1937.

Sharp, Kimberly Clark. *After the Light.* New York: William Morrow, 1995.

Silverstein, Shel. *The Giving Tree.* New York: Harper Collins, 1986.

—————. *The Missing Piece.* New York: Harper & Row, 1976.

Simpkinson, Anne and Charles, & Solari, Rose, eds. *Nourishing the Soul.* New York: HarperCollins, 1995.

Simpkinson, Charles and Anne, eds. *Sacred Stories.* New York: HarperCollins, 1993.

Smith, Jimmy Neil. *Homespun.* New York: Avon Books, 1988.

Stone, Ganga. *Start the Conversation.* New York: Warner Books, 1996.

Stone, Richard. *The Healing Art of Storytelling.* New York: Hyperion, 1996.

Tracy, Stephen. *The Story of the Odyssey.* Princeton, NJ: Princeton University, 1990.

Wallas, Lee. *Stories That Heal.* New York: W. W. Norton, 1991.

Weiss,M.D., Brian. *Many Lives, Many Masters.* New York: Simon & Schuster, 1988.

White, William. *Stories for Telling.* Minneapolis: Augsburg, 1986.

Williams, Terry Tempest. *Refuge.* New York: Random House, 1991.

Williamson, Duncan and Linda. *A Thorn in the King's Foot.* Harmonsworth, England: Penguin, 1987.

—————. *May the Devil Walk Behind Ye!.* Edinburgh, Scotland: Cannongate Publishing Limited, 1989.

Wolterstorff, Nicholas. *Lament for a Son.* Grand Rapids, MI: William B. Eerdmans, 1987.

Worden, J. William. *Children and Grief.* New York: Guilford, 1996.

—————. *Grief Counseling and Grief Therapy.* New York: Springer, 1991.

World Wide Web. "The Language of Traveller Storytellers." www.arts.gla.ac.uk/www/english/comet/starn/crit/language.htm.

Young-Eisendrath. Ph.D., Polly. *The Gifts of Suffering.* New York: Addison-Wesley, 1996.

Youngs, PhD, Bettie B. *Gifts of the Heart.* Deerfield Beach, FL: Health Communications, 1996.

Copyrights and permissions

The author gratefully acknowledges the following publishers and other copyright holders for permission to reprint their copyrighted materials. The contributors hold the rights on all unpublished stories and excerpts. All those interviewed graciously gave permission for their comments to be included in the book. If any copyrighted materials have been included without permission or correct acknowledgement, the proper credit and corrections will gladly be inserted in future editions.

Excerpts from audiotape "The Creative Handling of Grief," © by John Claypool.

Excerpts from *A Broken Heart Still Beats* by Anne McCracken and Mary Semel, © 1998 by McCracken & Semel. Reprinted by permission of Hazelden Foundation, Center City, MN.

Excerpt from *The Prophet* by Kahlil Gibran, © 1923 Alfred A. Knopf, a Division of Random House, Inc.

Excerpts from *Writing for Your Life* by Deena Metzger, © 1992 Deena Metzger. Reprinted by permission of HarperCollins Publishers, Inc.

"Why" and excerpts from *Of Death and Recovery,* © 1993 by Vern Hotchkiss.

Excerpts from *Sacred Stories: A Celebration of the Power of Stories to Transform and Heal,* edited by Charles and Anne Simpkinson. © 1993 by Charles and Anne Simpkinson. Reprinted by permission of HarperCollins Publishers, Inc.

Excepts from *The Gift of Story* by Clarissa P. Estes, © 1993 Ballantine Books, a Division of Random House, Inc.

"A Fable," © Jeannette Isley.

Excerpts from *Seven Choices – Taking the Steps to New Life After Losing Someone You Love* by Elizabeth Harper Neld, Ph.D., © 1990 Clarkson N. Potter, a Division of Random House, Inc.

Author's note

I sincerely hope *Spinning Gold out of Straw* has helped you to make sense of the events in your life. As a board member of the Healing Arts Special Interest Group of the National Storytelling Network, I invite you to visit our website at www.healingstory.org to discover more ways to heal and grow through stories. Join with others who are experiencing this healing power.

Life is a journey, and stories can guide us along the way. By telling our personal stories, we can celebrate all of our life events, the joyous and the difficult, as well as the simple beauty of everyday. Please contact me to share your stories and your healing experiences. We have so much to learn from each other as we seek to find meaning in everything we encounter.

If you have the courage to tell the stories that others need in order to find hope, I know the stories you need to hear will come to you.

Peace and blessings,

Diane Rooks
c/o Salt Run Press
151 Santa Monica Ave.
St. Augustine, FL 32080
diane@storyjourney.com
www.storyjourney.com

Contact the following organizations to learn about groups in your area:

The Compassionate Friends
P.O. Box 3696
Oak Brook, IL 60522-3696
630-990-0246
877-969-0010 (toll free)
www.compassionatefriends.org

National Storytelling Network
101 Courthouse Square
Jonesborough, TN 37659
423-913-8201
800-525-4514 (toll free)
www.storynet.org

Spinning Gold out of Straw: How Stories Heal

Quantity	Price
_____ @ $15.95 each	_____
Shipping and Handling ($4 for first book, $2 for each additional book)	_____
Tax (FL residents add 6% / $.96 per book)	_____
Total	_____

To place your order,

Call: 904-829-1754

Fax: 904-826-0449

Email: saltrunpress@storyjourney.com

Mail check / money order (payable to Salt Run Press):
Salt Run Press
151 Santa Monica Ave.
St. Augustine, FL 32080

Shipping information:

Name _____

Address _____

City _____State ____Zip _____

Country _____ Phone _____

E-mail _____

☐ Please have the author autograph the book as follows:

_____

☐ Please send information about programs and workshops